TONY GOLDSMITH

Prelude to Change

Hong Kong of the 1950s

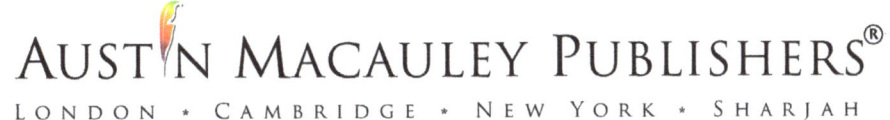
AUSTIN MACAULEY PUBLISHERS®

LONDON • CAMBRIDGE • NEW YORK • SHARJAH

A CIP catalogue record for this title is available from the British Library.

All of the events in this memoir are true to the best of the author's memory. The views expressed in this memoir are solely those of the author.

ISBN 9781035876402 (Paperback)
ISBN 9781035876419 (Hardback)
ISBN 9781035876426 (ePub e-book)

www.austinmacauley.com

First Published 2024
Austin Macauley Publishers Ltd
1 Canada Square
Canary Wharf
London
E14 5AA

Dedication

To my lovely wife, Sue, for her love and support, 'my girl next door' who encouraged me to write and get this book published. Sadly, she never got to see the final published version of this book. She died in September 2024 after long years of illness. Her braveness, warmth and humour inspire me still.

Dedicated with heartfelt thanks to Mr Tony Leong, Associate Specialist in Ophthalmology and his wonderful team at St Richard's Eye Clinic. Thank you for saving the sight in my right eye, so that I can go on taking pictures.

Acknowledgements

To my wife, Sue, who has been such a help as always
in being the best ever critic of my work.

Author's Note

The photographs in this book were taken by me from 1956 to 1959 with a Zeiss Ikon bellows camera whilst I was stationed on Hong Kong Island with the Royal Air Force. Prints and colour slides were stored until the technology was available for me to scan all images into digital format to produce this book on my home computer, using Photoshop. For the sake of completeness, I have used a few online library images, and I have noted where this has been done. All other photographs were taken by me.

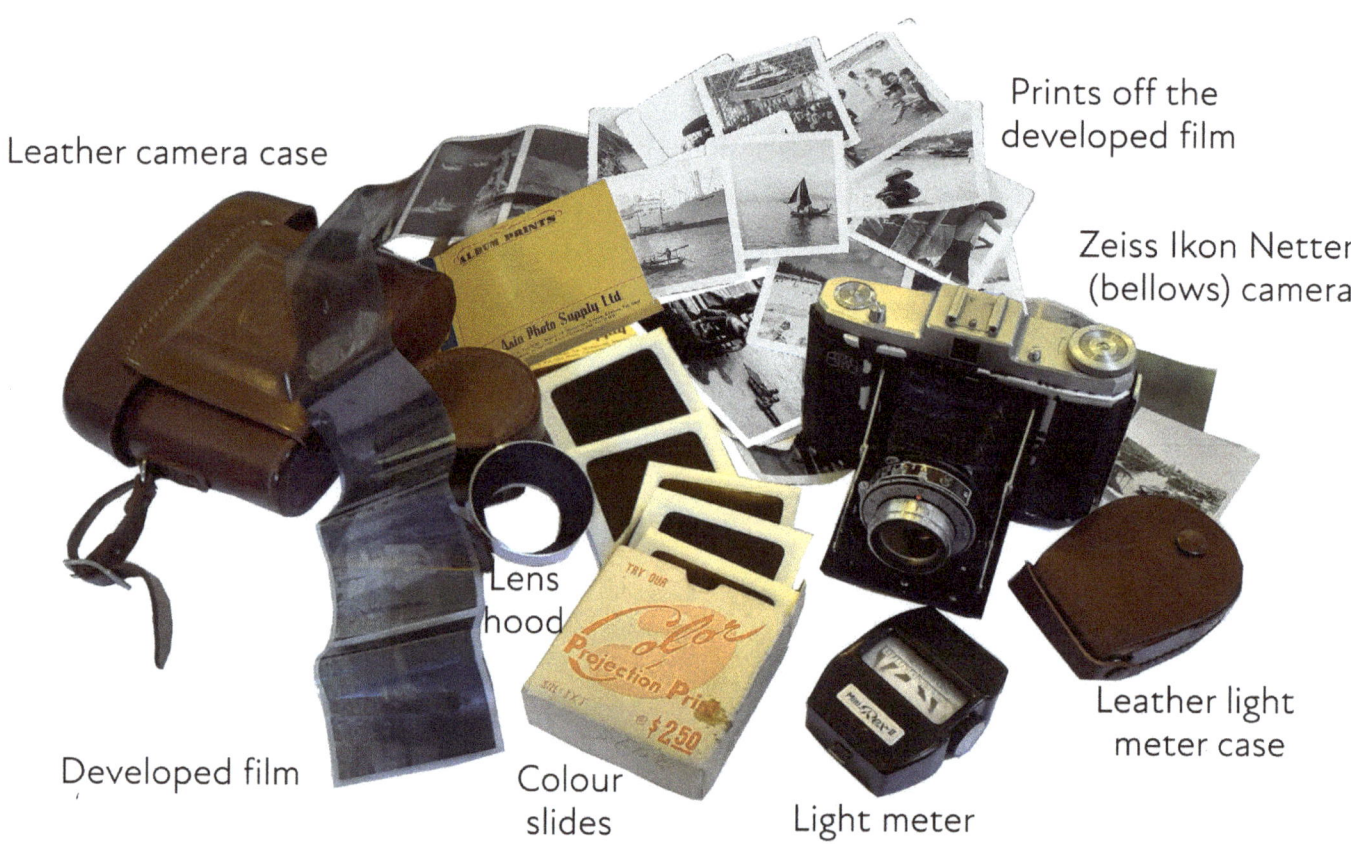

Leather camera case

Prints off the developed film

Zeiss Ikon Netter (bellows) camera

Lens hood

Developed film

Colour slides

Light meter

Leather light meter case

What the 1950s amateur photographer used

Contents

Introduction

As this is a very personal account, I decided to introduce myself at the front end of this book. My name is Tony Goldsmith, and this is what I looked like when I served with the RAF during the 50s in Hong Kong and what I look like now at the ripe old age of eighty-five.

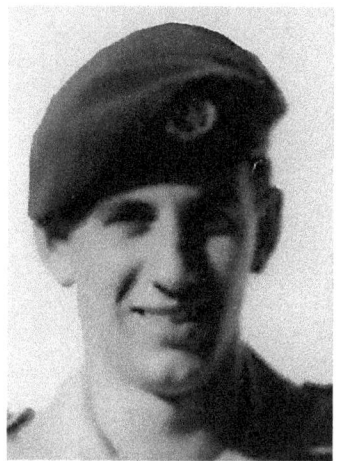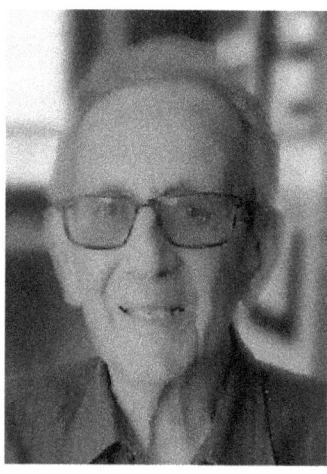

Left: SAC Goldsmith, RAF Wireless Operator
Right: Tony Goldsmith, retired structural engineer

This is really a co-contributor's introduction, because the young lad that I was in my late teens serving in Hong Kong was in so many ways not the old guy I am today. He had, for instance, no intention of putting his photographs into a book one day. He was merely taking pictures to send home to his family to let them share in the fascination he discovered in what he found in Hong Kong at that time. It was almost by accident that they were kept safe for the much older version of me to realise, having scanned them into my computer, just what a broad picture of life at that time in Hong Kong they represented, and how well they adapted to being enlarged using the wonders of modern technology in the form of Adobe Photoshop, which I had taught myself to use after my retirement.

The younger version of me led a much more carefree life with none of the illnesses that befall most of us as we age and no more to worry about than doing the job asked of him, after which his time was his own to enjoy swimming, playing soccer with his friends, setting off on his motorcycle to explore more of Hong Kong and take more pictures or perhaps take in a movie at the camp cinema, 'The Astra', or downtown in Victoria. For a young man with few responsibilities but to perform his work to the best of his ability and training, his worries were few.

For the older version of me, some of the detail has been fascinating to rediscover, such as the metal drinking cup that the smiling boy carries to supply drinks of water or that a small girl rowing her mother and siblings in their family's sampan had only one leg. It had been my policy not to photograph when people objected, but I am pleased to say that most of the time, there was no objection to my photography. With such cooperation from ordinary Chinese people, I was usually able to capture the candid shots of life at that time in Hong Kong. Perhaps what the younger and older versions of me have very much in common is a fascination for how other members of our global community live. It is my hope that my fascination for these images will give equal pleasure to others and provide a picture in their minds of what I, as a young man, tried to convey to my family back in England, all those many years ago.

With over sixty years between my service in Hong Kong and now, I apologise for a lack of recall regarding where in Hong Kong most pictures were shot or in what year, or in some cases the activity being carried out. Some of my readers might be able to enlighten me in this regard, for which I would be extremely grateful.

What I do well recall, however, is the wonder and awe I felt at being given the opportunity to travel to Hong Kong. While other guys on our flight out played cards to while the time away, I spent every moment with my eyes looking down from the aircraft's small window to catch every glimpse of the differing terrain over which we flew. That sense of awe and wonder did not abate when we reached Hong Kong, and I acquired a second-hand camera to record my experiences there.

Any form of historical account can only exist in the mind of the author, whether a first-hand account or one gleaned from academic research. So I am aware that the Hong Kong of the 1950s that I have so nostalgically embedded in my mind is not necessarily that of those who had been born there or who had chosen to live there. These were, in the main, Chinese folk who had fled communist China to seek a life less overshadowed by political oppression.

As a very young man living at a time when, for most people in the world, travel to foreign parts was rarely experienced whether for work or for pleasure, I shall be forever grateful that my service with the RAF afforded me that relatively rare privilege. Like most British young men, I was called up to do national service after reaching the age of 18. My burning ambition at that time was to use that as an opportunity to travel. After finishing my basic training, I realised that the trade of wireless operator offered one of the best chances of being posted overseas. Learning to read and

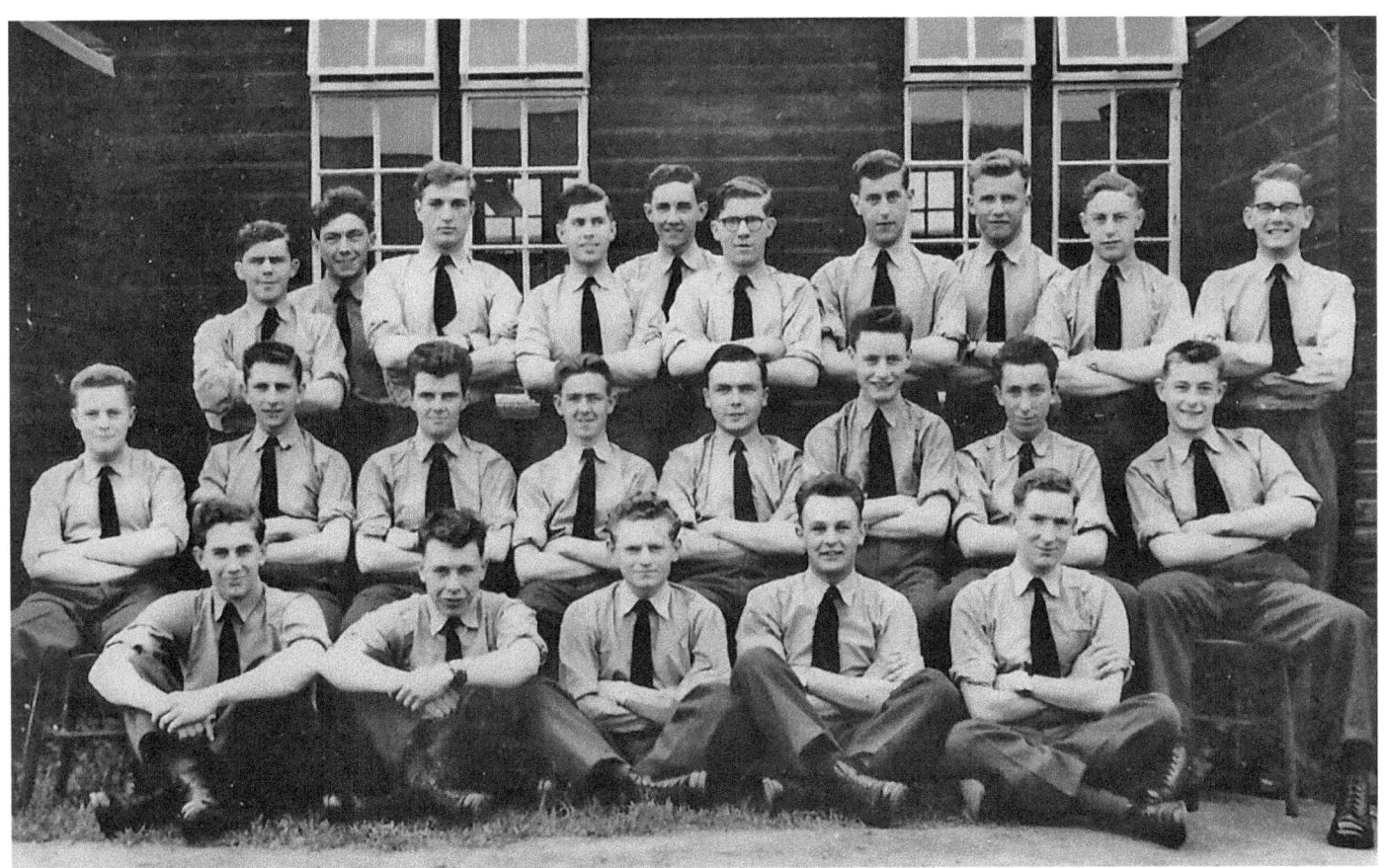

The author (bottom left) and other National Service lads of WOP 19 who shared a billet at RAF Compton Bassett, Wiltshire. Taken June 1956. We had all trained to become RAF wireless operators. Most would be posted to various operational flying stations in UK and overseas, whereas a few of us opted for further training at RAF Wythall near Birmingham. The guy in the middle row far right is the late actor Derek Fowlds. I met Derek and some of our guys at an airbase in Libya, after the first leg of our journey to Hong Kong.

send signals by Morse code was not the most interesting training that I could have chosen to do and would certainly lead to few job opportunities when I left the RAF. But I stuck with it at the RAF's huge training centre at Compton Bassett in Wiltshire and volunteered for specialist training at RAF Wythall, near Birmingham, to achieve my dream of overseas travel.

It took the RAF nine days to fly myself and a few other 'wops' (wireless operators) as we were now called, out to Kai Tak airfield from Lyneham airfield in the UK. The four-engine Hastings aircraft was very noisy, vibrated a lot and was not pressurised, so when we flew over the mountains of Turkey en route to night-stop in Iraq, we all had to put on oxygen masks. Because these old propeller-driven aircraft flew relatively low, there were land and seascapes to be seen when we were below the cloud base. I could see below us fields, forests, snow-covered mountains, rivers, and deserts, as we edged our way at a snail's pace each day south over Europe then eastwards over the Libyan desert. We then looped north to fly over the Turkish mountains so that we could avoid any confrontation with Egypt, with whom relations were not particularly friendly at that time. Then more sea and desert, as we flew south for night stops in Iraq and Pakistan and down to Sri Lanka, or as it was known then, Ceylon.

Many miles of blue ocean followed as we crossed to Changi in Malaysia (then still called Malaya). Not too many years before, Changi had been an infamous Japanese prison camp for Allied prisoners of war. By the time we reached Changi, without exception, all of us RAF transportees were suffering from diarrhoea. No more flying the next day for us. From our overnight billet hut, we tramped next morning to the camp's medical hut, all of us looking and feeling very, very, sorry for ourselves, with stomach cramps and the ever-present fear of 'not making it' in time to the loo!

We were greeted by an RAF medical orderly, who asked, "Just out from UK? Hmm. Thought so. Takes about six or seven days after leaving the UK. It's the change in climate – see? Changes all the bacteria in your tummies. Here you are – each take a bottle of this jollup." With that, the orderly issued each airman with a large bottle of kaolin mixture. "Guaranteed to bung you up in time for take-off tomorrow," he assured us. "Off you go."

With that, we all trooped out in single file back towards our billet, each carrying a large bottle of murky brown kaolin mixture. The ridiculousness of what we must have looked like as we shuffled slowly back in single file to our billet, each with his bottles of jollup, struck me as hilarious, despite sharing the misery of griping pains and general disability that only a severe dose of 'Montezuma's revenge' can endow. We had been told that Changi was a fascinating place for a stop-over, but for us it was back to our beds and regular doses of that disgusting medication as we wallowed in the misery of trying to recover from our 'gippy' tummies.

The next leg took us to Saigon for a brief refuelling stop then on again towards Hong Kong over the South China Sea. Suddenly, I could see huge waves directly below us. Clearly the cloud base almost touched down to the sea. With a roar of the engines, the plane was brought up into a steep climb to avoid crashing into those treacherous high seas directly below us. It was flying by the seat of the pants if ever there was. Soon after, the sergeant whose job it was to feed and occasionally inform us came back and told us that the cloud base over Hong Kong's Kai Tak airfield was too low for us to land and that we were diverting for a one-night stay at Clark Field, the US base in the Philippines. Here, we RAF guys experienced just how different life in the American forces was to our own.

At that time, RAF food was only just bearable and would get worse for us when we reached Hong Kong, where breakfast bacon would taste of fish due to local pigs being fed on fish waste. All our breakfast fried eggs would be dried up, having been cooked in large numbers sometime before being served onto our plates. A decent fry-up meal could, however, be bought in the NAAFI (Navy, Army and Air Force Institutes) when things got too bad, and of course the restaurants and chow-stalls of Victoria and Kowloon served the most delicious Chinese and other foods. All this we had still to discover. At Clark Field the next morning we were agog when the cooks asked us how we would like them to cook our eggs and to see available all sorts of lovely fresh fruit juices to drink with a plate of food that we RAF guys could only normally dream of.

When we continued on to Hong Kong that morning, we were told that landing at Kai Tak would be a 'bit tricky', especially with a side wind. The runway was short and surrounded by either sea or mountains. The pilot would have to manoeuvre in and finally lose height quickly, so that we would miss the sheer rock cliffs at the side of the runway. What nobody had mentioned was that, prior to our landing, there had been a total of 72 fatalities between 1948 and 1951, due to three failed attempts to land at Kai Tak airport. Luckily, due to the skill of our RAF pilot, we landed safely and the adventure I had so looked forward to had begun.

I would find Hong Kong so fascinating and different to anything I had known back in England. I believe that my pictures capture that interest I found, and it is my hope that you enjoy looking at them as you journey back in time with me – as much as I have enjoyed refreshing my memories of that time and what was then the beautiful and largely unspoilt territories of Hong Kong island and the Kowloon peninsula.

Hong Kong's New Runway – Catalyst For Change

Our outward journey had taken nine days in an RAF Hastings aircraft. Fortunately for us passengers, we were oblivious to the fact that Hong Kong's Kai Tak landing strip was very short, enclosed by a rock face on one side and the sea on the other, making it extremely difficult to land a large plane on. I was to learn later that between 1948 and 1951 there had been a total of three crash landings, resulting in 72 people being killed.

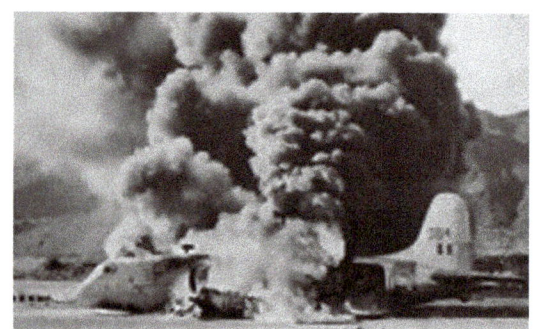

RAF Hastings crash of 1953 (library picture)

My first view of a Hong Kong citizen out of my plane window was a female quarry worker carrying rocks in big baskets hanging from a yoke across her shoulders.

During that first year in Hong Kong, I witnessed the building of a new Kai Tak runway stretching out into the sea. It opened in 1957 and was soon enabling large jet airliners to land in Hong Kong, albeit that it still had a reputation for being one of the most difficult to land or take off from, as seen below, with a Boeing 747 flying between tall buildings. In time it would become one of the busiest airstrips in the world. Kai Tak's capacity to handle the numbers of passengers towards the end of Britain's colonial rule became insufficient, so in 1998 a new, larger airport, free from Hong Kong's then mass of high rise-buildings, was opened on the island of Chek Lap Kok.

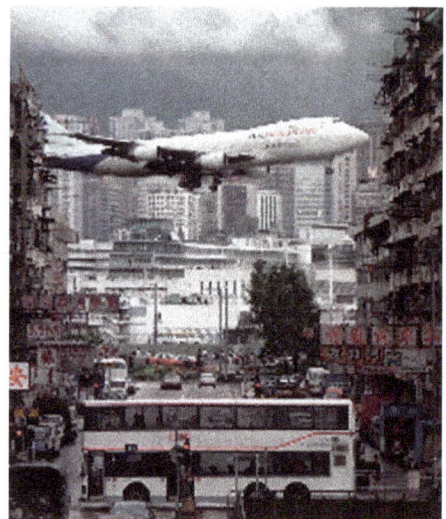

(Library picture)

The timing of the completion of a runway at Kai Tak would, over the next four decades, allow Hong Kong to play host to businessmen, architects and other professional people. Those trained and skilled in construction management and the building trades were also invited in to work on the rapid development of Hong Kong's buildings and infrastructure that would change its skyline dramatically. In conjunction with this massive material development of Hong Kong came the easing of hostility between Britain and mainland China, with tentative steps towards restoration of diplomatic links and what was to become an explosion over the following decades in manufacturing and trade.

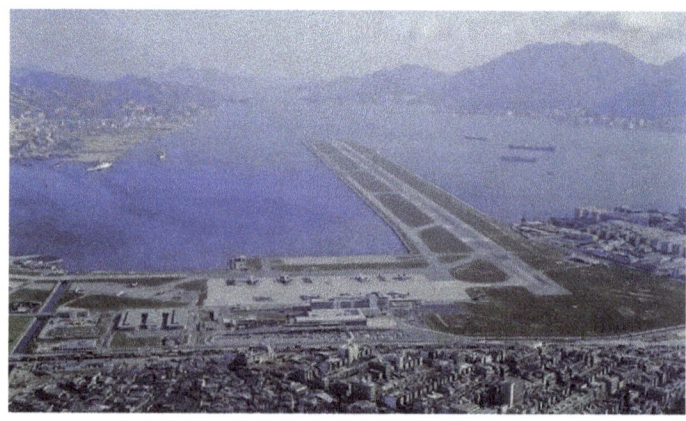

Kia Tak's new airstrip, opened in 1957 (library picture)

A Colony of Contrasts

I arrived in Hong Kong in 1956 as a wireless operator skilled in the art of intercepting weak Morse signals over static from countries that the United Kingdom was at that time not on friendly terms with, such as Communist China. I would be stationed at RAF Little Sai Wan at the eastern end of Hong Kong Island.

Hong Kong's population had swollen to 2.2 million because of the upheaval of the civil war that had taken place in mainland China between communists and nationalists. Shaukiwan district was reportedly the most populous area in the world and a place our camp bus drove through on its way to our narrow mountain's edge road to our RAF camp. My photographs here show Shaukiwan's main street (top) and typical makeshift dwellings housing the massive overspill of families (second picture down). Regularly such dwellings would be swept away by typhoon rains. Such was the fate at one time of the only road into our camp, seen here (third picture down) being cleared of landslide material.

By contrast (bottom), I show a typical downtown nightclub where Chinese girls would dance or chat with servicemen in return for buying them a drink of what was probably just coloured water. They wore the traditional Chinese cheongsam, but much shorter than generally worn and with splits each side almost to their hips. They probably did such work to support their families. On the island's tallest mountain, The Peak, lived millionaires in luxurious houses and as you will see, there were beautiful beaches and a Europeans-only golf course. The Hong Kong government had, however, just started the task of building high-rise accommodation to solve the colony's housing crisis.

On the following pages, I hope that readers will see more clearly how the Hong Kong of yesteryear differed so much from the modern metropolis it is today.

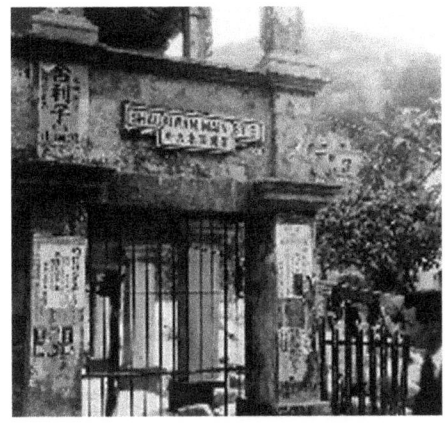

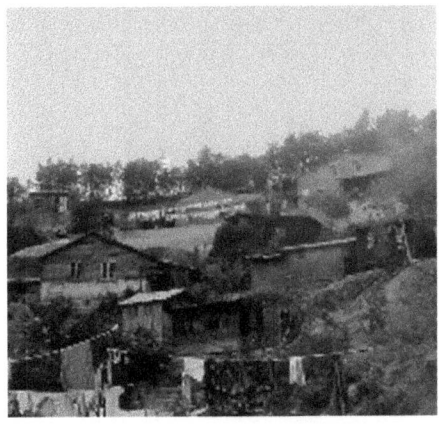

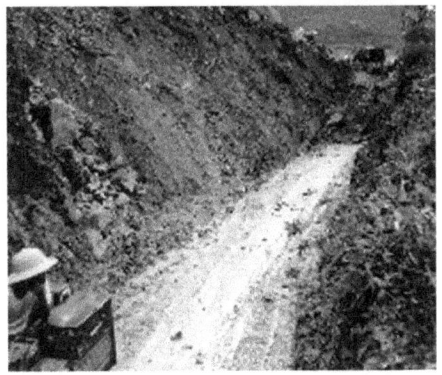

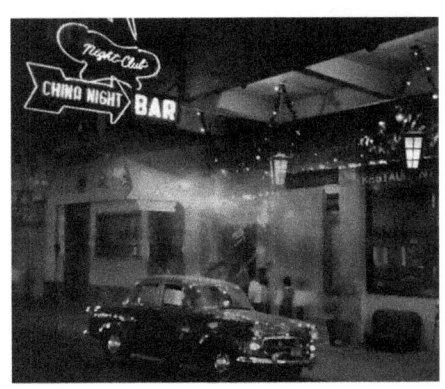

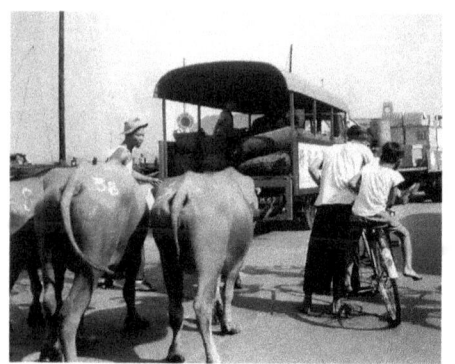

Waiting to board a ferry

Overcrowding and inadequate housing were prevalent in the Hong Kong of the nineteen-fifties, due to a massive influx of Chinese immigrants who had fled from the civil war on mainland China and later when the Communists gained total control in 1949. As the picture inside the fishmonger's shop reveals, there was support for the Communists within Hong Kong. Many families lived either in hillside shacks or on board sampans.

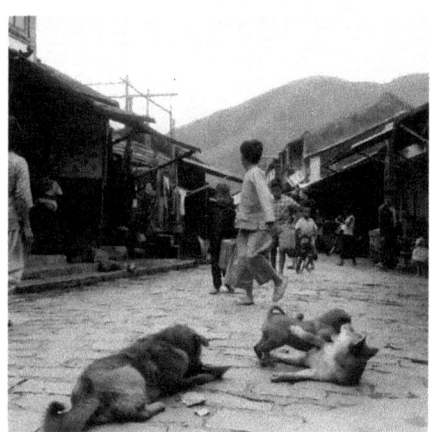

Kids on way to school

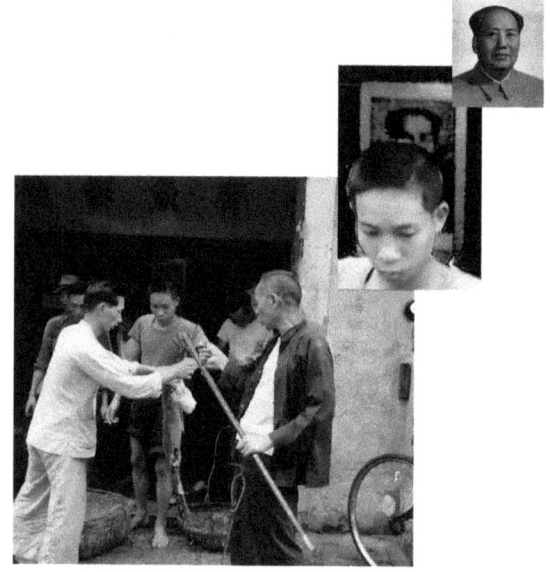

Fishmonger's shop
A blow-up of the picture inside the fishmonger's shop reveals a likeness of the Communist Chinese leader Mao Zedong

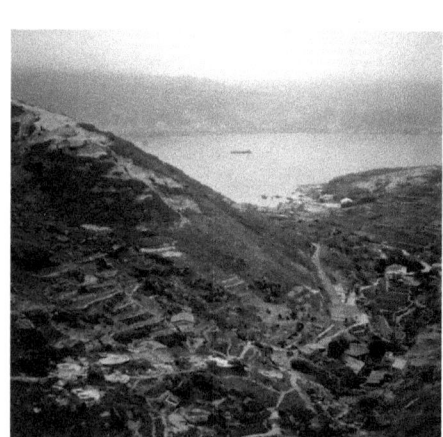

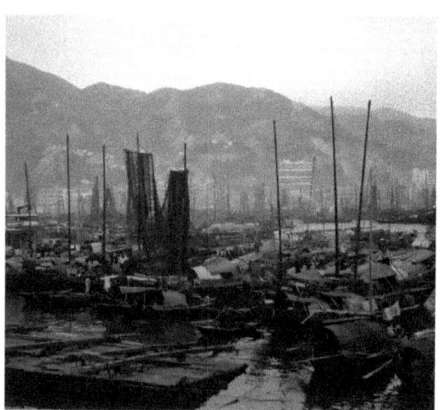

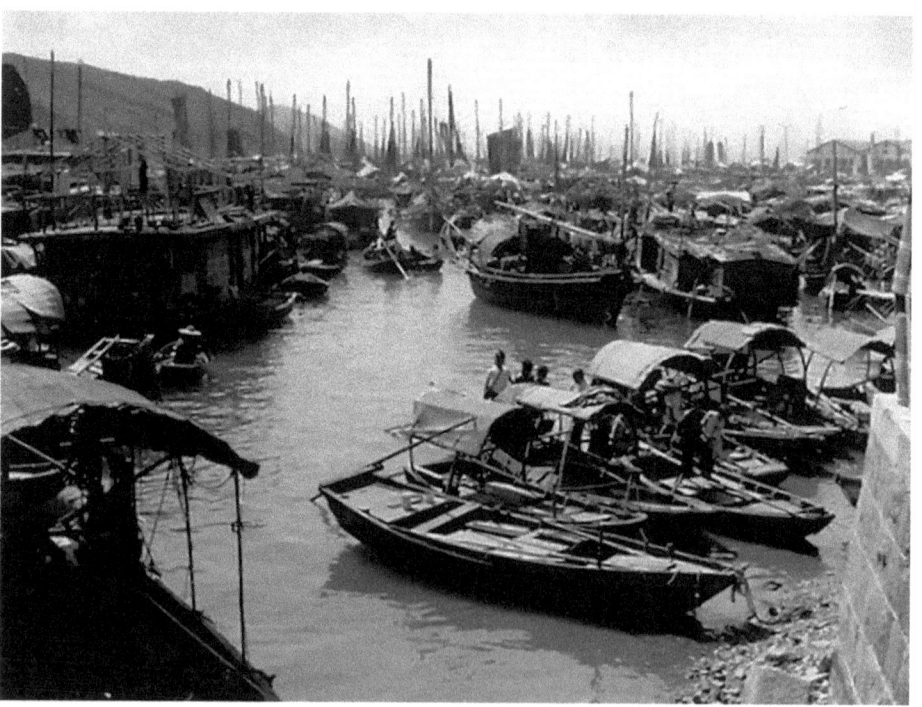

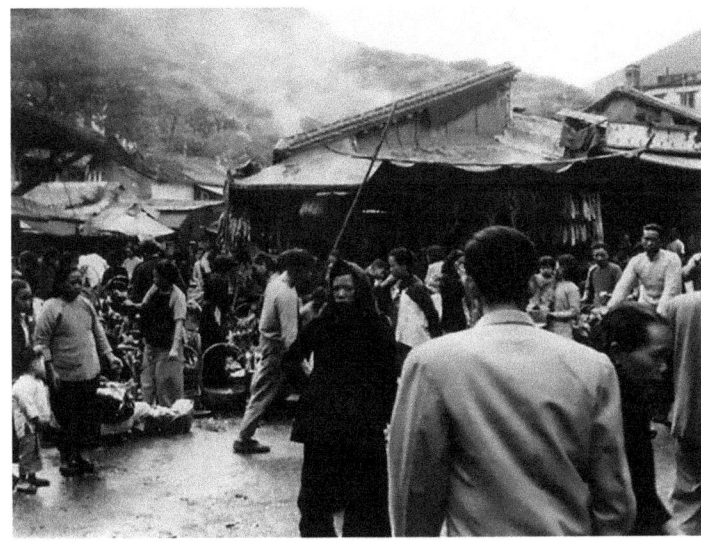
A Crowded Market-place

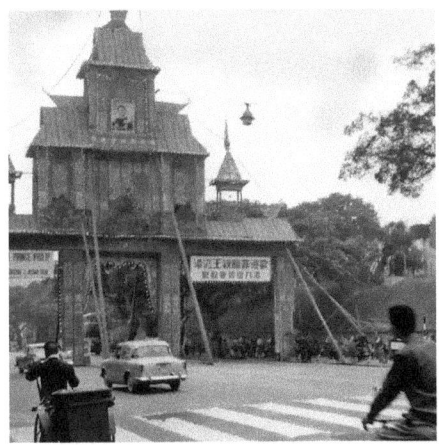
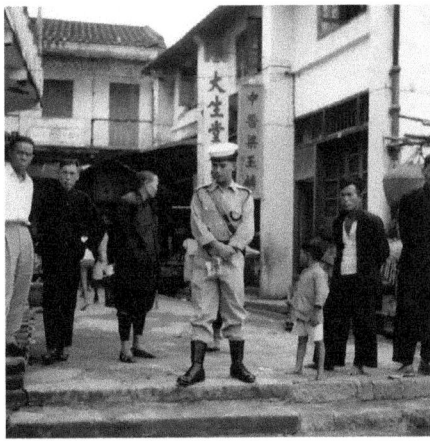
Left: Royal Visit of Prince Philip – March 1959
Right: Awaiting the Water Taxi
Note how footwear varies showing differences of tradition and status.

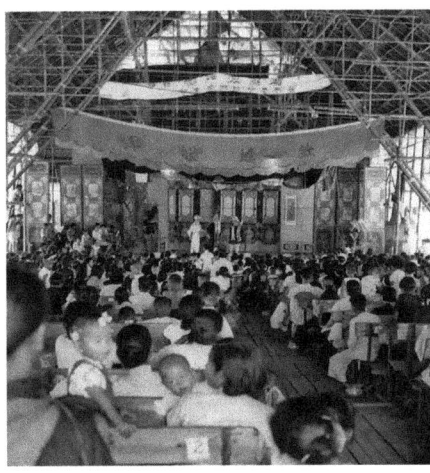
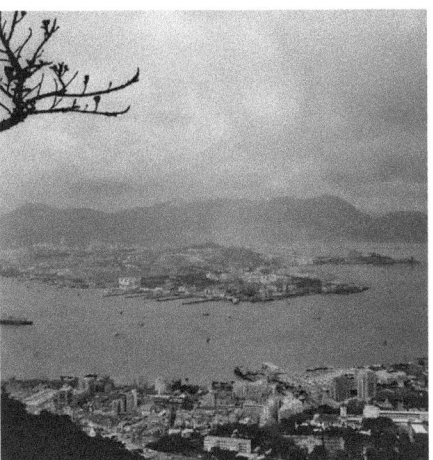
Left: Travelling Theatre
Right: Looking down from The Peak Towards Kowloon
A view that only the more wealthy Hong Kong folk could enjoy from their homes.

Looking back now, I can see contrasts in the sheer beauty and tranquillity of Hong Kong Island away from the hustle and bustle of its commercial centre, Victoria. There was also the difference between centuries-old wooden junks and modern-day ships. So too the styles in dress, from Chinese men and women in mainly black loose top-and-trousers to made-to-measure European style suits from the many Indian tailor-shops, or, for the ladies, stylish variations of the traditional cheongsam.

Traditional Chinese theatres contrasted with more modern cinemas and nightclubs. There was also the seeming calm of Hong Kong life whilst, below that surface, operated the Triad gangs and unrest over poverty and overcrowding that led to the 1956 riots in Kowloon, when sixty people died and many were injured, before calm was restored by the army. On the island we had little knowledge of all these Communist-led disturbances, only that our borders with Communist China were constantly patrolled, on land and at sea to stem the ever-present flood of families into Hong Kong. Once I saw a Gurkha platoon, with their pack mules, returning from a border patrol in the New Territories.

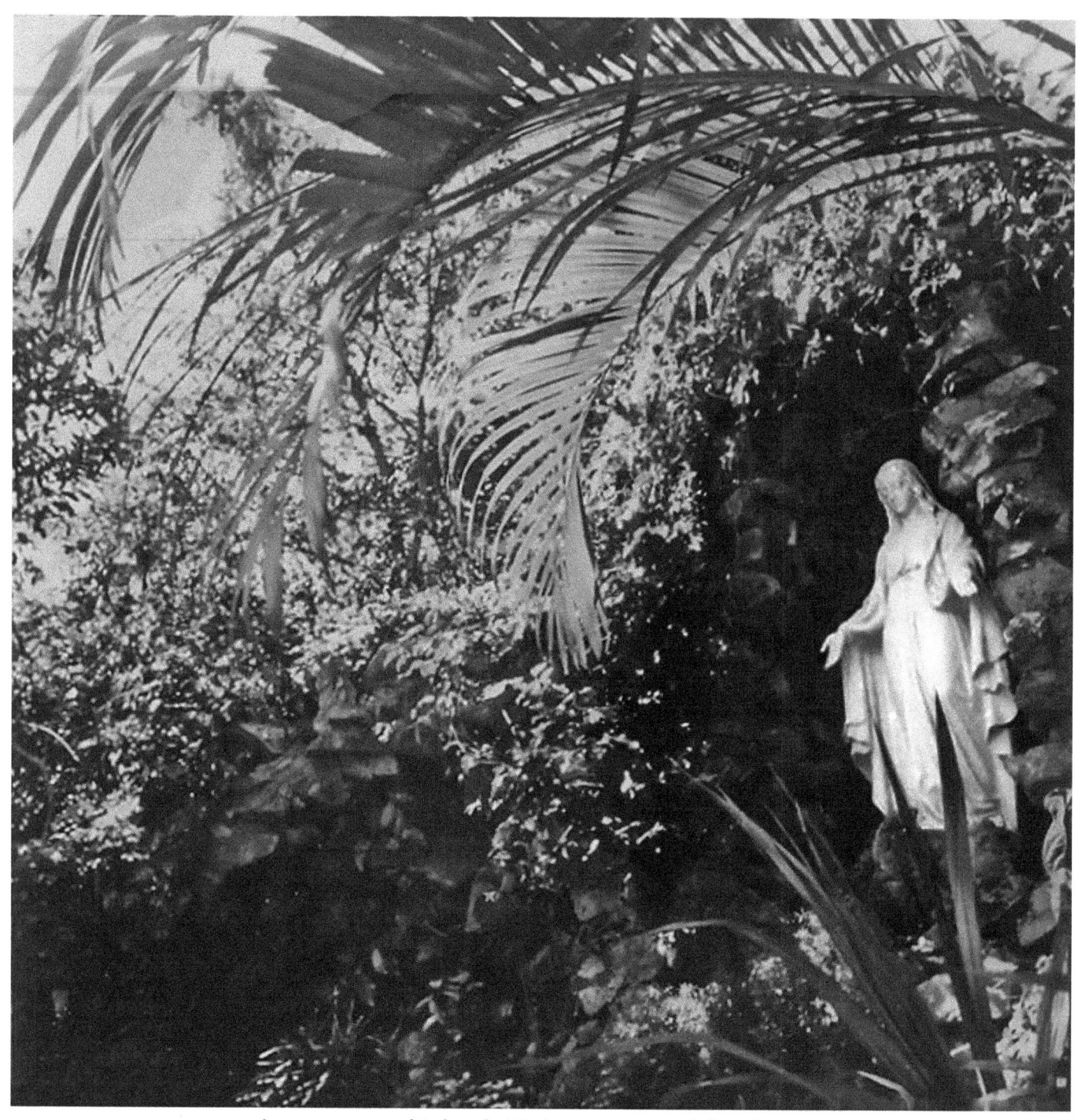

I came across this lovely Madonna statue while riding my
motorbike on the South side of Hong Kong Island.

Much of my exploration of Hong Kong was done by means of getting around on my old ex-police motorbike which was a Norton side valve, originally intended for being coupled to a sidecar. Being totally very young and foolish, I would navigate the Island's twisty narrow roads with little thought of my own safety in mind and would lean the motorbike at times so far over that the exhaust pipe would scrape on the road.

I would at times, be dressed in only shorts, shirt and sandals and riding round the beautiful island of Hong Kong, as it was then, was totally exhilarating – unless I came off my motorbike, where fresh grit had been laid to compensate for where a bend in the road had been cambered in the wrong direction, as many were.

Eventually, I had to accept that for my own safety I should sell my motorbike.

Mountain Graveyard

Another unexpected discovery by motorcycle. Note the roof of the Tiger Pagoda Hong Kong Island's Tiger Balm Garden on the left with its tall Tiger Pagoda, was an impressive landmark in the 1950s. Sadly, in 2004 this very traditionally Chinese building became yet another casualty of the overpowering pressure of urban development.

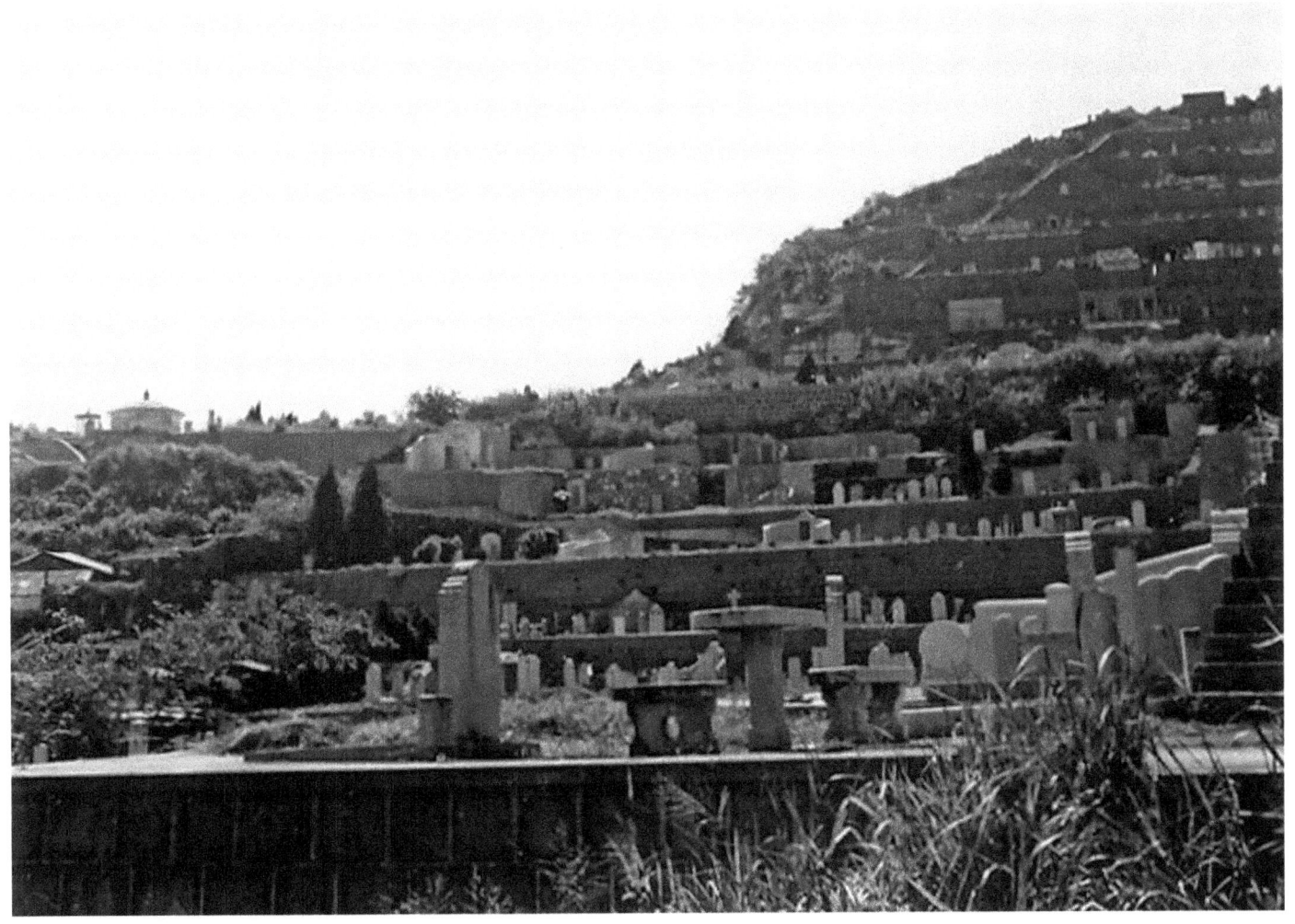

A Shipwreck Story

In 1957, Typhoon Gloria scored a direct hit on Hong Kong on the evening of 21st September. The waves sweeping across our bay were huge. Next morning, I looked out from the balcony of my barrack block to see that a large ship had run aground on the rocky headland to the North of our camp, on the mainland side of the approaches to Victoria Harbour.

I took my camera down to the foreshore of our camp and was able to attract the attention of a family on a sampan fishing just out to sea. On the boat were a man, his wife, and their daughter. They most likely lived on their boat and would have spent the night in one of Hong Kong's typhoon shelters. I spoke no Cantonese and they no English, but by waving some Hong Kong dollars and pointing to the grounded ship, I was able to strike a deal for them to take me over to it – a journey of several miles across a busy shipping lane.

My pictures tell the story of my adventure that day. I was able to board the stricken ship and meet the Dutch ship's officers who, unlike the crew members who had scrambled ashore, stayed on board to prevent the ship being claimed as a salvage prize. Lucky for me, the sampan family also brought me back!

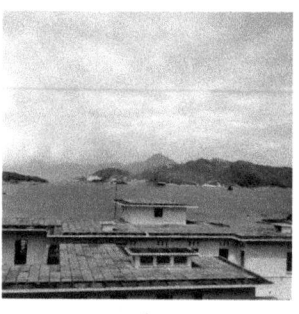

1

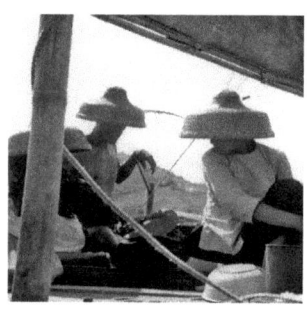

2

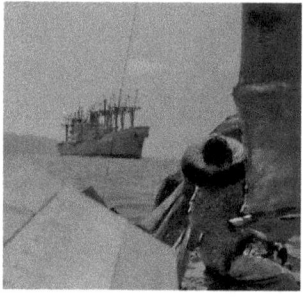

3

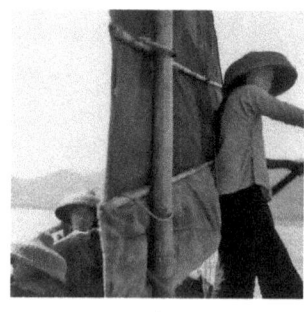

4

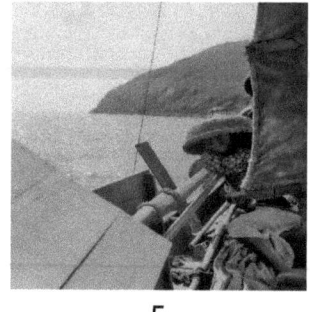

5

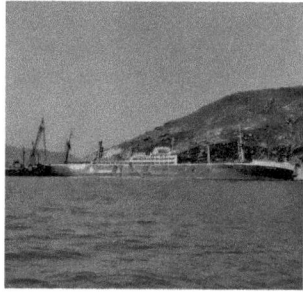

6

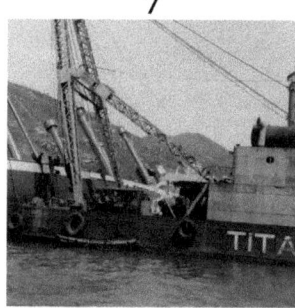

7

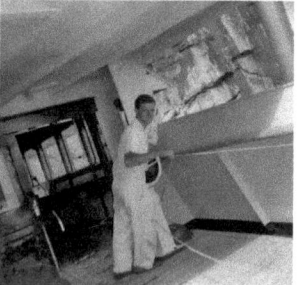

8

9

Hong Kong's Boats and Ships

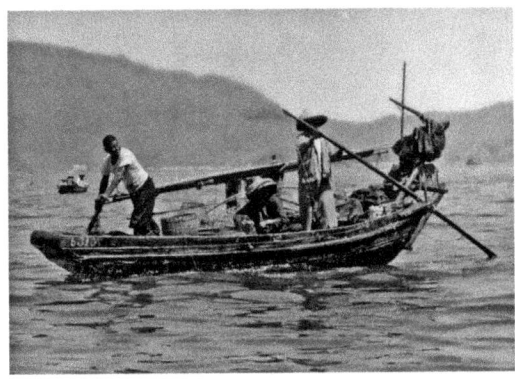 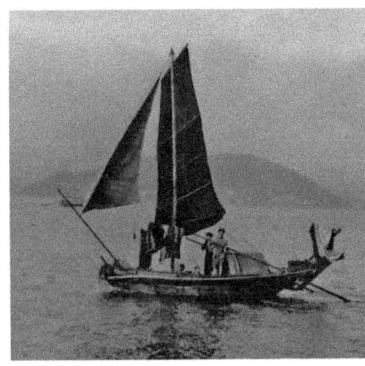 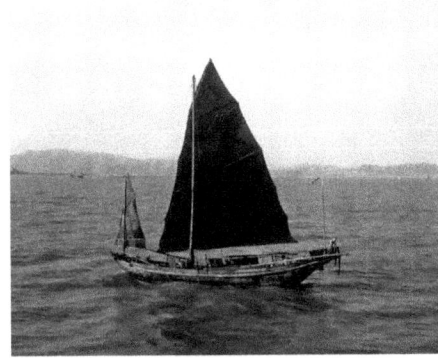

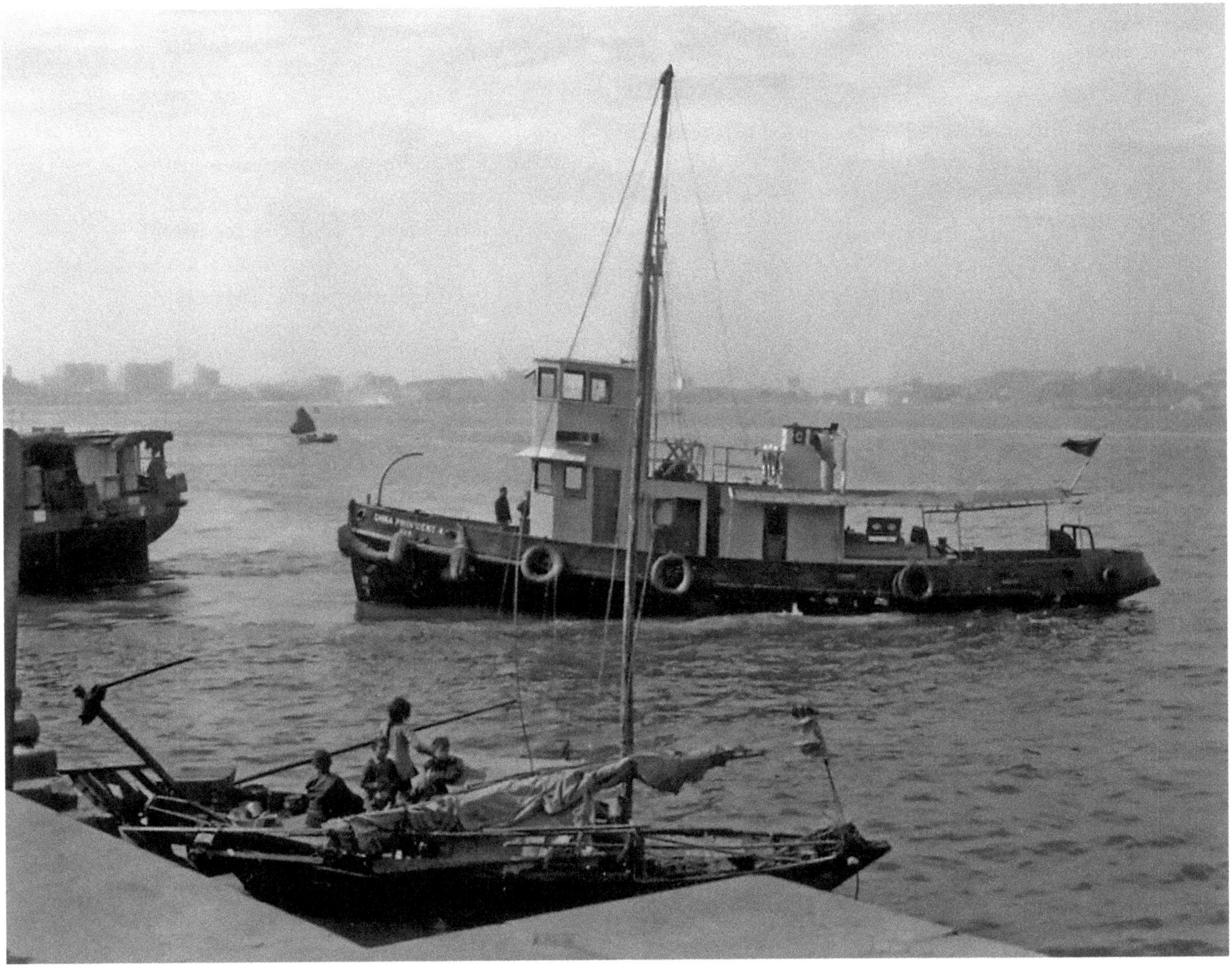

Here we see the contrast between traditional wooden boats using sail and manpower and a modern steel-hulled tug-boat powered by a powerful diesel engine.

Star Ferry

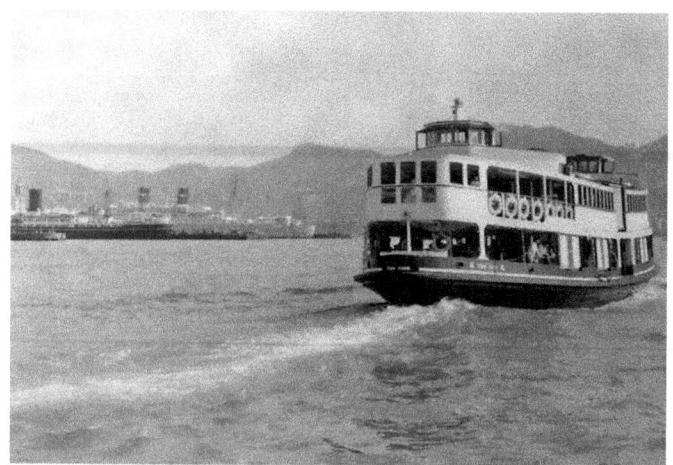

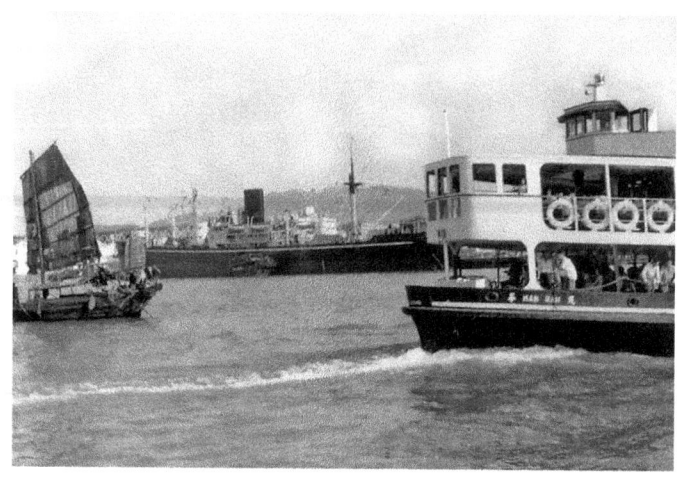

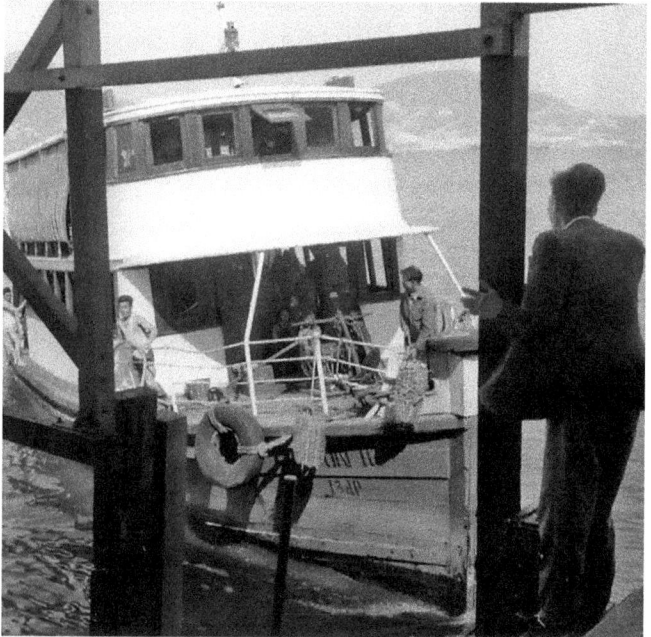

Top: This was our main link between the island and Kowloon side, as we called the mainland.

Left: Commercial Traveller Hong Kong style

Bottom: Hong Kong's many shallow drafted sampans provided transport, living accommodation and a means to catch fish

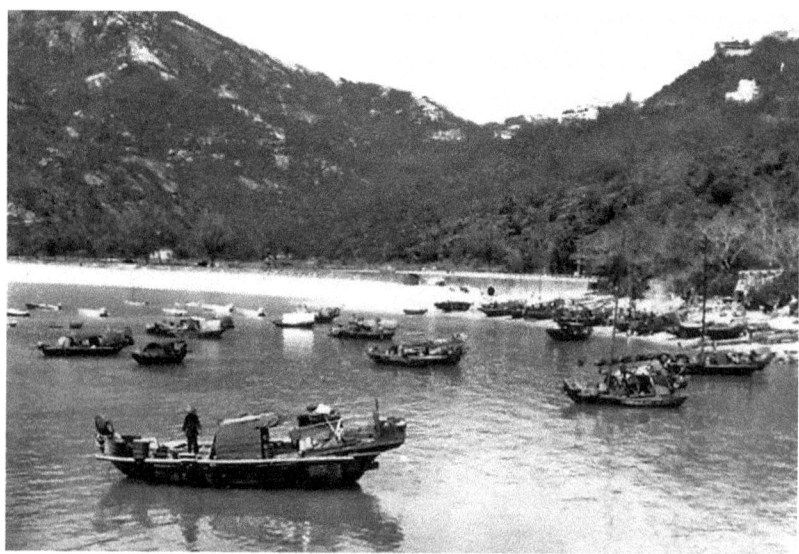

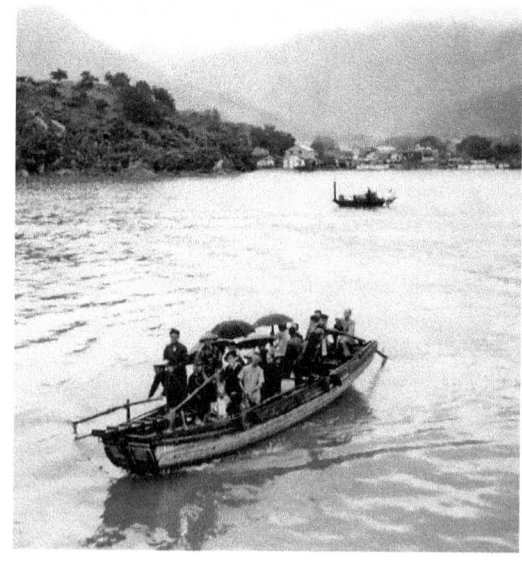

With Red China then having virtually no navy, the US Navy had complete domination over the South China Sea. Hong Kong was frequently host to large US carriers like USS Coral Sea.

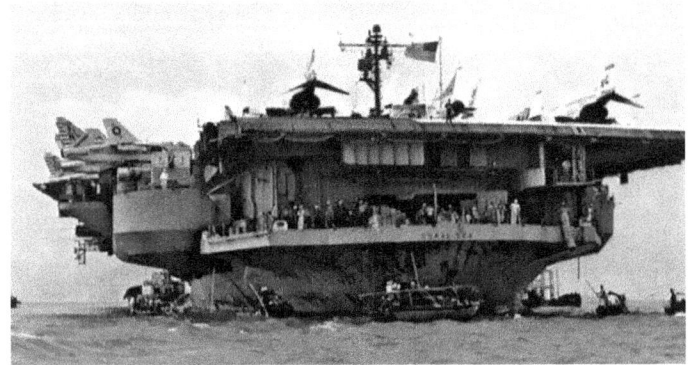

USS Coral Sea (library picture).

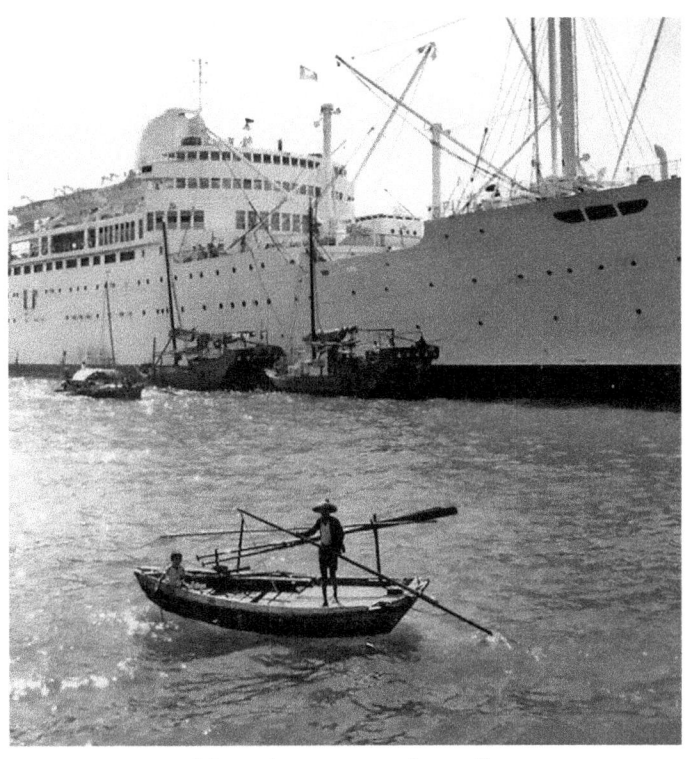

Vessels great and small.

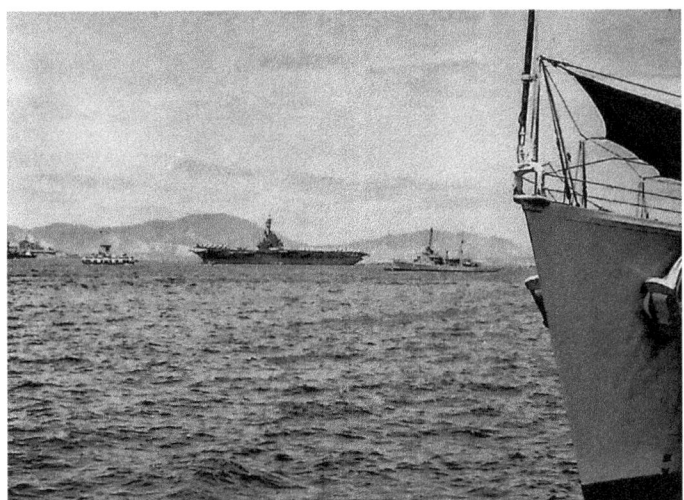

US Carrier in Victoria Harbour.

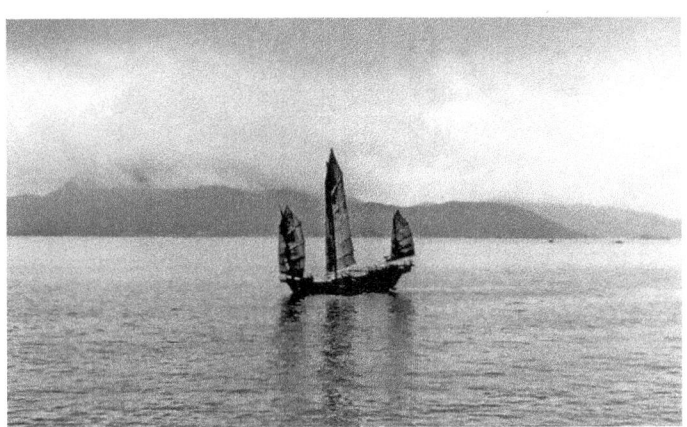

Passing junk on a misty morn.

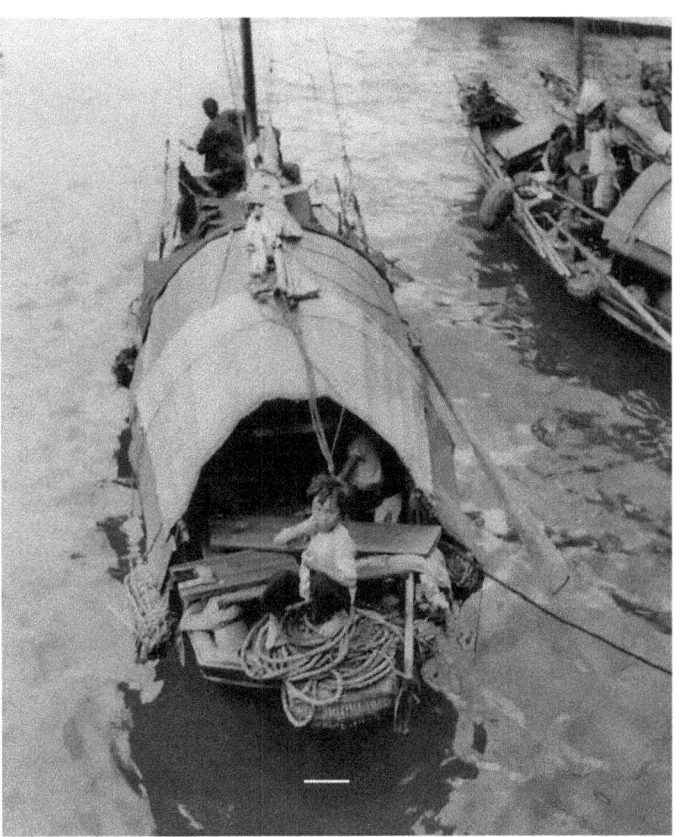

Young sampan dweller.

Hong Kong's Sampan Fishing Families

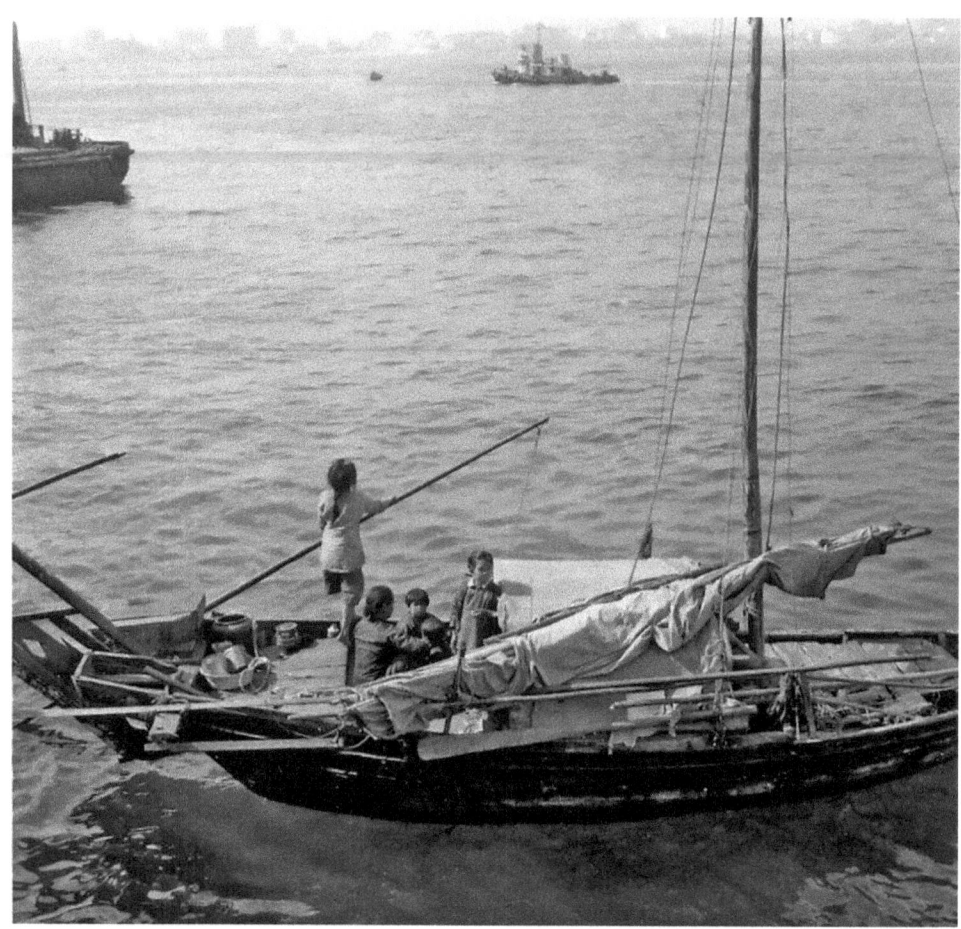

Note that the young girl at the oar has lost a leg.

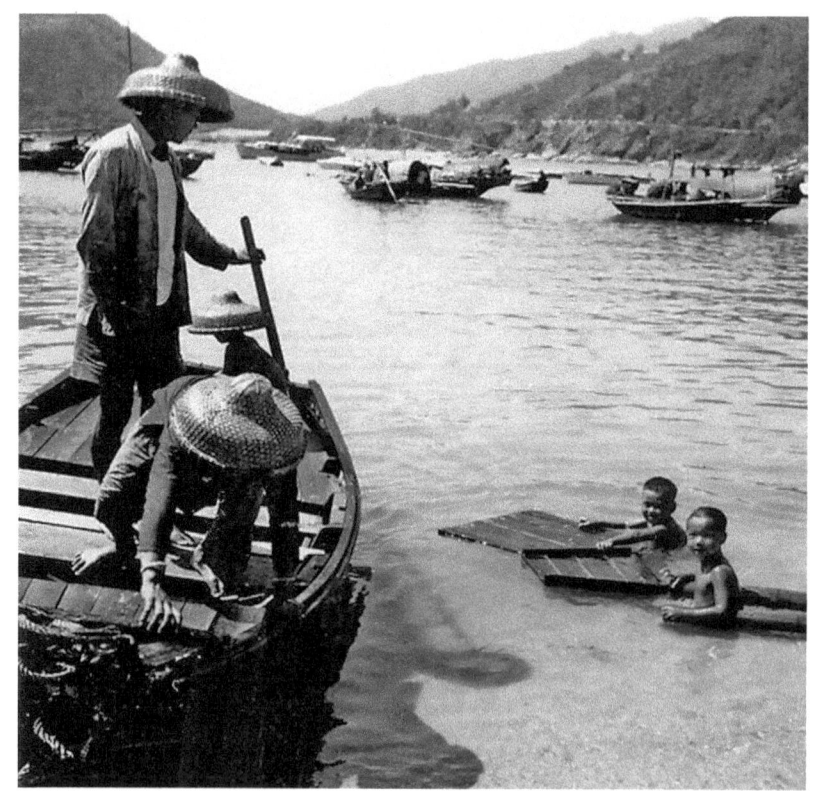

Story of Chinese Junks

Typically, perhaps, what we mainly know of old sailing ships in Western culture is almost entirely confined to a knowledge of how big ships like galleons were built. Ships such as the Mary Rose or Nelson's Victory can even be studied in detail at Portsmouth. We know how they were sailed, how they made voyages of discovery and trade and how they were used in battle.

But there is a history of sail that arguably eclipses the exploits of Drake or Nelson. It is the history of the Chinese junk. At the pinnacle of their use as vessels for the expansion of China's trade, exploration and means of waging war, Chinese junks were larger, more technically advanced and yet arguably simpler to sail, with the Chinese invention of a ship's rudder and latticed sails, than anything developed by European ship builders in the early days of sail. Their hulls contained watertight compartmentation and were built using rabbeted interlocked and caulked joints between planks that gave them lightness and strength without having to use thick hardwood planking, as employed for instance on a British man-of-war. Some junks were reportedly very big. Although claims that they could have been up to one hundred metres long are being challenged by modern-day marine engineers who point out that the stresses imposed on any long ship can be such that large ocean waves can break even steel vessels in two, there can be no doubt that the skills employed by Chinese ship builders resulted in stretching the boundaries of marine construction. Junk design dates from around 200 BC, at a time when in Northern Europe the open clinker-built long boat, such as would later be used by the Vikings, represented state-of-the-art boat construction.

Then, 500 years ago, of a sudden, these magnificently large ship ships were gone. For reasons of economic policy, the ruling Ming administration had China's whole fleet of massive junks destroyed. The building of wooden junks did of course continue but not at anything like the scale and grandeur of before.

The Romans were notorious for stealing ideas and technology. For instance, they got the concept of the arch from an ancient civilisation, the Etruscans who came from around Tuscany. From the arch the Romans developed the dome. Similarly, the Romans are credited with the building of keeled framed ships, but this concept came originally from the Carthaginians, whom the Romans eventually conquered in battle. It was the Romans, however, who took this form of ship construction to its limit, as evidenced by the remains found of a massive Roman barge The Caligula, with an estimated length of 103 metres. Whether this huge vessel could have endured the type of massive swells that can break a longship in half in deeper waters than the Mediterranean would be debatable.

From these early beginnings, European big ship design featured a keeled and framed skeleton onto which, in the case of ships of war, thick hardwood planking was fixed. Such ships not only were required to sail fast under many square metres of sail but were also designed to act as massive gun platforms, capable of supporting rows of heavy cannons and strong enough to endure battering from enemy broadsides.

In 1840, at the start of the first Opium War, the lighter Chinese junks, operated by local sailors less skilled in the art of warfare as practised in Europe, came up against British frigates. They were no match for these, and the British forces prevailed. After two opium wars, the island of Hong Kong and the mainland area known as the New Territories were forcibly leased to the British Crown.

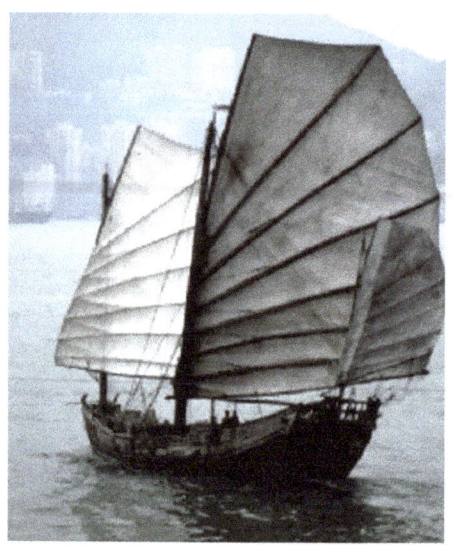

Three-masted junk typical of those we saw regularly coming to and fro between Victoria Harbour and ports on the Chinese mainland (library picture).

The library picture above of a three-masted working junk, so typical of the ones we could see daily from our RAF camp at Little Sai Wan, illustrates beautifully how the design allowed a large vessel with an equally large area of sail to be handled by a very small crew, due to its latticed sail configuration. Soon after, just as the whole character of Hong Kong would change from having a relative few tall buildings, make-shift dwellings and sampans that provided families with a place to live and work, so did its ships. Soon the timber junks, so familiar to us servicemen, would disappear.

It seemed that, more often than not, such vessels were powered along through the straits between the island and the mainland by diesel engine. The story went that these were in fact diesel motors taken from the many Japanese tanks that presumably the Japanese army would have abandoned after the surrender of Japan. It seemed to me a logical assumption. My good mate Barry, however, delighted in teasing me about this notion and would murmur as we sunned ourselves on the sea wall of our camp:

"Just listen to the throb of that Japanese tank engine, Tony."

"Shuddup, Barry," I would lazily reply.

Could the picture below be a rare picture of a man and wife curving planks to incorporate into the hull of one of the last, if not the last, junk built in Hong Kong? (Although curving of planks would equally apply to the building of sampans.)

Using steam to curve planks up to 150mm thick was the accepted way for European ship builders. Unlike the European hardwood ships, junks used firs, pine, and camphor timber. The planks were skilfully jointed together by steam caulking and rabbet jointing.

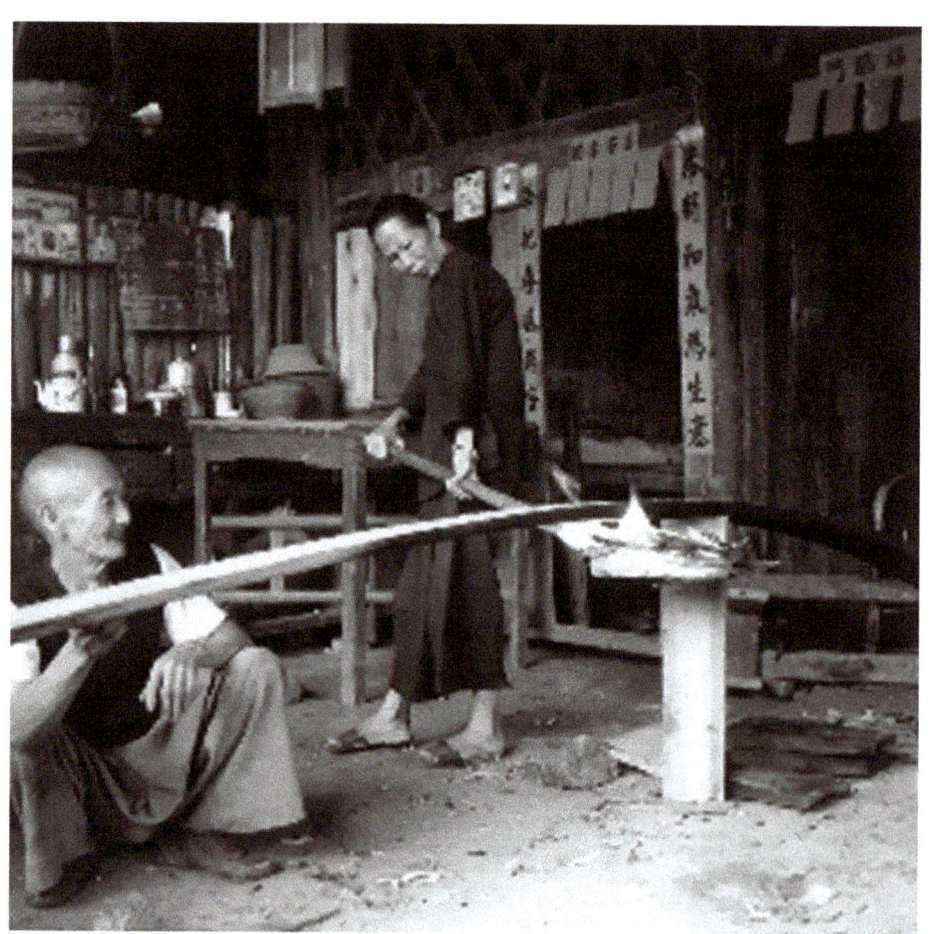

Curving of planks

PRELUDE TO CHANGE: HONG KONG OF THE 1950S

Racing a junk under sail – a day to remember

On one occasion I was asked by a corporal who had an interest in dinghy sailing if I would like to sail as crew to bring over a dinghy from RAF Kai Tak to our RAF camp at Little Sai Wan, where a new yacht club building had been built to serve as the station's sailing club facility.

It would, as it happened, serve civilians more than service people, because gradually our jobs were being phased out to be taken over by civilian personnel working directly for GCHQ.

It sticks in my memory as one of those magical days. My corporal captain was a skilled yachtsman, and we were sailing the same west-to-east course as a three-masted junk plying its trade of carrying goods to and from Hong Kong and Red Chinese mainland harbours.

As in so many similar situations in the world, ordinary folk were just getting on with their lives regardless of what politicians were doing. No doubt the junk-master felt the same competitive stimulus to out-sail the impertinent little dinghy tacking along a similar course to his own, before he could go on to sail to whatever small harbour or offloading point he was headed for, perhaps outside of Hong Kong's territorial waters.

It was so totally bizarre and great fun. I cannot recall who had out-sailed who, before we reached our own destination at Little Sai Wan. It did not really matter. Suffice to say, we had got a huge buzz out of our 'race' through the beautiful straits between Hong Kong Island and the New Territories, and so, no doubt, had the Chinese sailors aboard the junk. Even if they had been fitted with an engine, they had not used it, and it was sail against sail all the way.

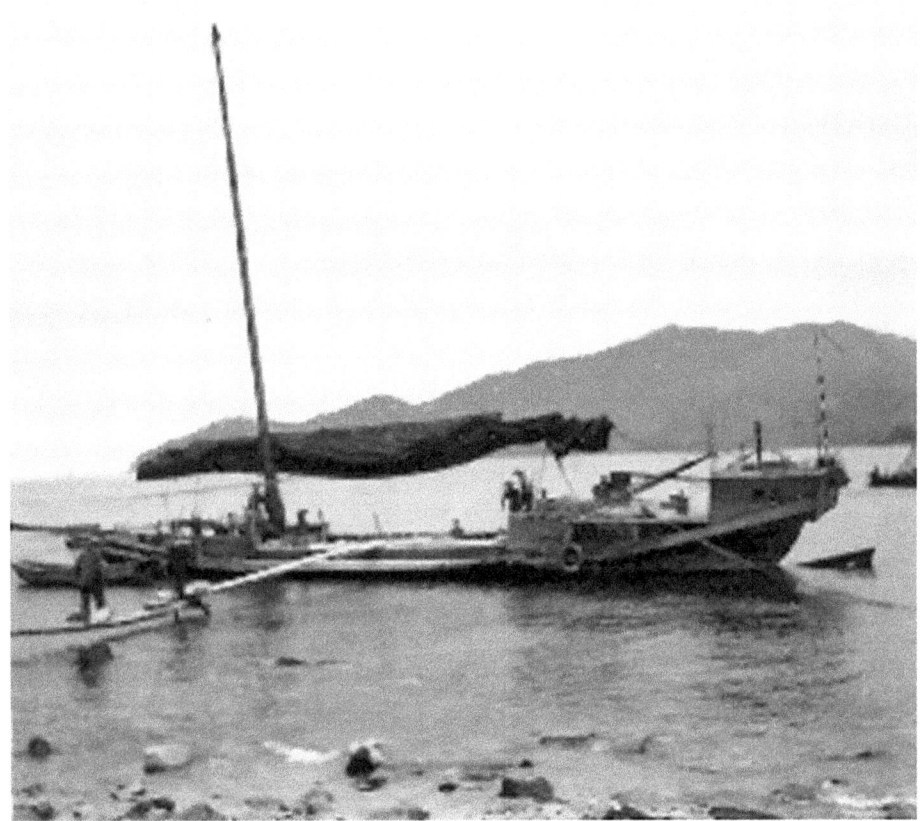

Junk being loaded or offloaded at a makeshift harbour, somewhere away from the main harbour of Victoria. What was happening in this picture who can tell, but the vessel had been loaded almost to the waterline.

Hong Kong's Last Junk Builders

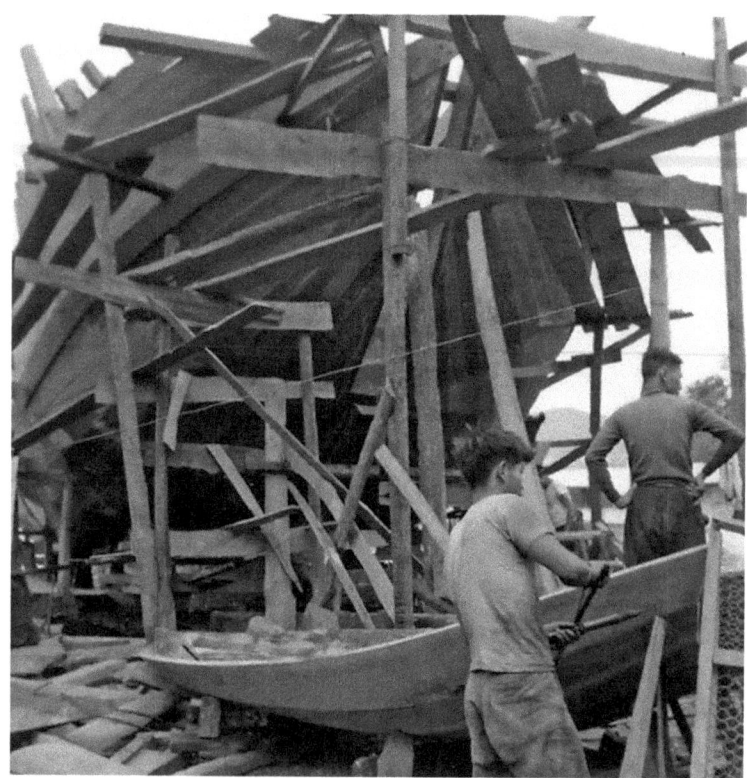

Carpenters at Work Sawing the Planks – Top Dog and Under Dog (circa 1956 or 1957). Could this be the very last working junk to be built in Hong Kong before steel ships took over from them? Was the tourist boat 'Duckling', originally a shrimp boat, really the last Hong Kong working junk to be built? Or were these perhaps the very last photographs to be taken of a traditional working junk being built?

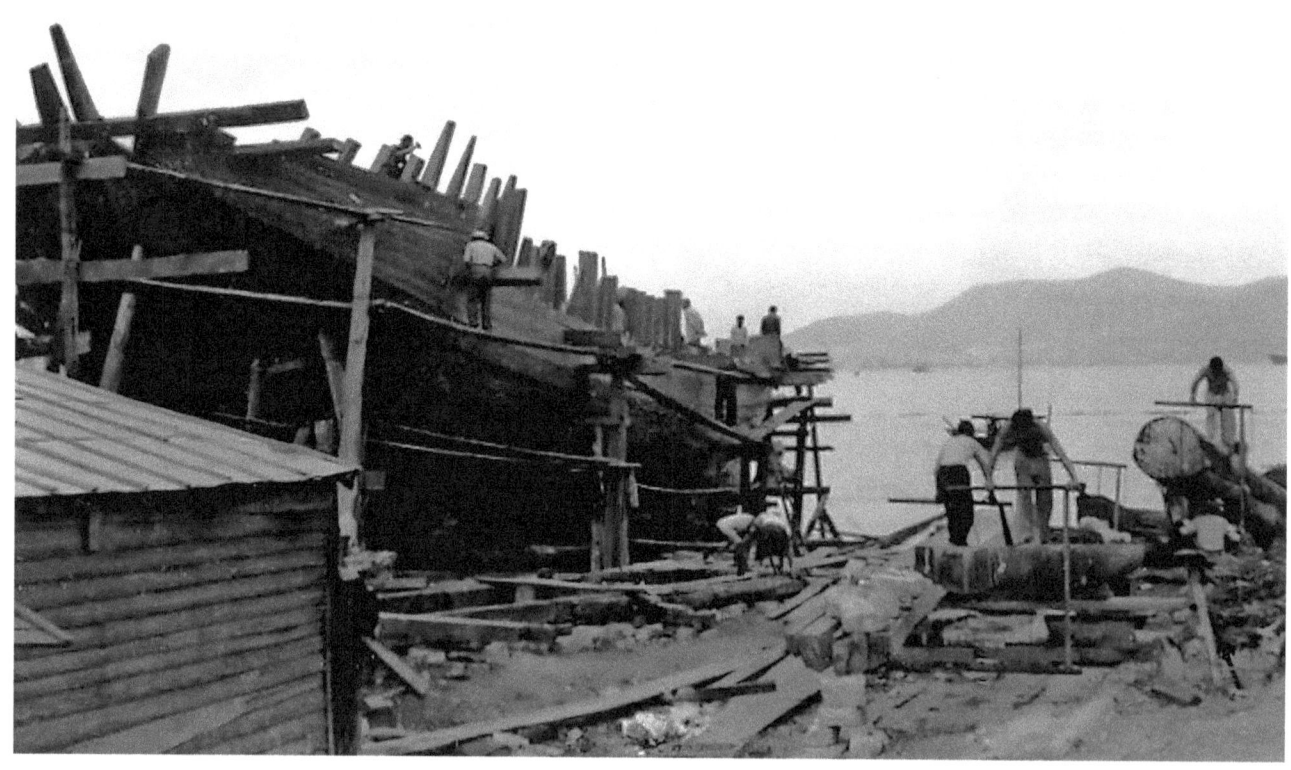

PRELUDE TO CHANGE: HONG KONG OF THE 1950S

Hong Kong in Glorious Colours

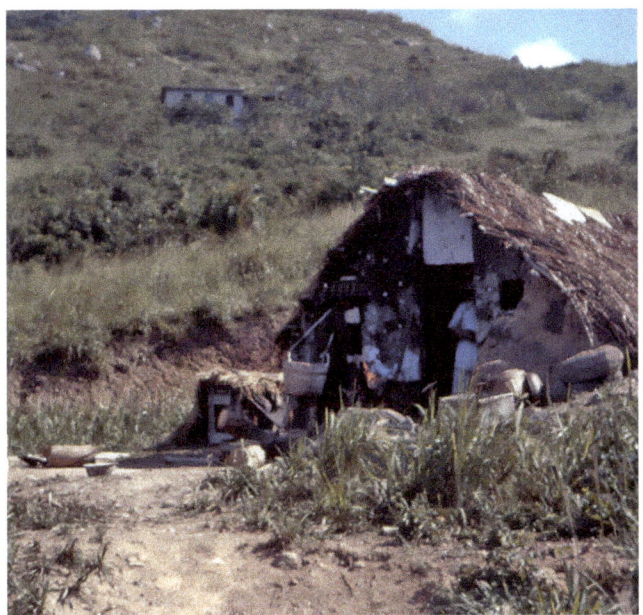
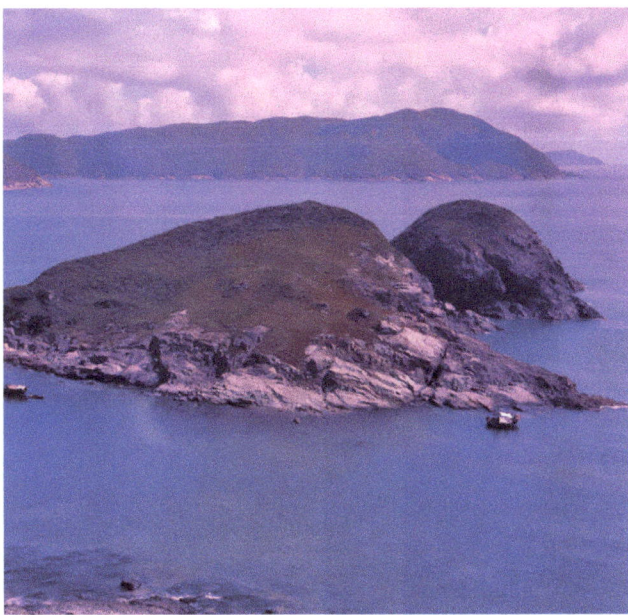
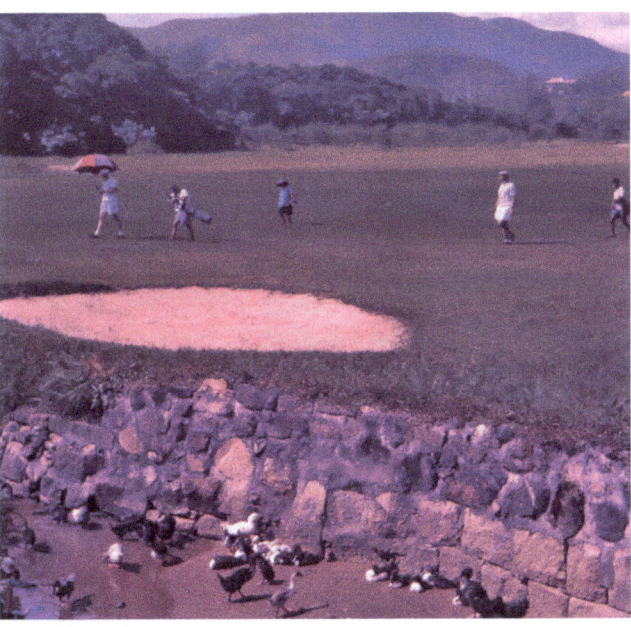
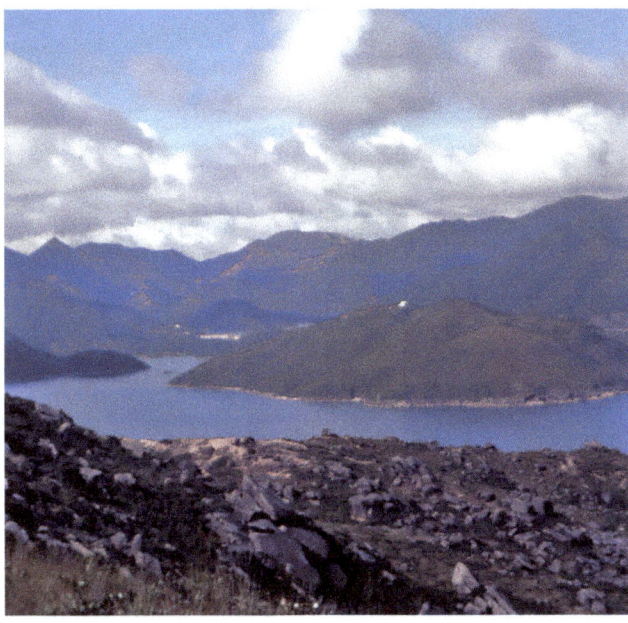

The lack of any air pollution in the 1950s rendered the beautiful island of Hong Kong a scenic paradise for a young amateur photographer out with his motorbike, looking for scenes to capture with his camera. These shots were originally taken as colour slides which were eventually scanned onto my computer.

Top left, we see the home of a 'hakka' woman. They cut grass, presumably to sell to farmers. They wore the traditional black 'pyjama suits' and had very wide-brimmed hats. Bottom left is a shot of the island's golf course. There were apparently no Chinese members – but they were allowed to work as caddies! On the right are two typically breathtaking seascapes.

Hong Kong of the 1950s had clear blue skies and a total lack of any air pollution, unlike its dangerously polluted air of today. This once so colourful enclave on the southern coast of mainland China has since paid a high price for the development that followed the 1950s. Sadly, fumes from power stations and the engines of cars, trucks and ships have changed its stunning natural beauty in ways that are now lost.

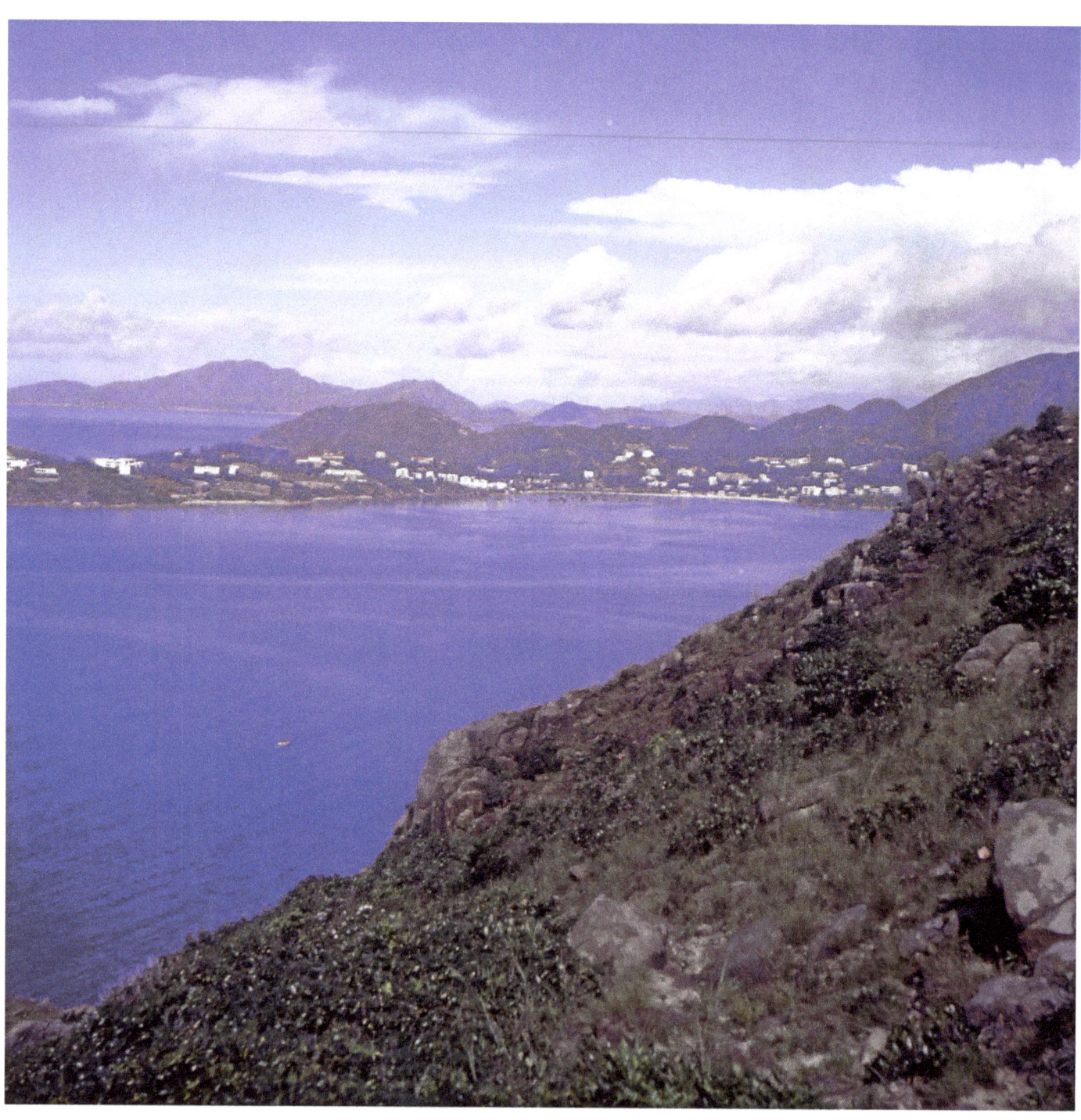

PRELUDE TO CHANGE: HONG KONG OF THE 1950S

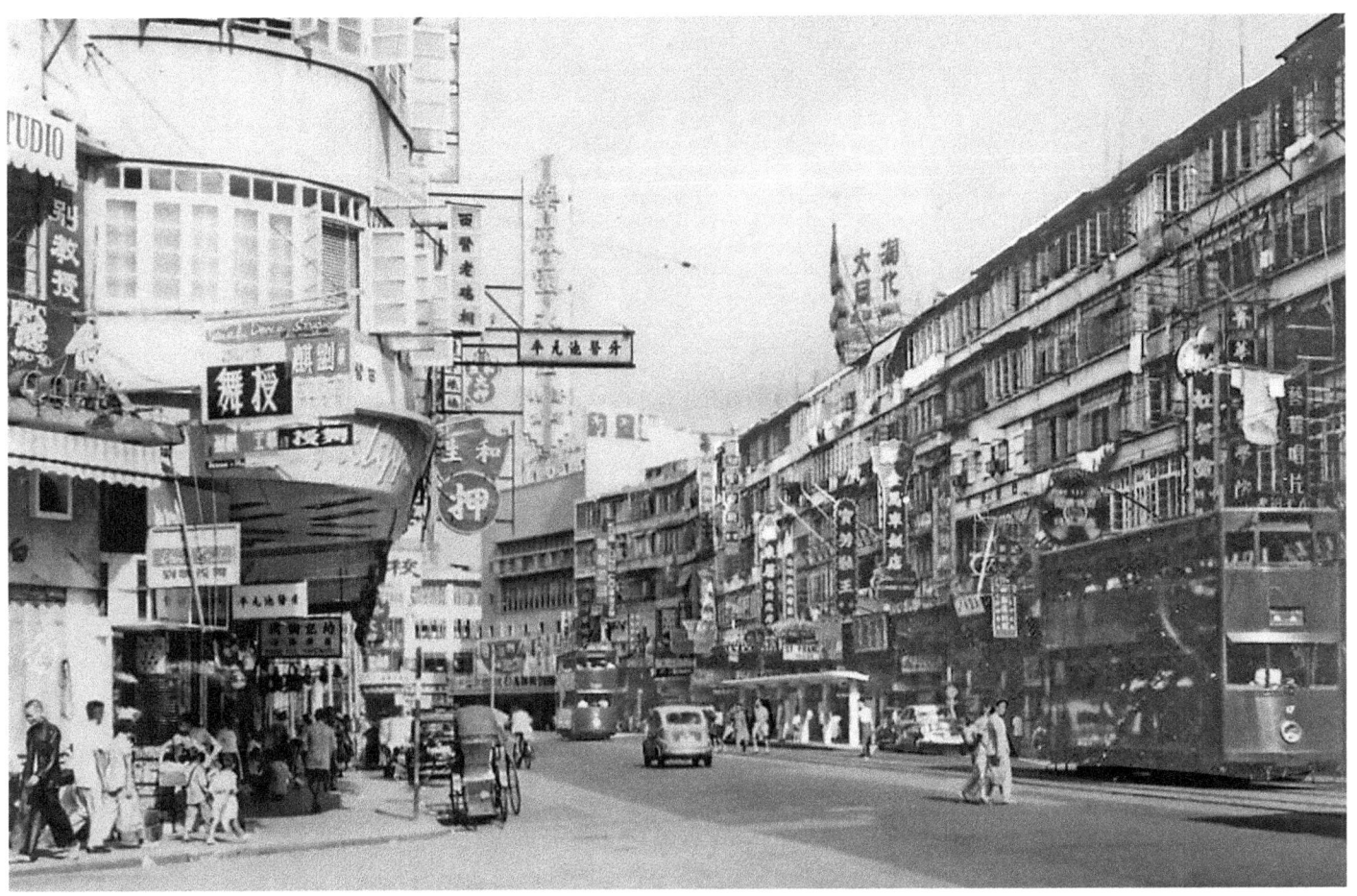

Typical 1950s Hong Kong street scene including tram cars and a rickshaw in the foreground.

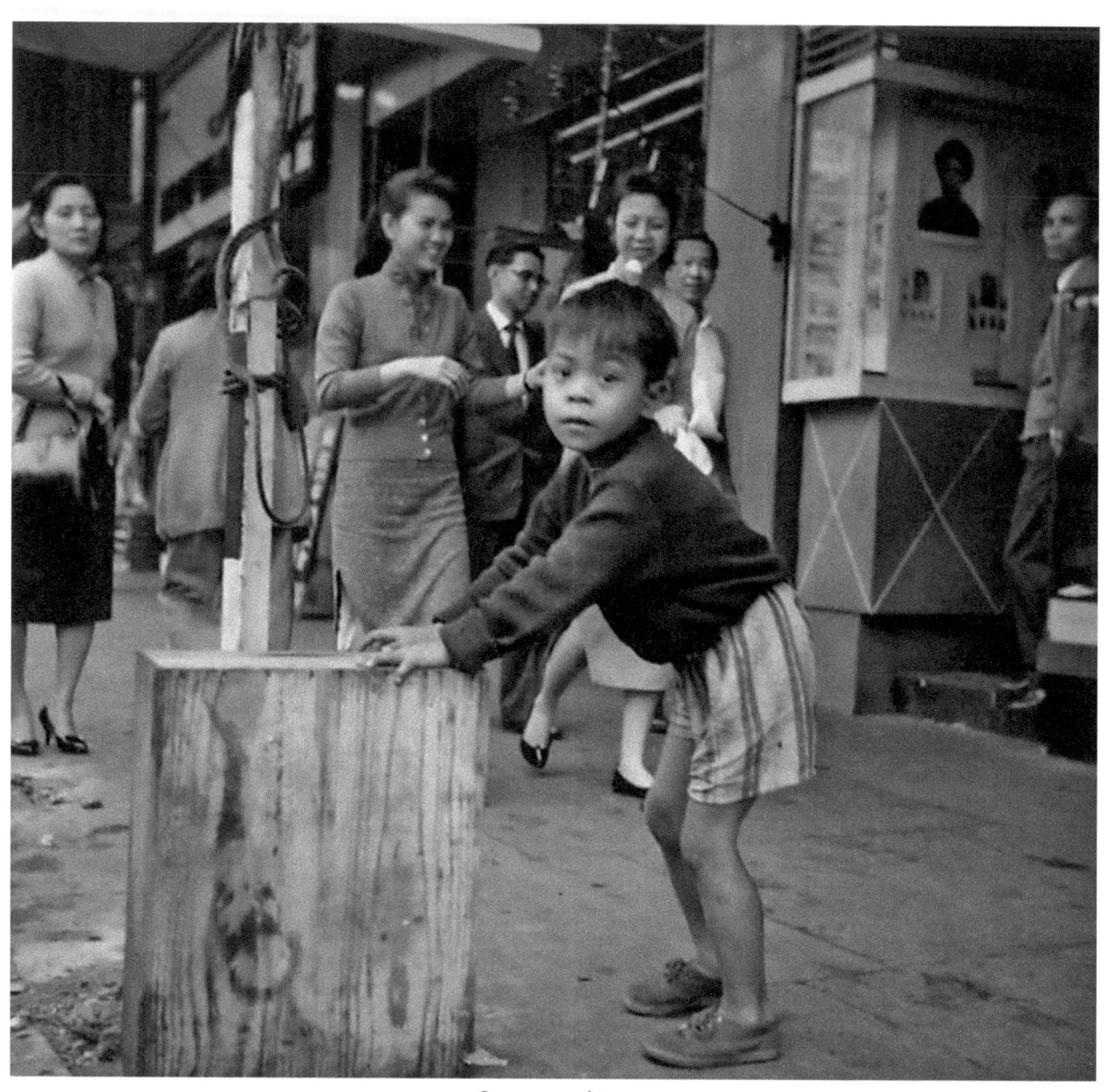

Street urchin.
Note also ladies wearing the traditional cheongsam.

PRELUDE TO CHANGE: HONG KONG OF THE 1950S

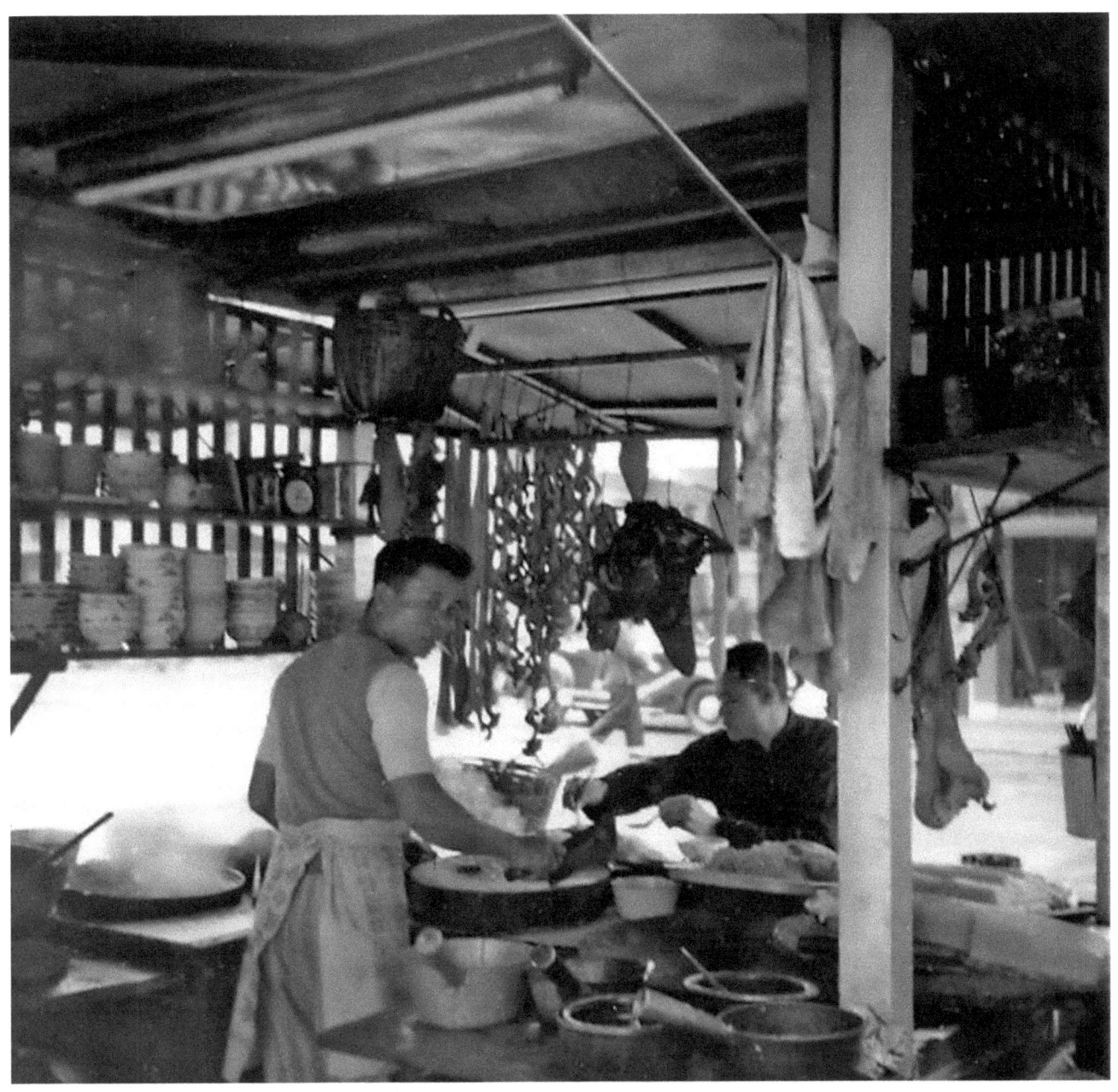

Chow stall owner and customer.
The Wanchai chow stalls were not only a good place to find and eat authentic Chinese food but also during the late evening to gather and chat to other servicemen, including visiting sailors off American warships.

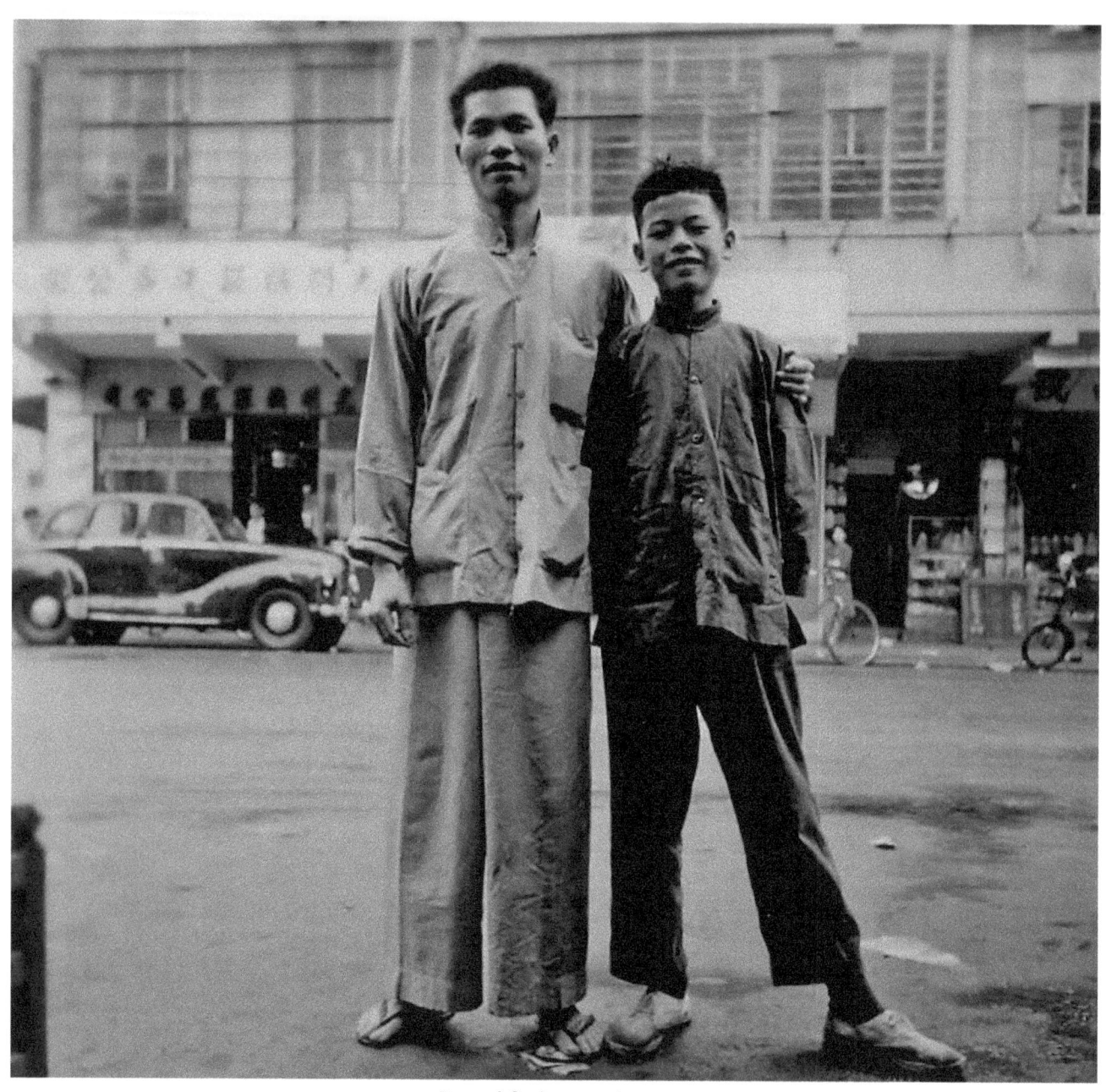

Proud father and son

PRELUDE TO CHANGE: HONG KONG OF THE 1950S

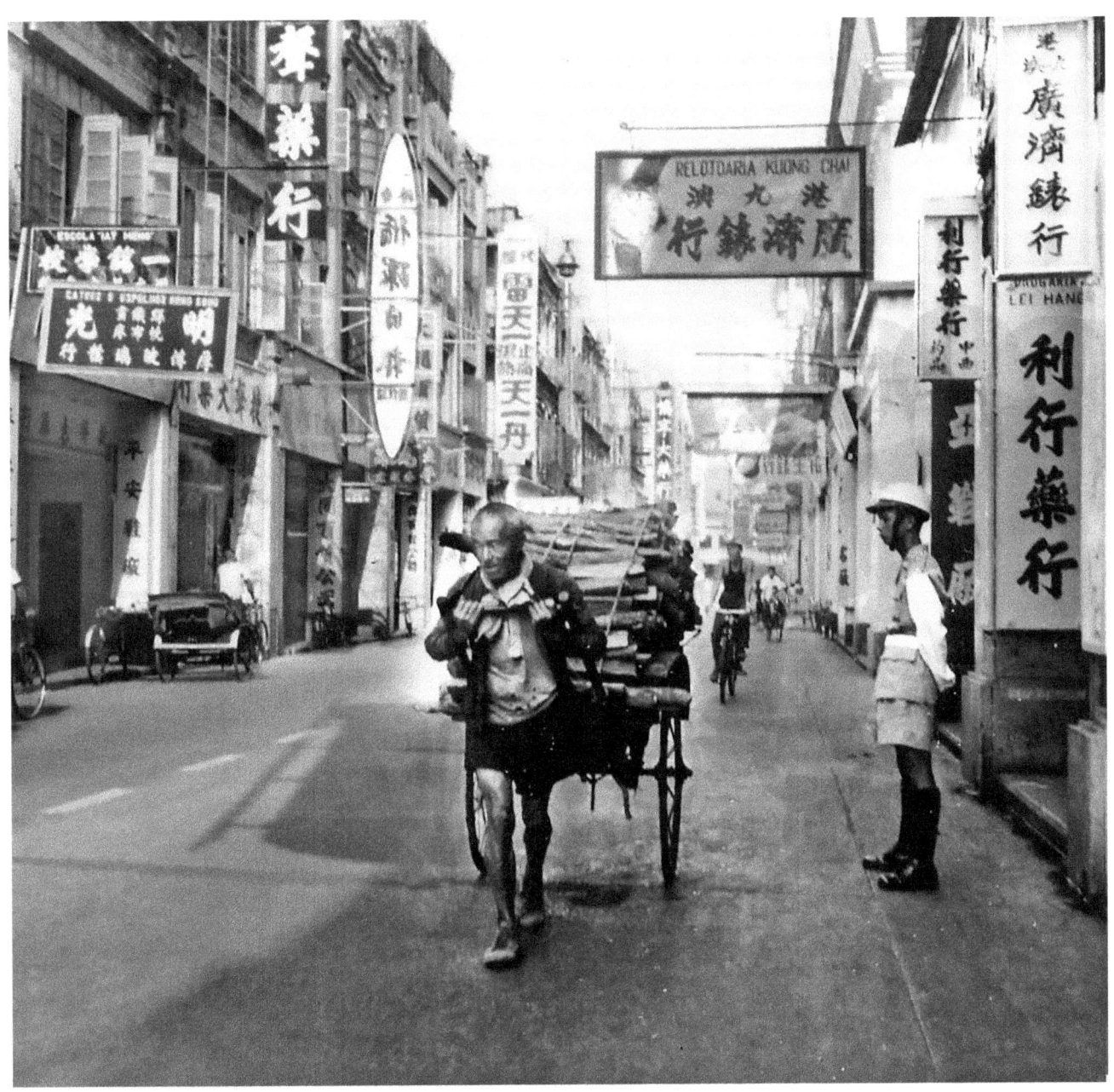

Rickshaw man pulling a load of what appears to be firewood. It is hard to guess his age, but doing such hard work would, I believe, have aged him a lot quicker than a less demanding way of earning a living. In stark contrast stands a British trained police constable doing a markedly less strenuous job.

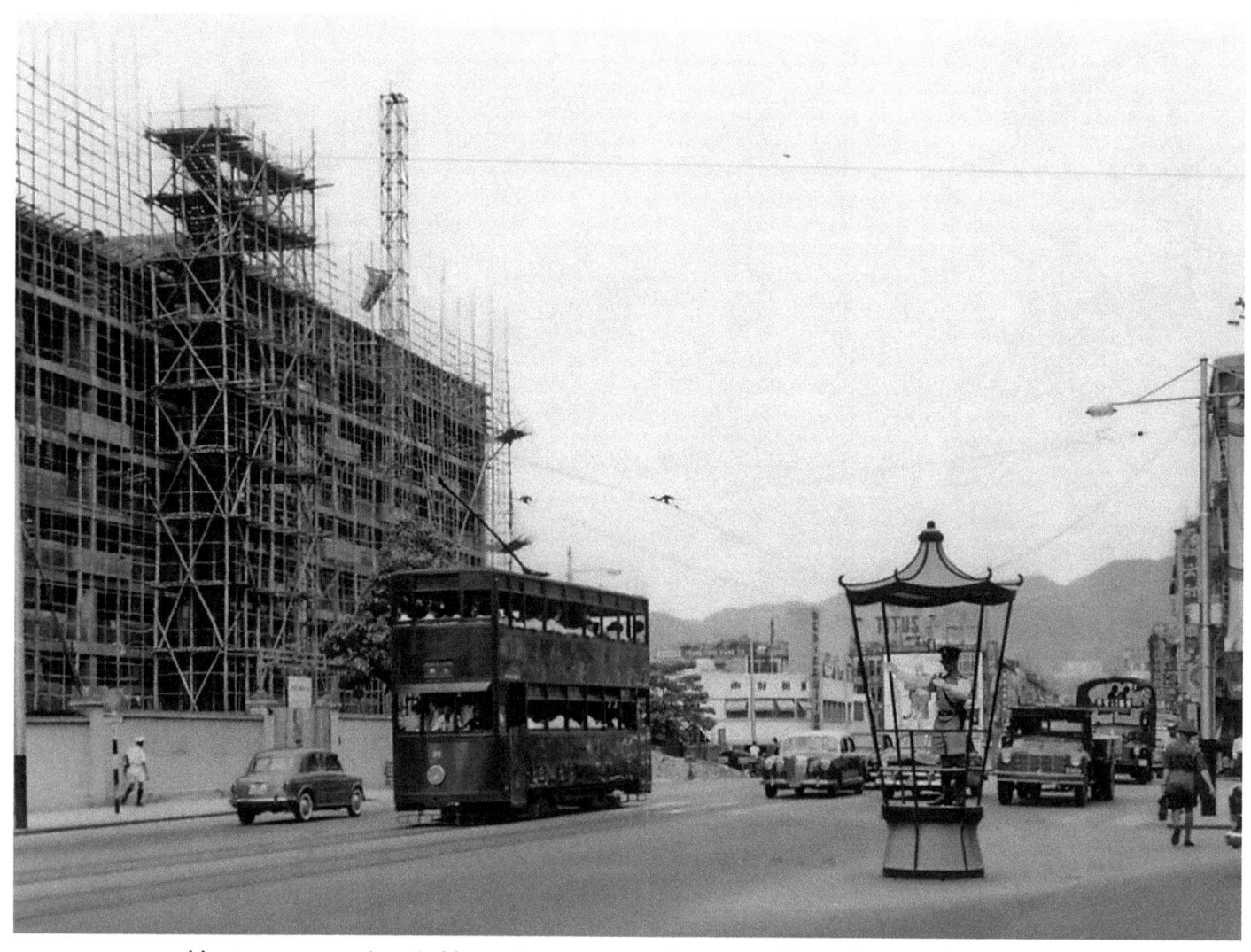

Here we see an iconic Hong Kong tram and a smart Hong Kong policeman on traffic control. The British way of politely queueing to get on a tram never really caught on in Hong Kong. It was always a matter of simply crowding on. The scaffolding for the high-rise building under construction was all composed of bamboo poles lashed together, as was the custom (and still is).

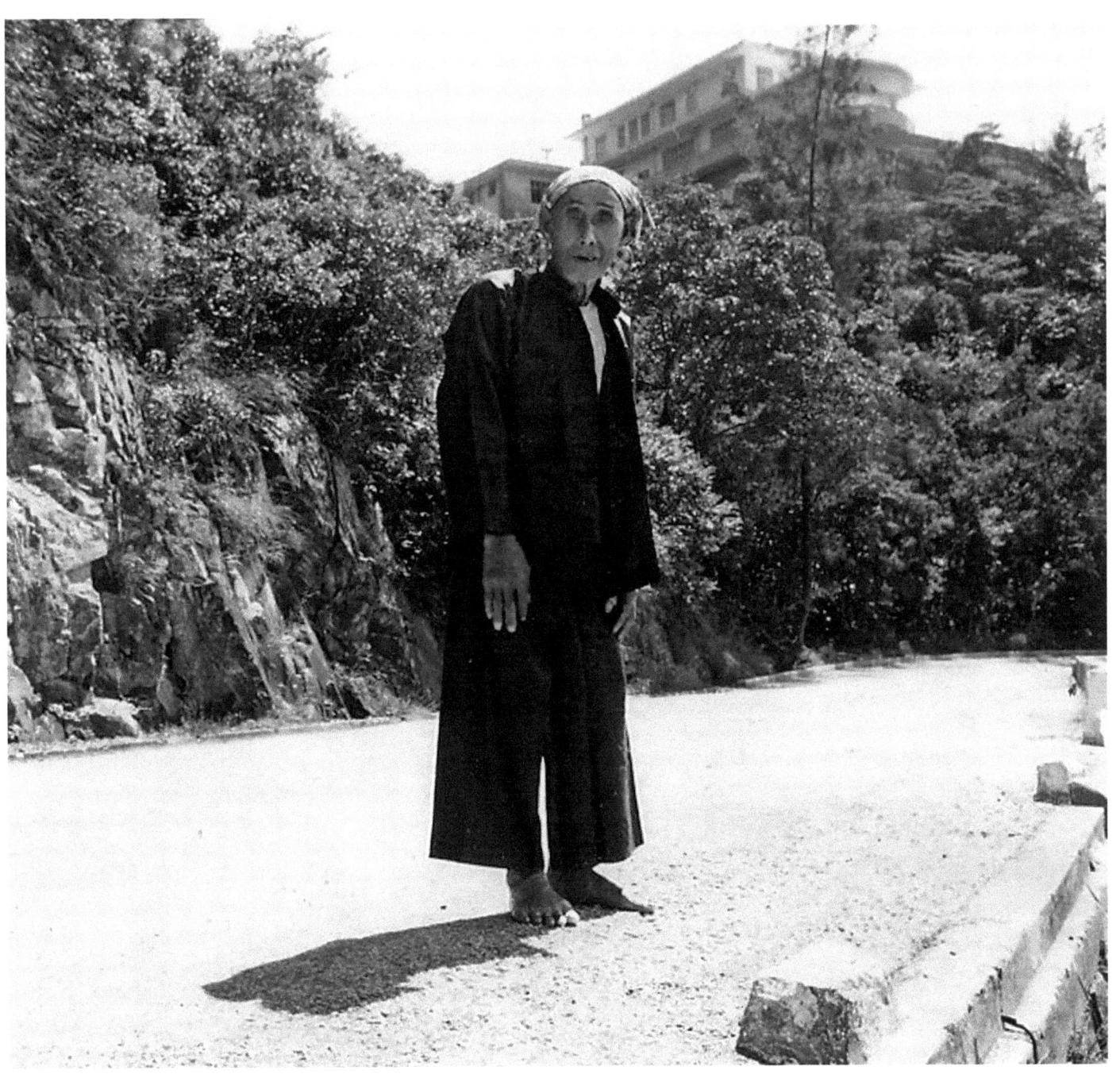

I reasoned that as this old man had taken the trouble to pose for me
to take his photograph, he deserved a whole page to himself.

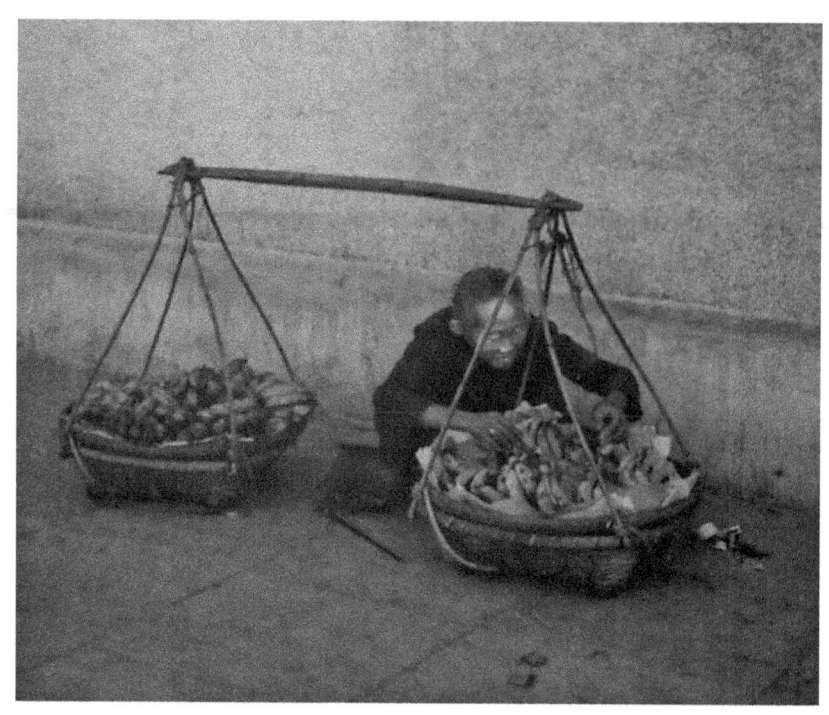

Street traders

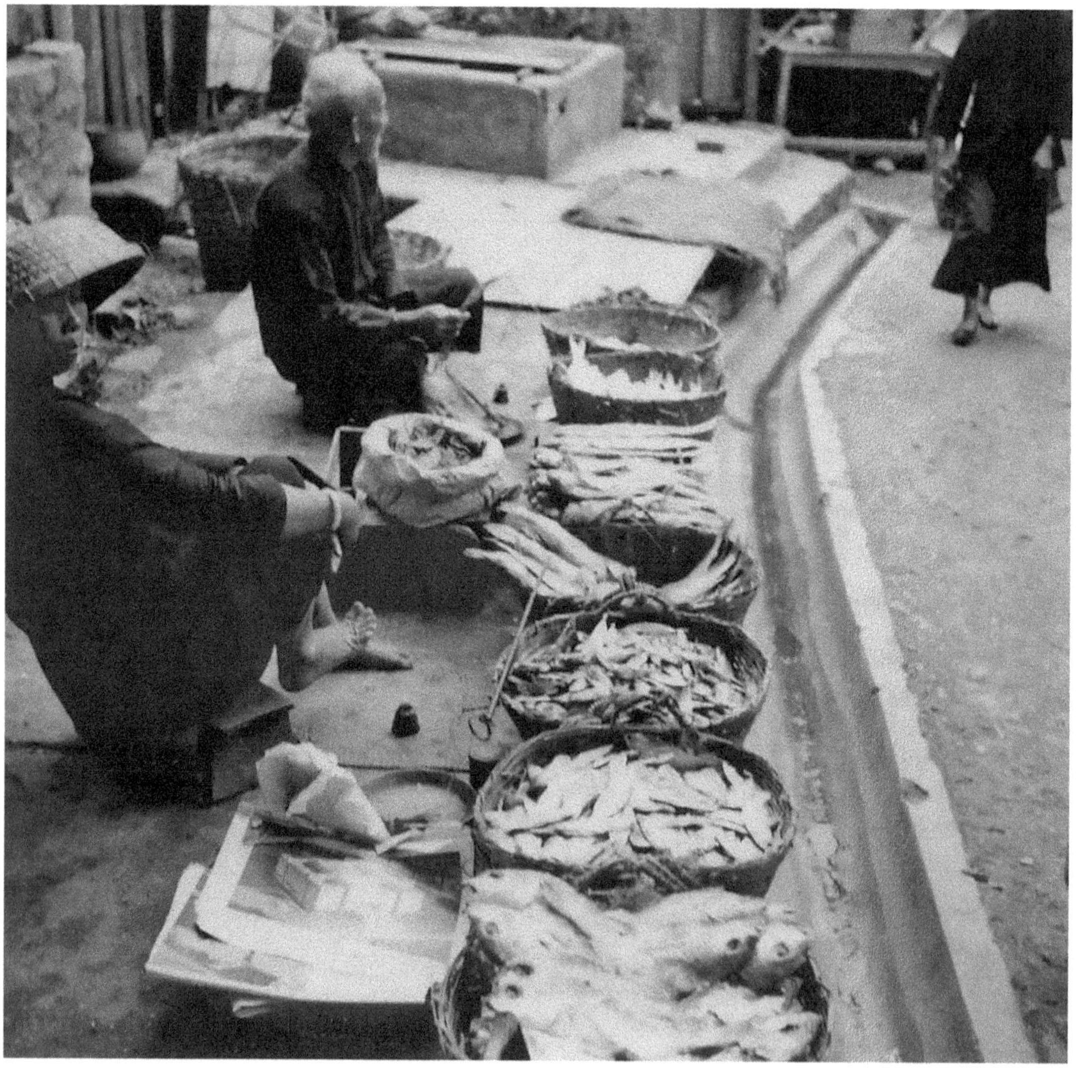

        PRELUDE TO CHANGE: HONG KONG OF THE 1950S

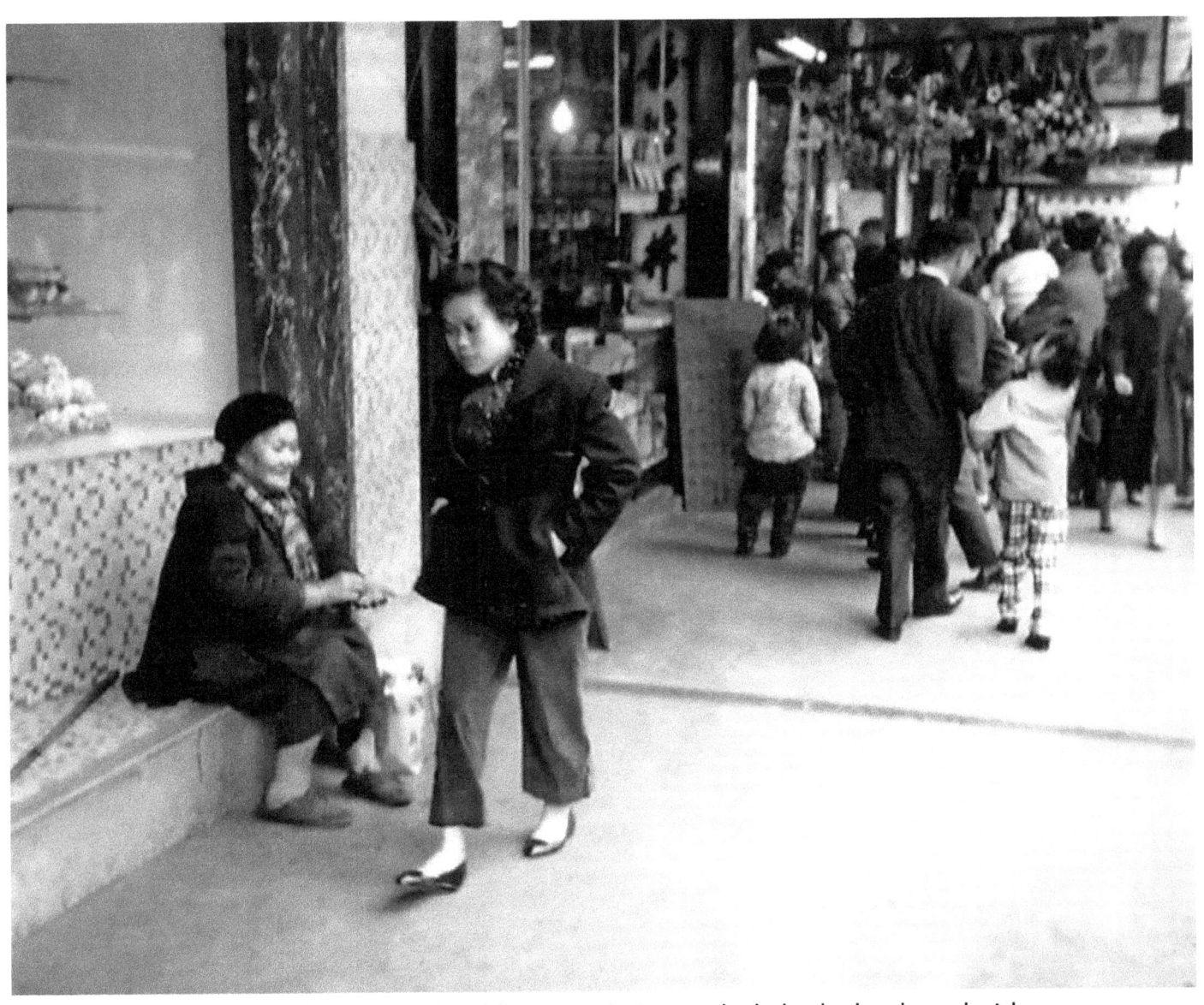

A picture that tells a story: the old woman sitting on the ledge looks pleased with some money she has just received. My guess is that the more affluent man with his little girl on his arm stopped to give the old lady some money, and his little girl is perhaps recalling the conversation that they had with her. Begging was very common in the 1950s and usually involved small, ragged boys sent out to beg by their parents. It was yet another sign of the more affluent Hong Kong side by side with the impoverished.

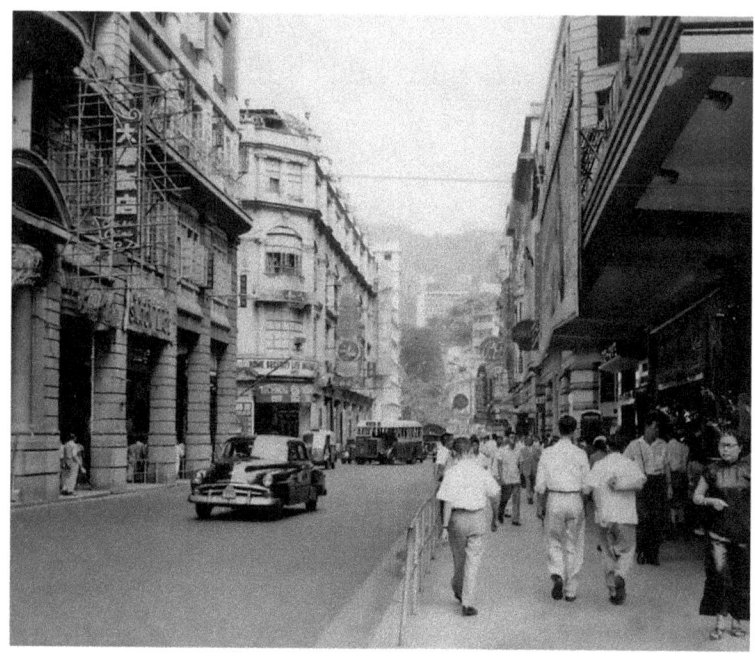

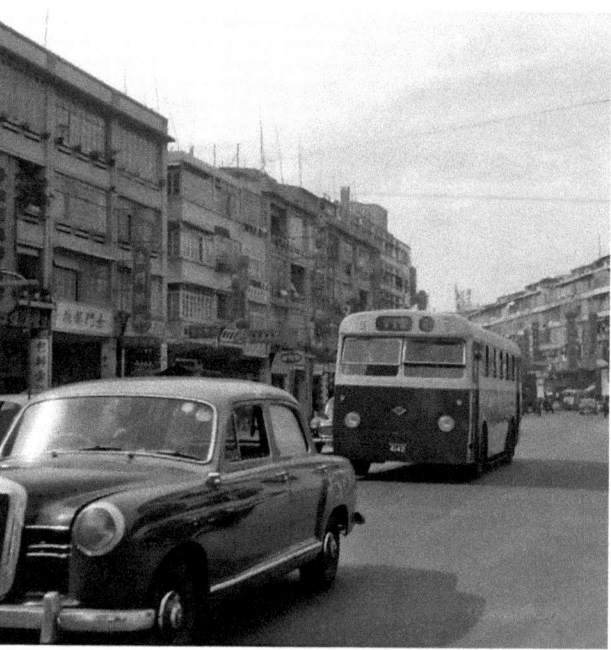

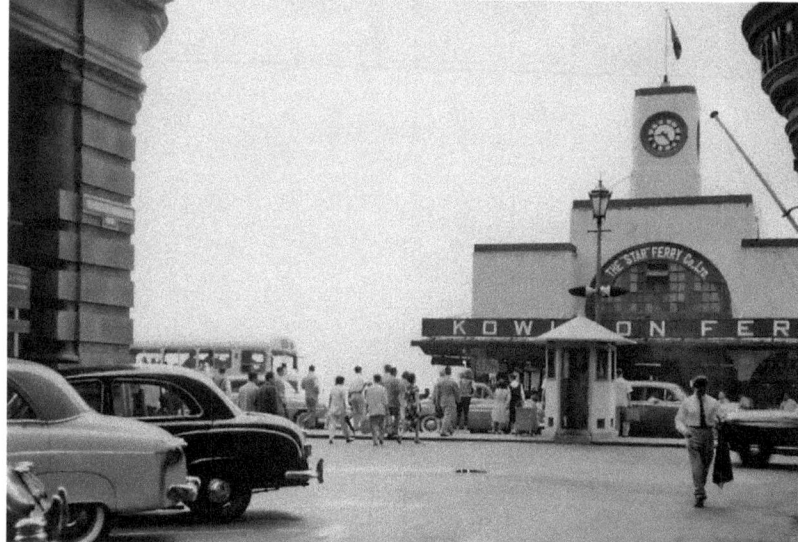

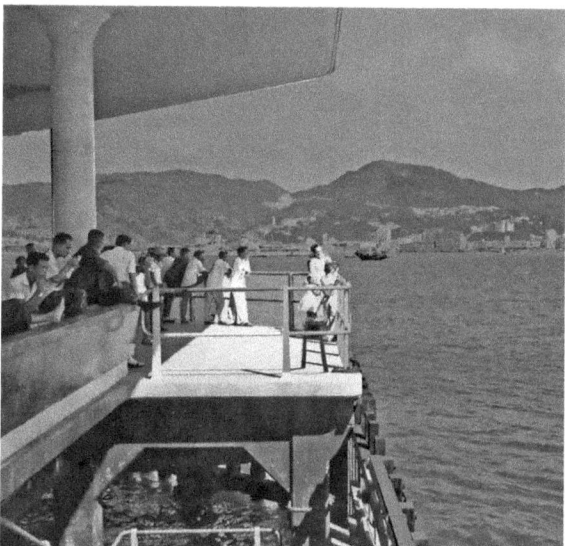

Passengers for the Star Ferry.

PRELUDE TO CHANGE: HONG KONG OF THE 1950S

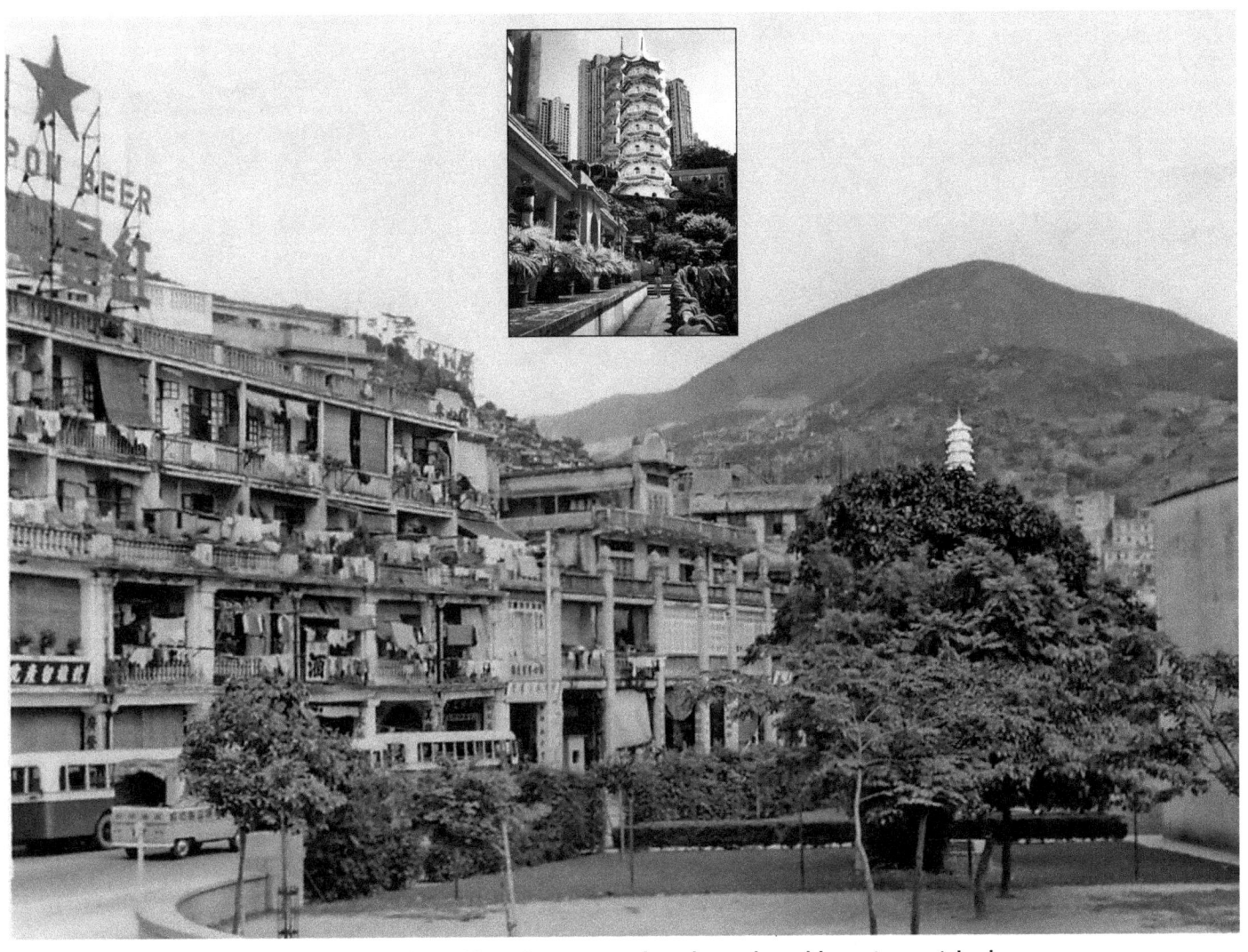

Main picture: Hong Kong's cramped and outdated housing, with the
iconic pagoda at the Tiger Balm Gardens in the distance.
Inset: library image of the pagoda prior to demolition for redevelopment in 2004.

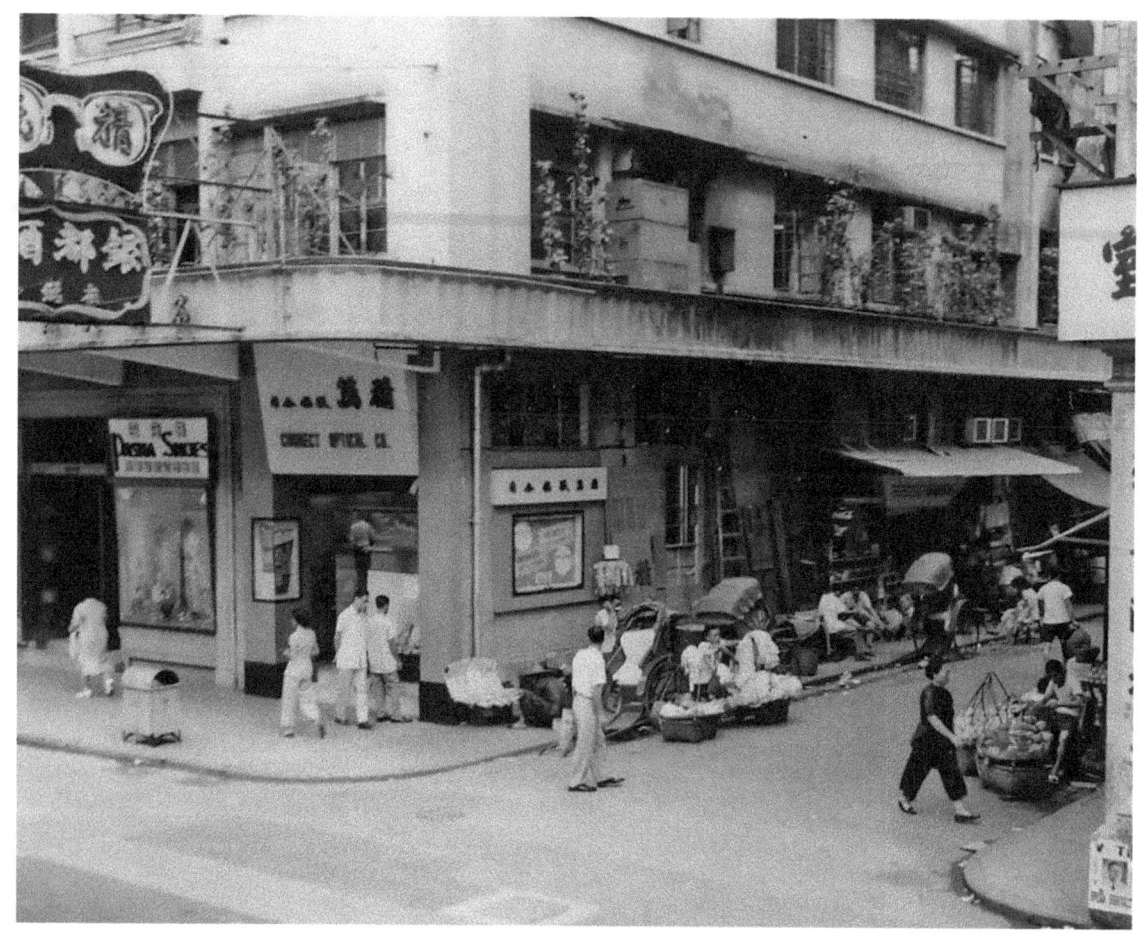

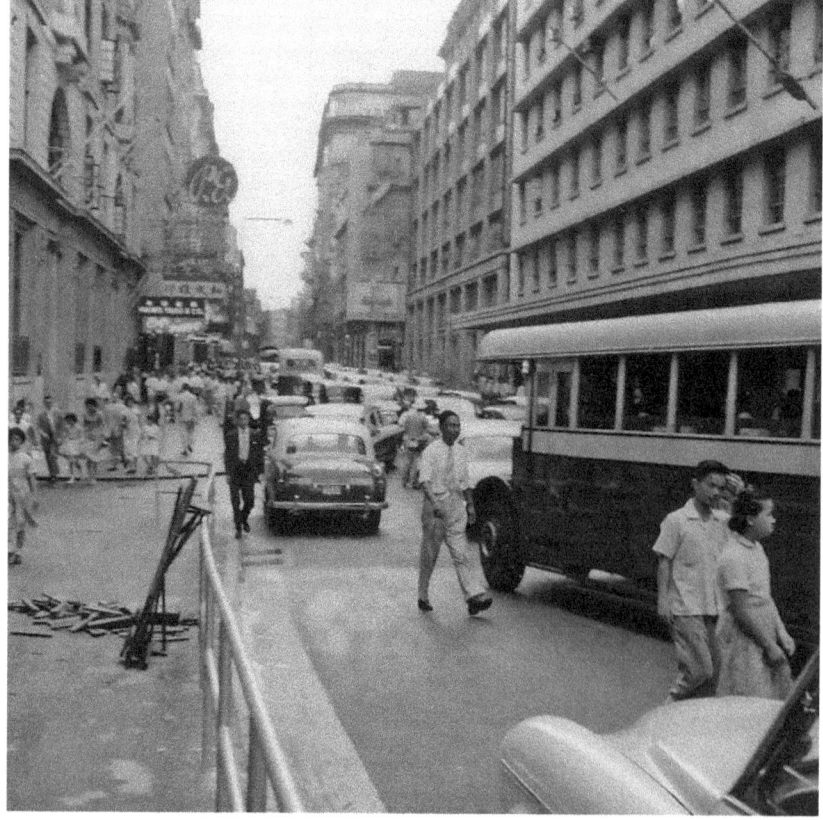

Hong Kong's streets were ever-bustling and ever-interesting, giving notice that its people, though often very poor, had the energy and commitment needed to one day turn this extraordinary place into one of the most affluent and enterprising centres of world commerce.

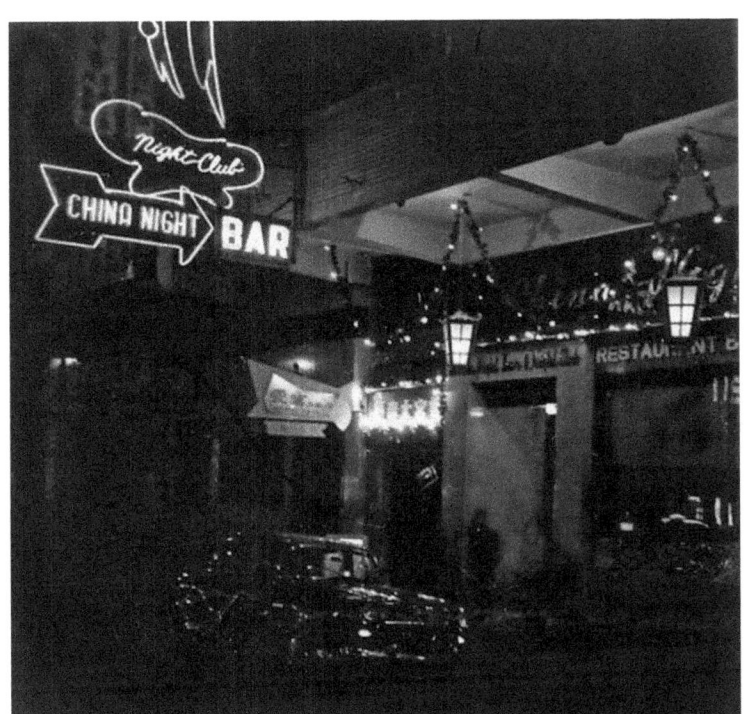

Left: "The World of Suzie Wong", one of Hong Kong's many bars
Below: Side by side with the poverty were the bright lights of a city undergoing change.

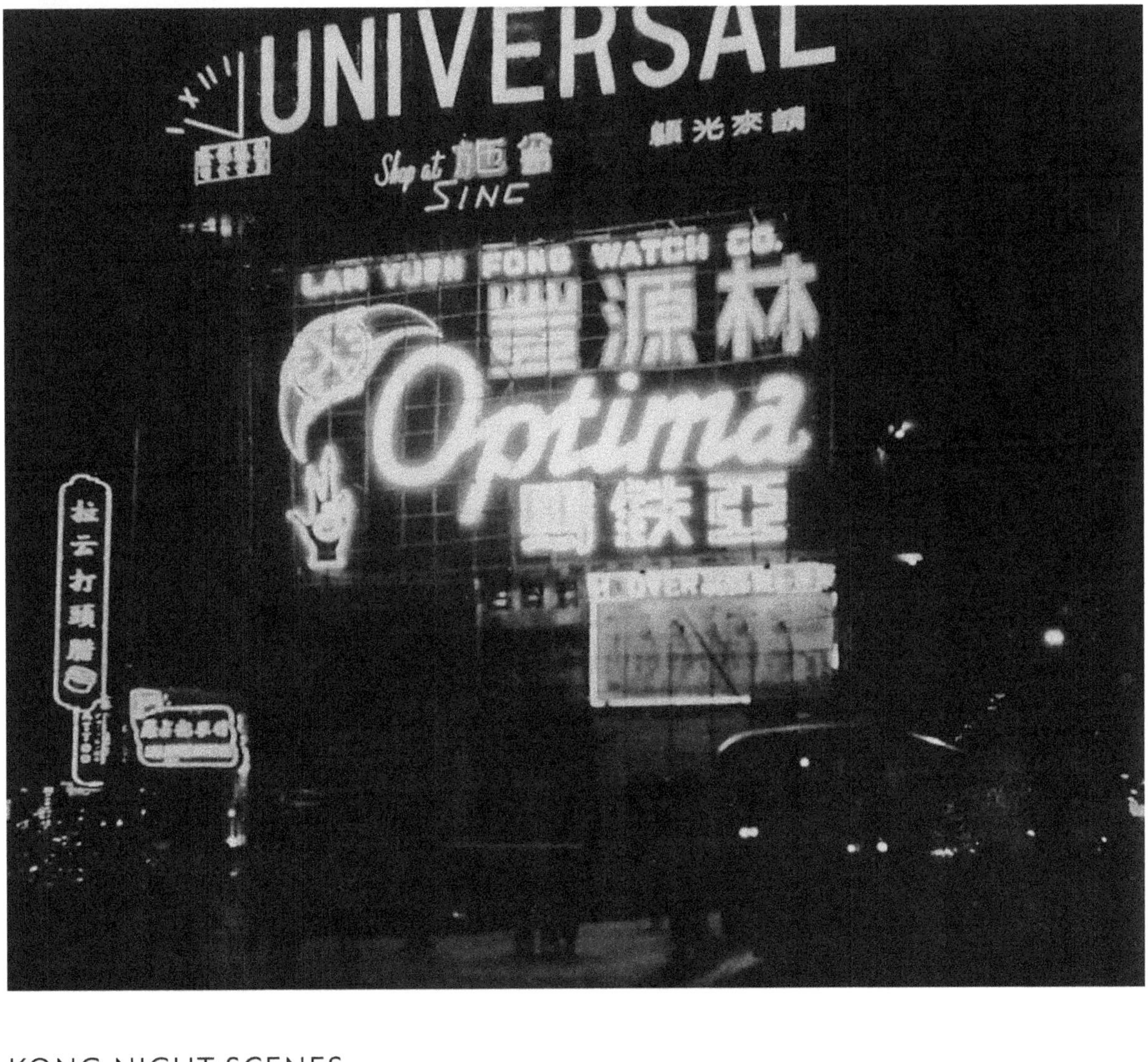

Coastal Scenes

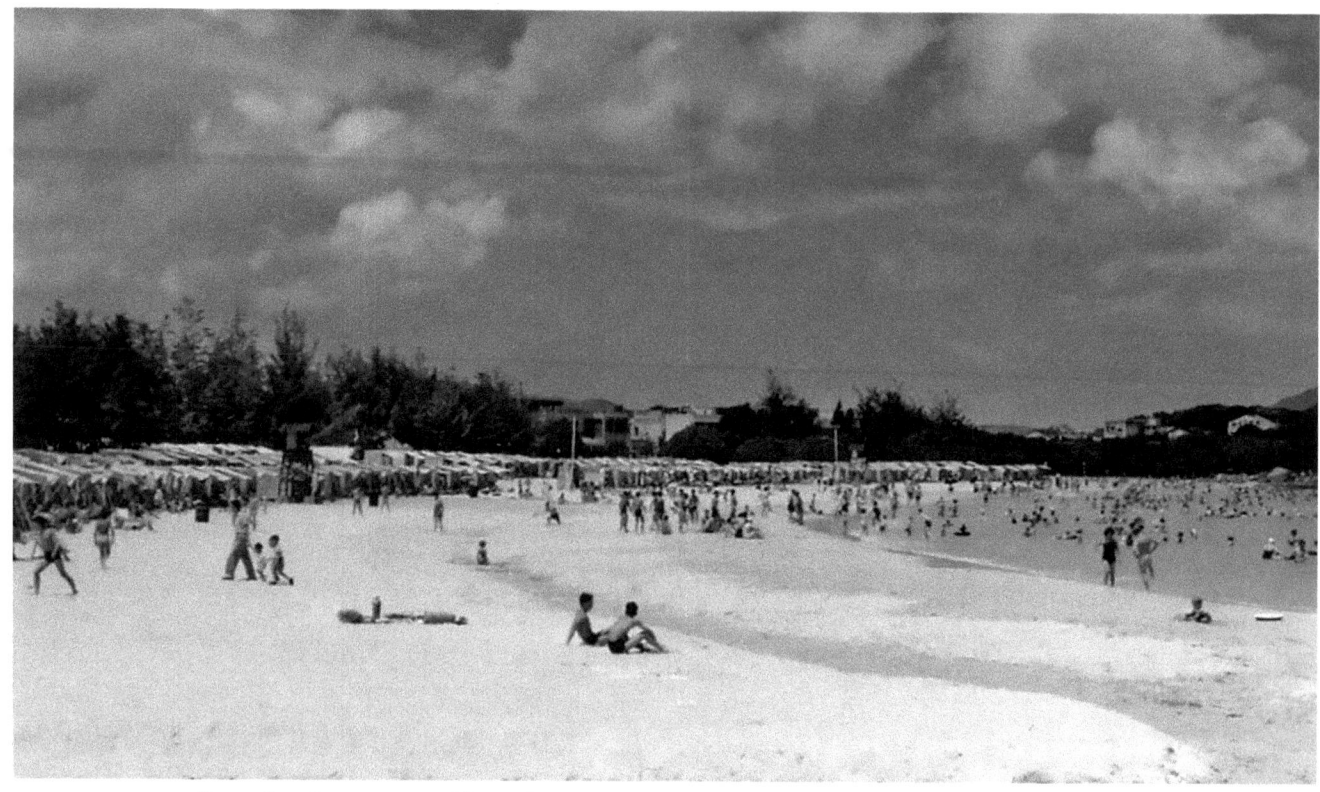

Repulse Bay: typical beach scene where the Europeans tended to like to swim and sunbathe and Chinese citizens of Hong Kong tended to stay out of the sun and play very noisy and exited games of Mah-jong.

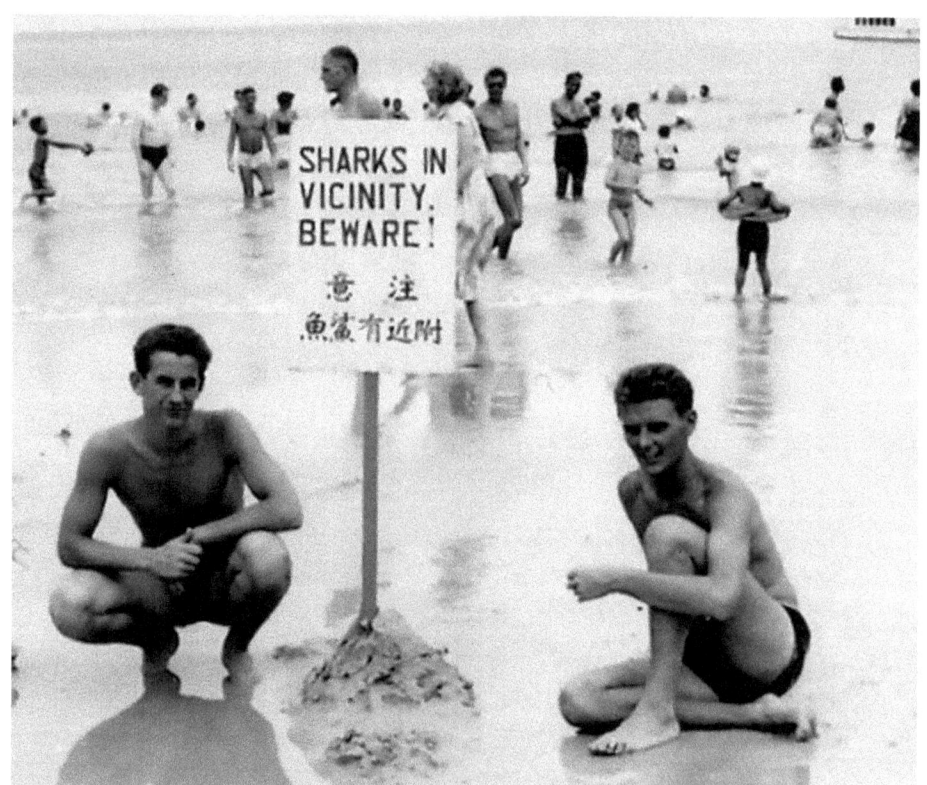

Yours truly on the left with my pal Neville at Big Wave Bay. Never did see any sharks.

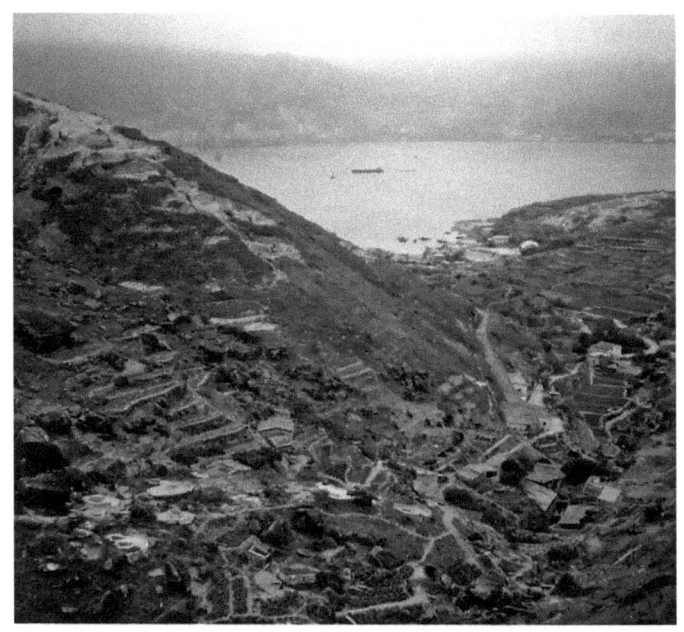

From our narrow road to camp, cut into the side of a mountain, we could look down onto small holdings stepped into the mountainside where perhaps pigs, fed on fish, would be bred. Our breakfast bacon tasted of fish! We had Australian operators working alongside of us and one morning when the orderly officer asked his perfunctory 'Any complaints?', an Australian voice piped up just after he had passed his table with 'Yeah – the bacon's lousy!' Which of course was quite true.

Big Wave Bay was RAF Little Sai Wan's camp playground. It was an energetic but enjoyable walk up and over the foothill of a mountain. It could also be accessed by road. We would regularly take a football over for a kick about, buy soft drinks at a beach bar, swim out to one of the rafts anchored offshore and of course sunbathe.

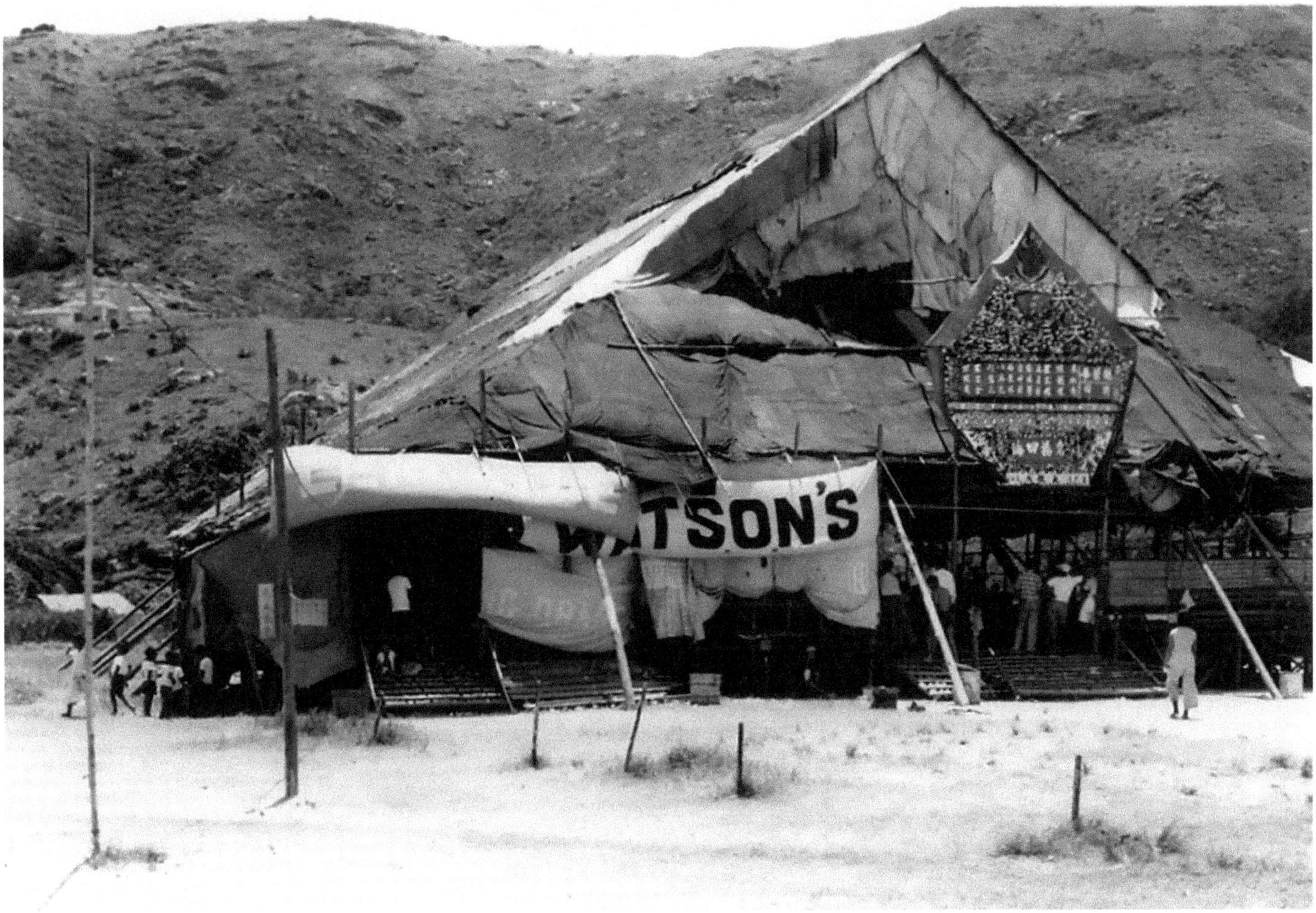

Travelling traditional Chinese theatre set up on the beach at Big Wave Bay.

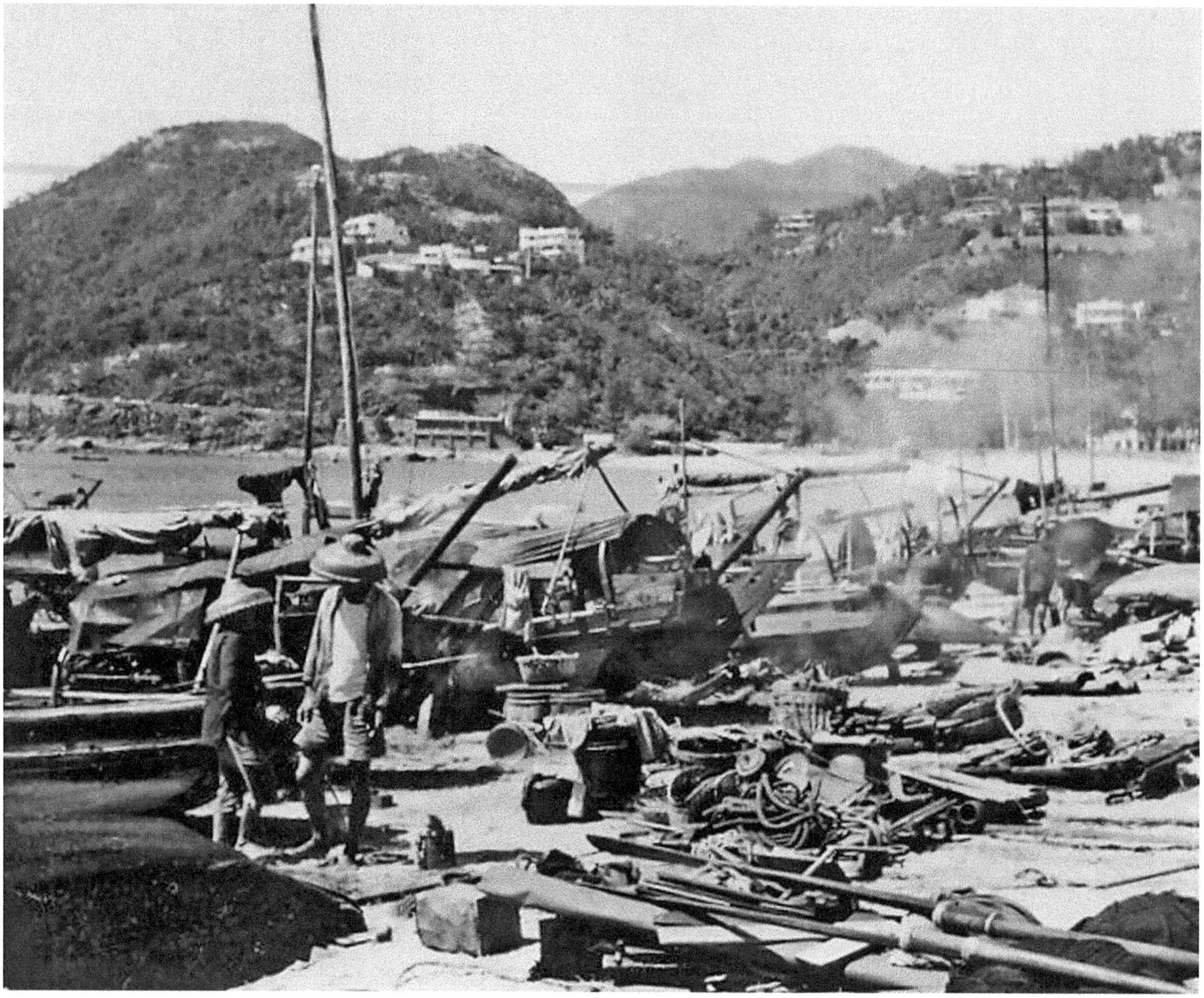

Aberdeen's Fisherman's Bay reeked of fish, and I would try to
hold my breath as I motorcycled round the bay.

With a group of us RAF lads, I visited the newly
opened Tai Pak floating restaurant at Aberdeen
Harbour in 1957. We sat round a circular table and
bowls of food were placed in the middle. Our strict
rule was to use only chopsticks to take food from
the middle. It was a case of learn to use chopsticks
or go hungry! I learnt very quickly!

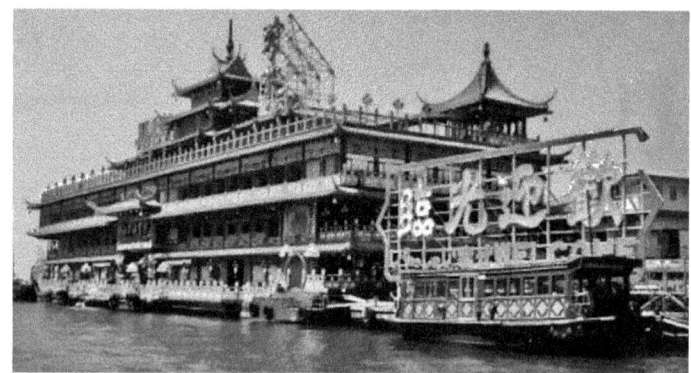

Tai Pak Floating Restaurant (library picture).

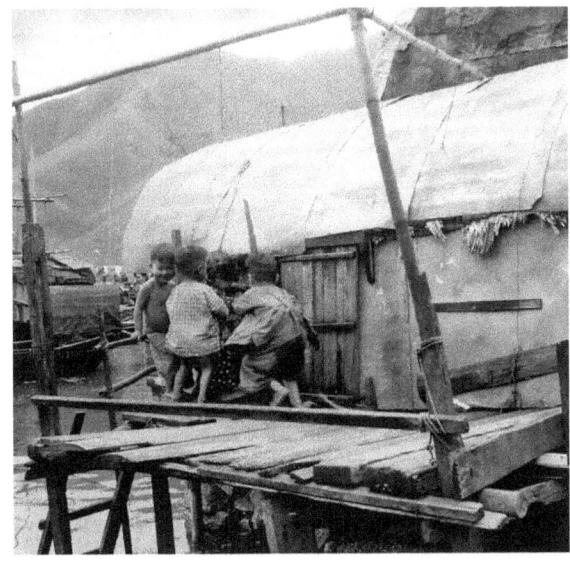
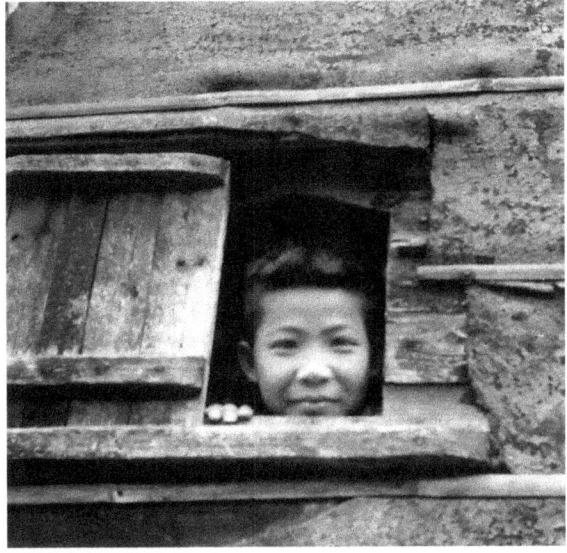
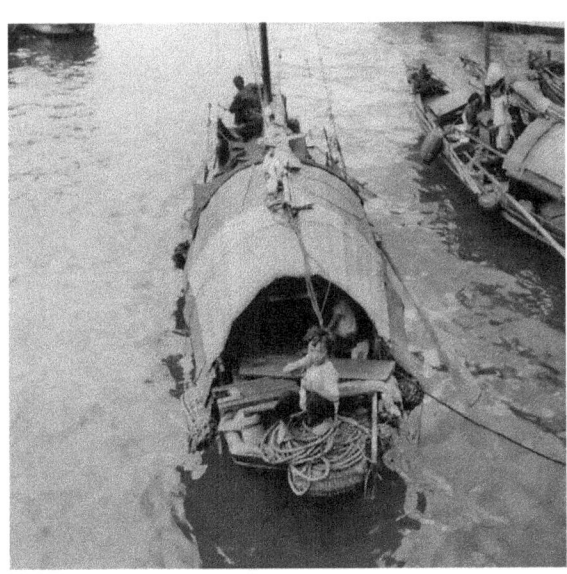
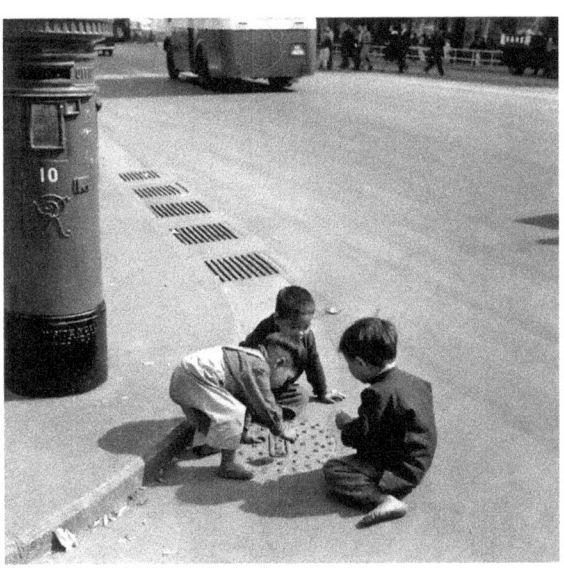
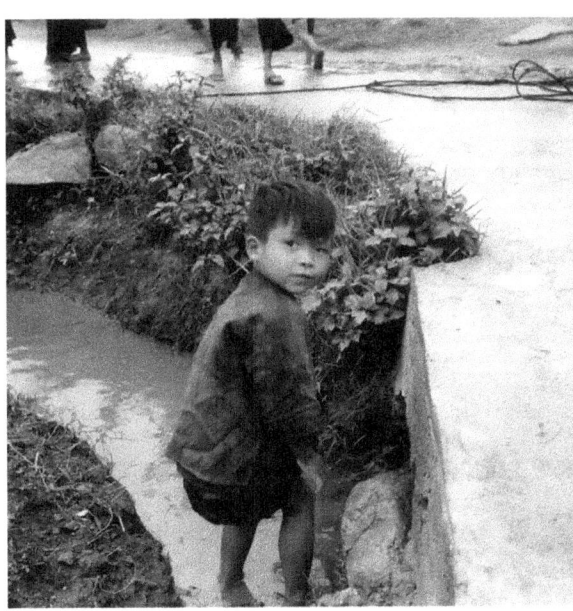
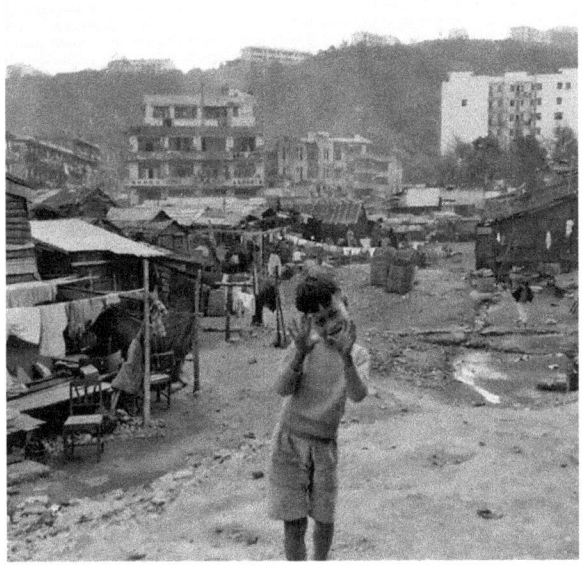

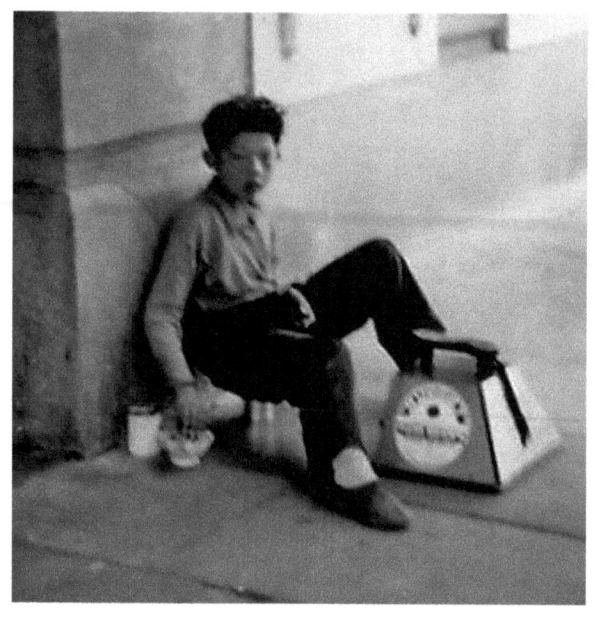
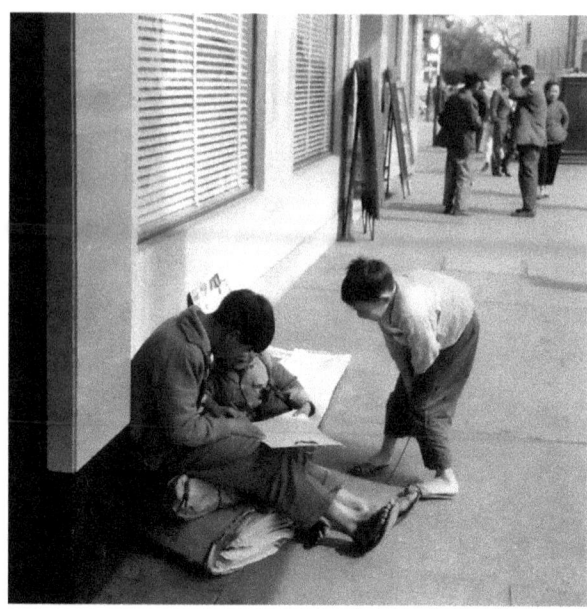
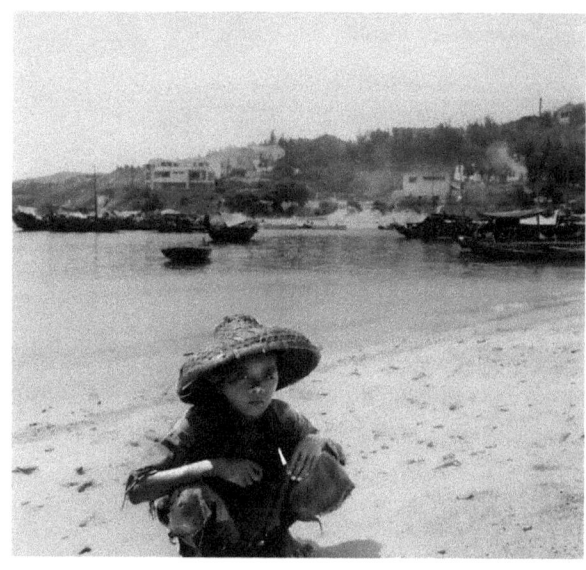
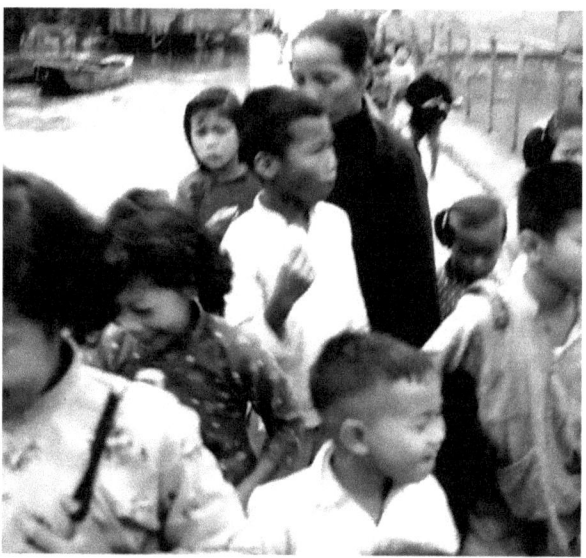
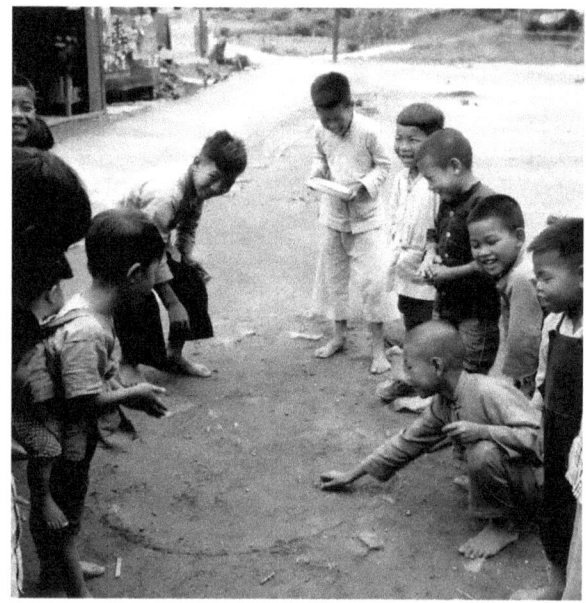
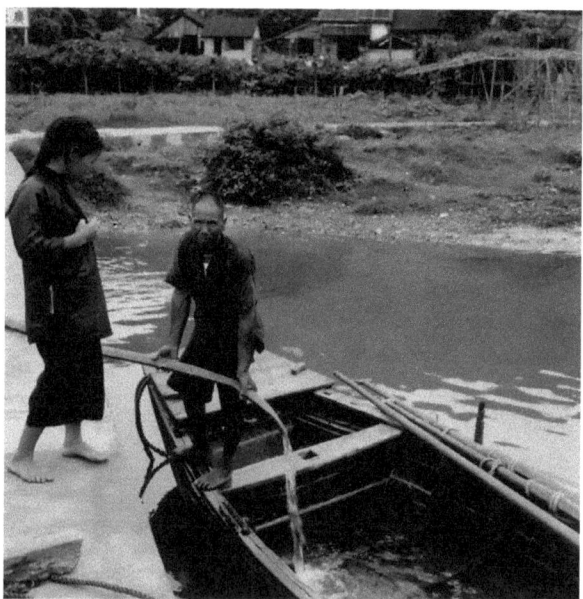

PRELUDE TO CHANGE: HONG KONG OF THE 1950S

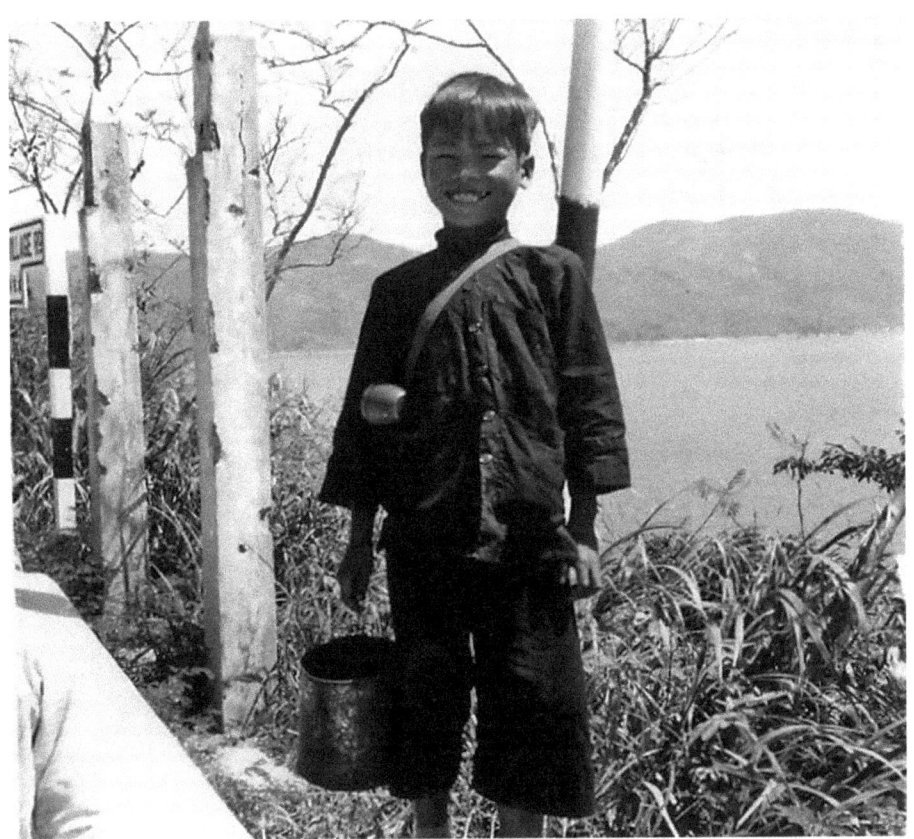

Young water carrier

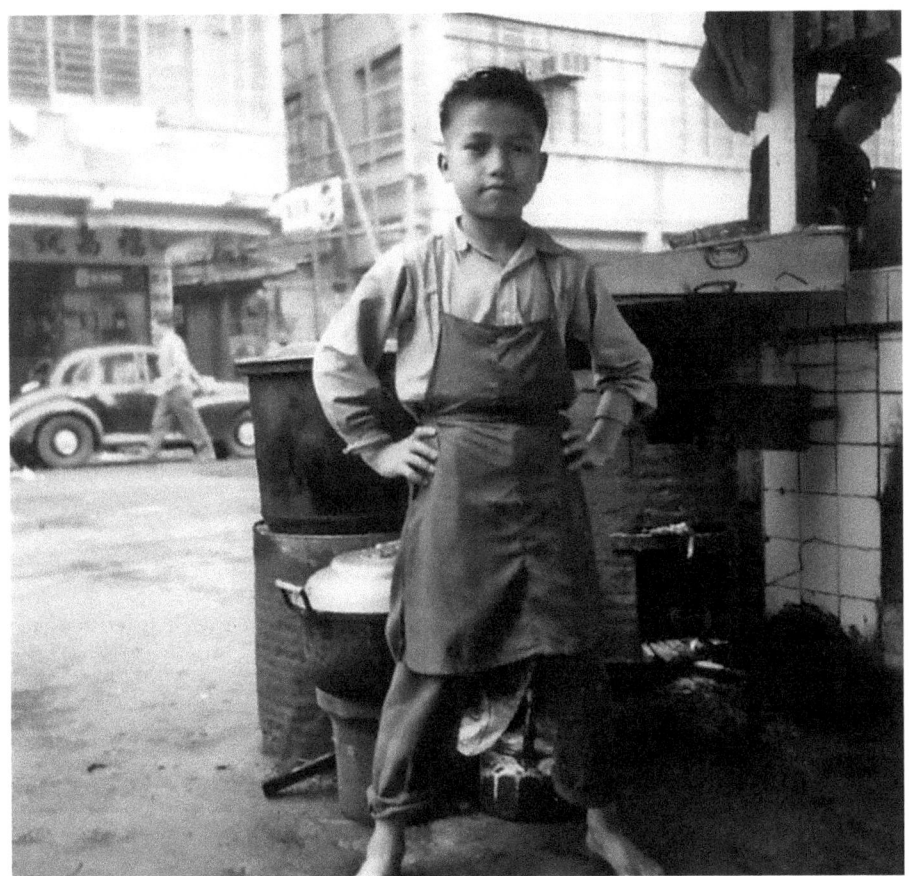

Young chow stall worker

Hong Kong at Work

These pictures look like some forms of food production. With the influx of many more people flooding into Hong Kong from over the border with Communist China, the Hong Kong government had the problem of trying to ensure sufficient employment and were therefore reluctant at that time to permit the importation of machines that would replace manual labour.

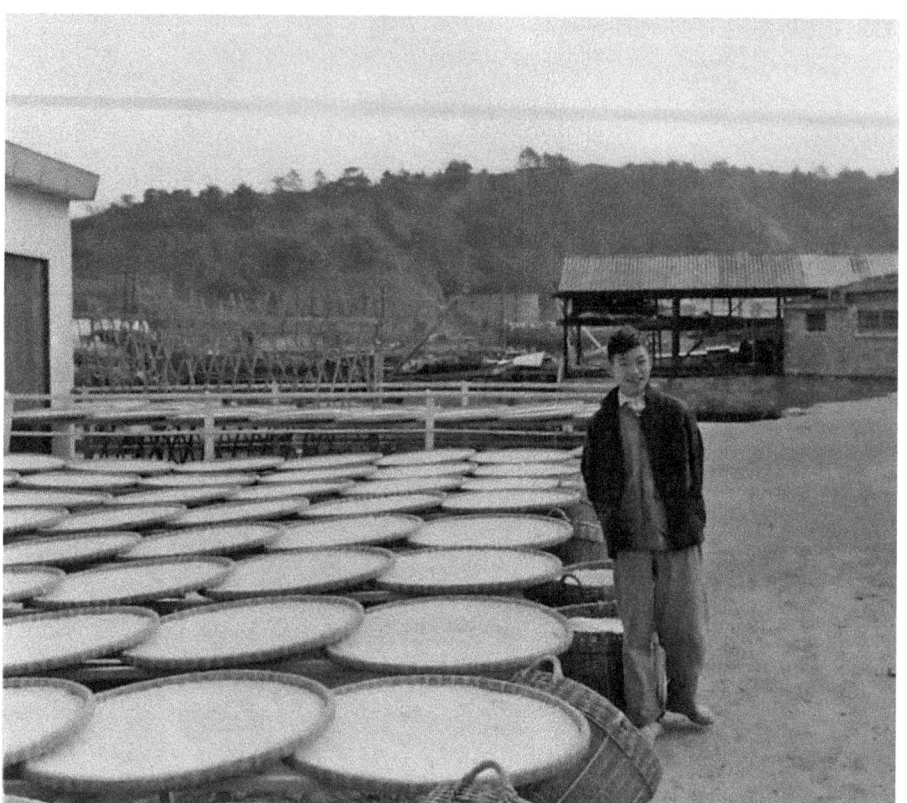

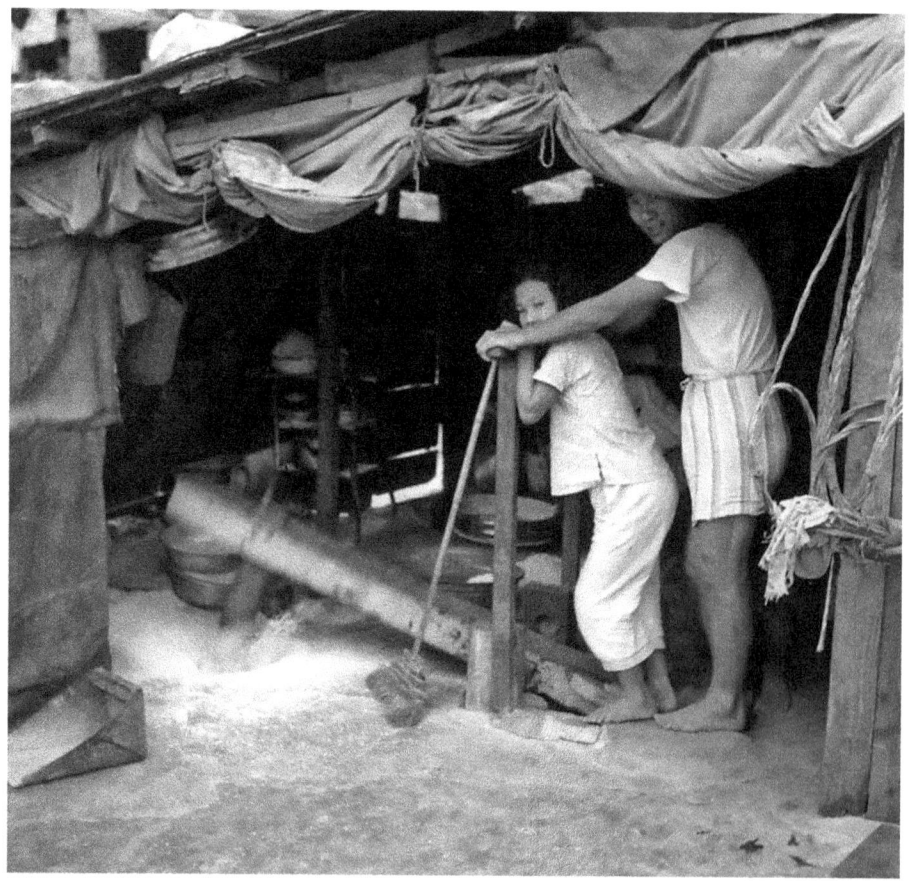

PRELUDE TO CHANGE: HONG KONG OF THE 1950S

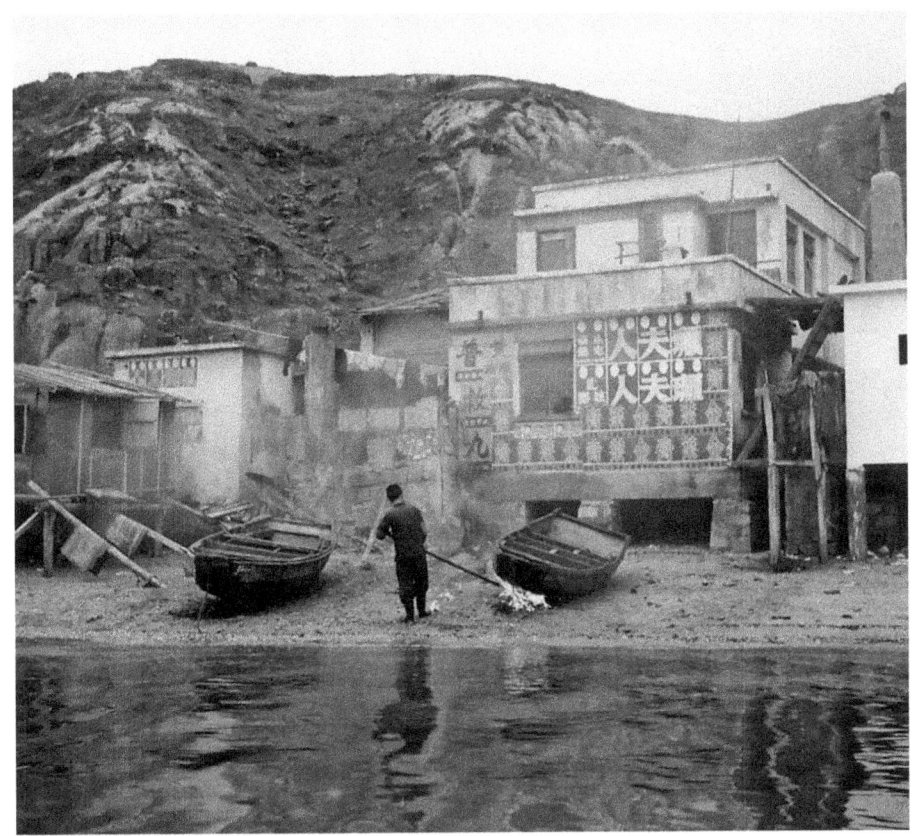

Re-caulking a boat.

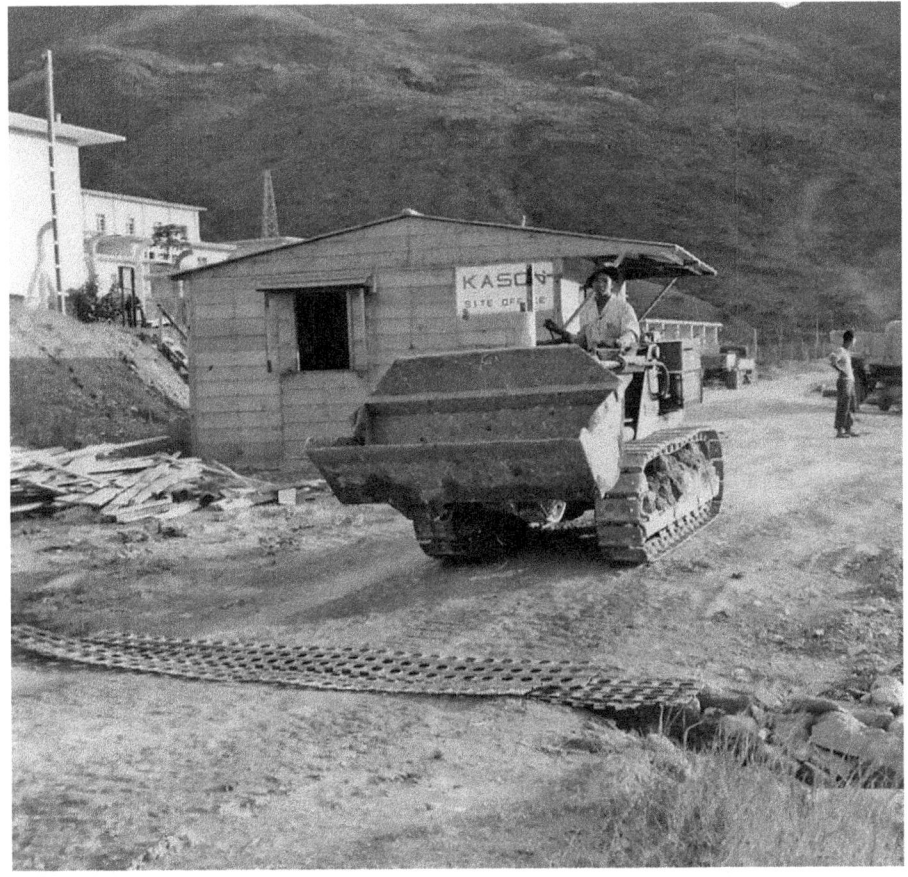

Right: Major land reclamation at RAF Little Sai Wan.

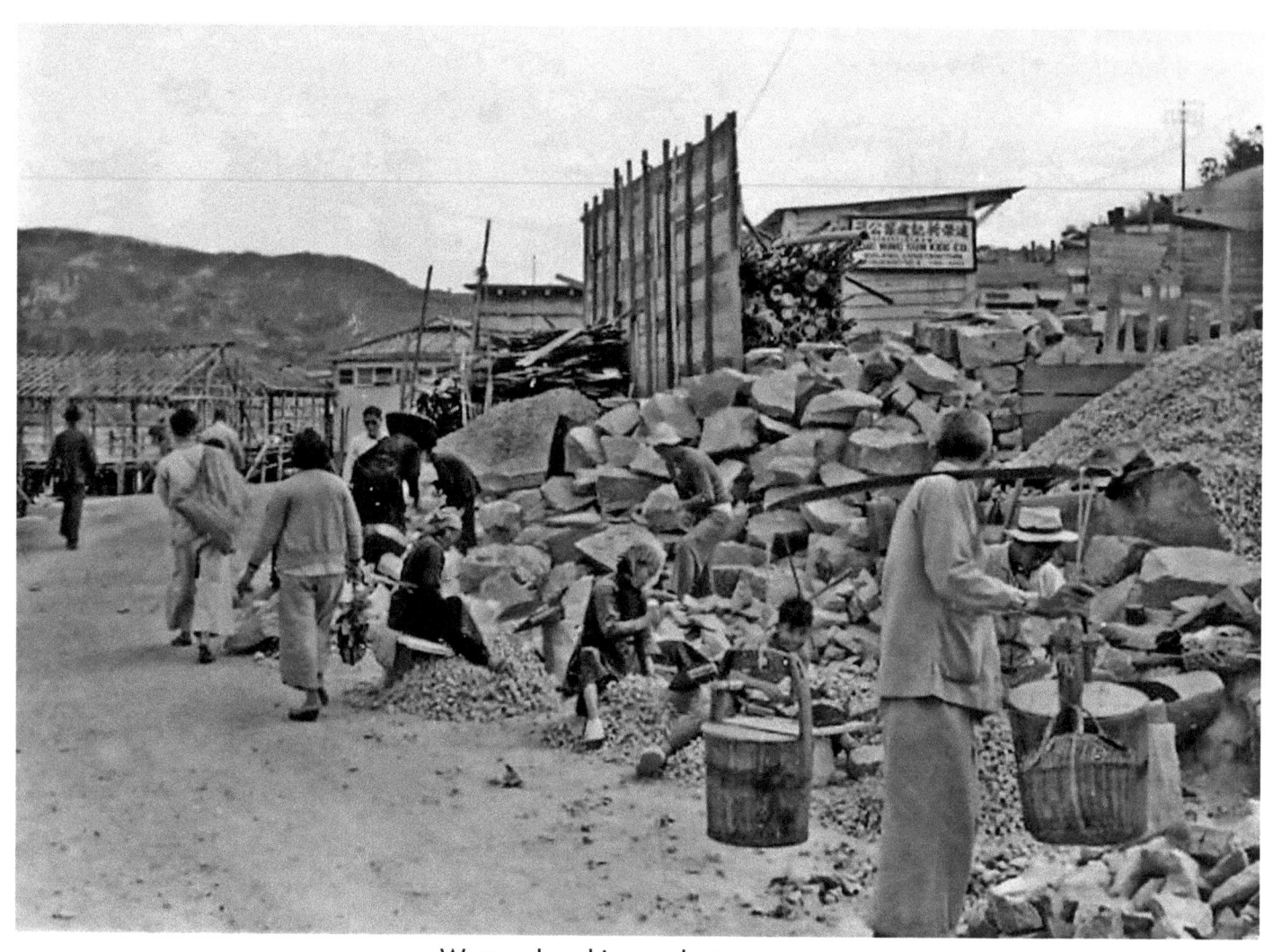

Women breaking rock at a quarry.

PRELUDE TO CHANGE: HONG KONG OF THE 1950S

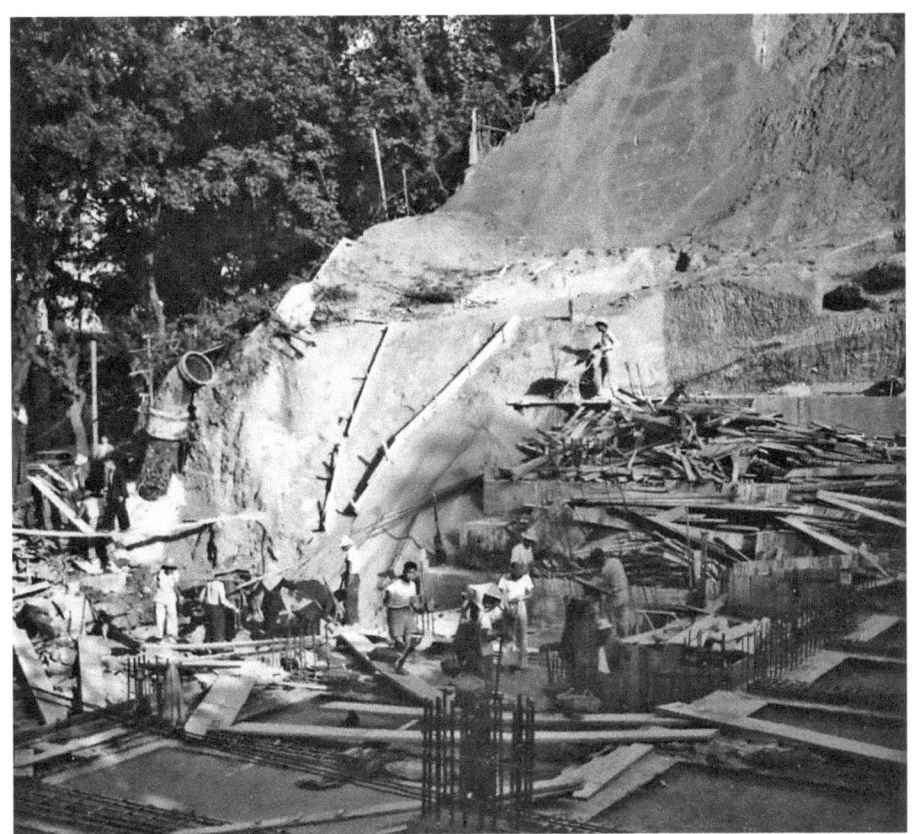

Construction site.

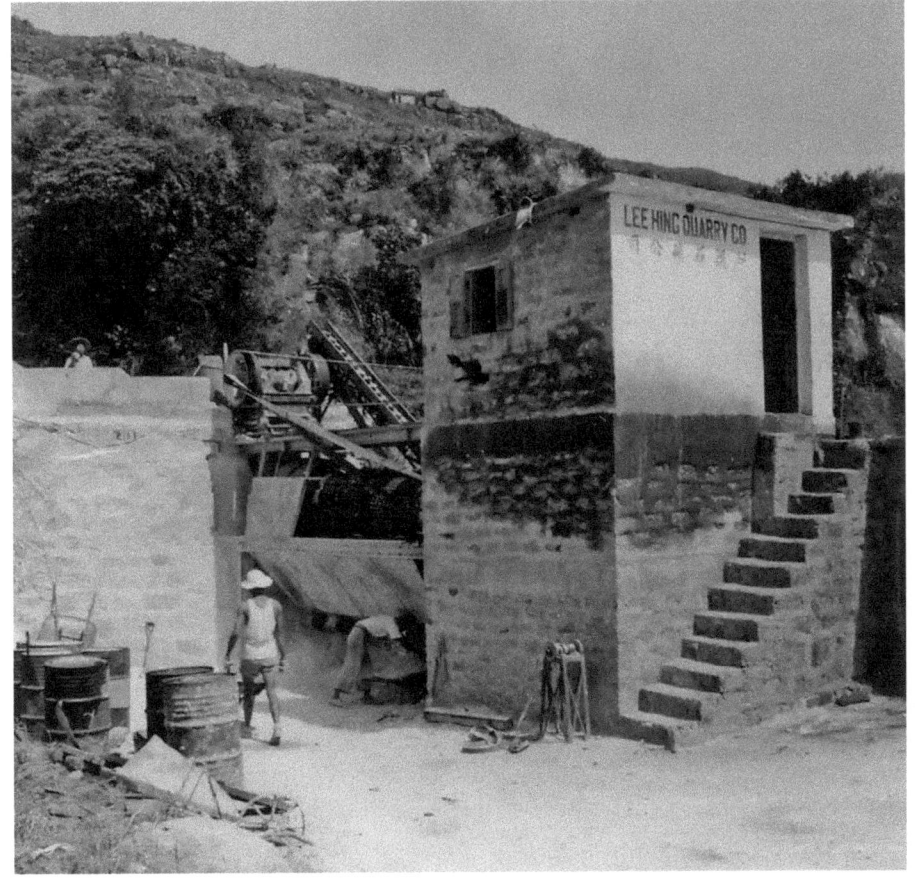

Entrance to a quarry.

Hong Kong's Pre-Modern Era Buildings

One of the great pleasures that I have experienced in finally sitting down at my computer to edit and present these pictures, taken so very long ago by me as a young serviceman, has been the opportunity that it has given me to look closer at the subject matter of them. Examining this picture again, I have realised just how it epitomizes the contrasting lifestyles of Hong Kong in the 1950s. In terms of buildings in the broader sense, we have the shanty town shacks of the poor in the foreground, stretching back to an old then a more modern tenement block, to the apartments above where no foul smells from lack of proper sanitation would spoil time spent out on a balcony having a drink on a balmy evening.

Perhaps most significant of all is the cheeky young lad who, though living in the squalor of shanty town, has such a wonderful cheeky grin as he mimics me taking his photograph. I have found so often in my travels that the poorest folk are so often the most cheerful and generous of heart.

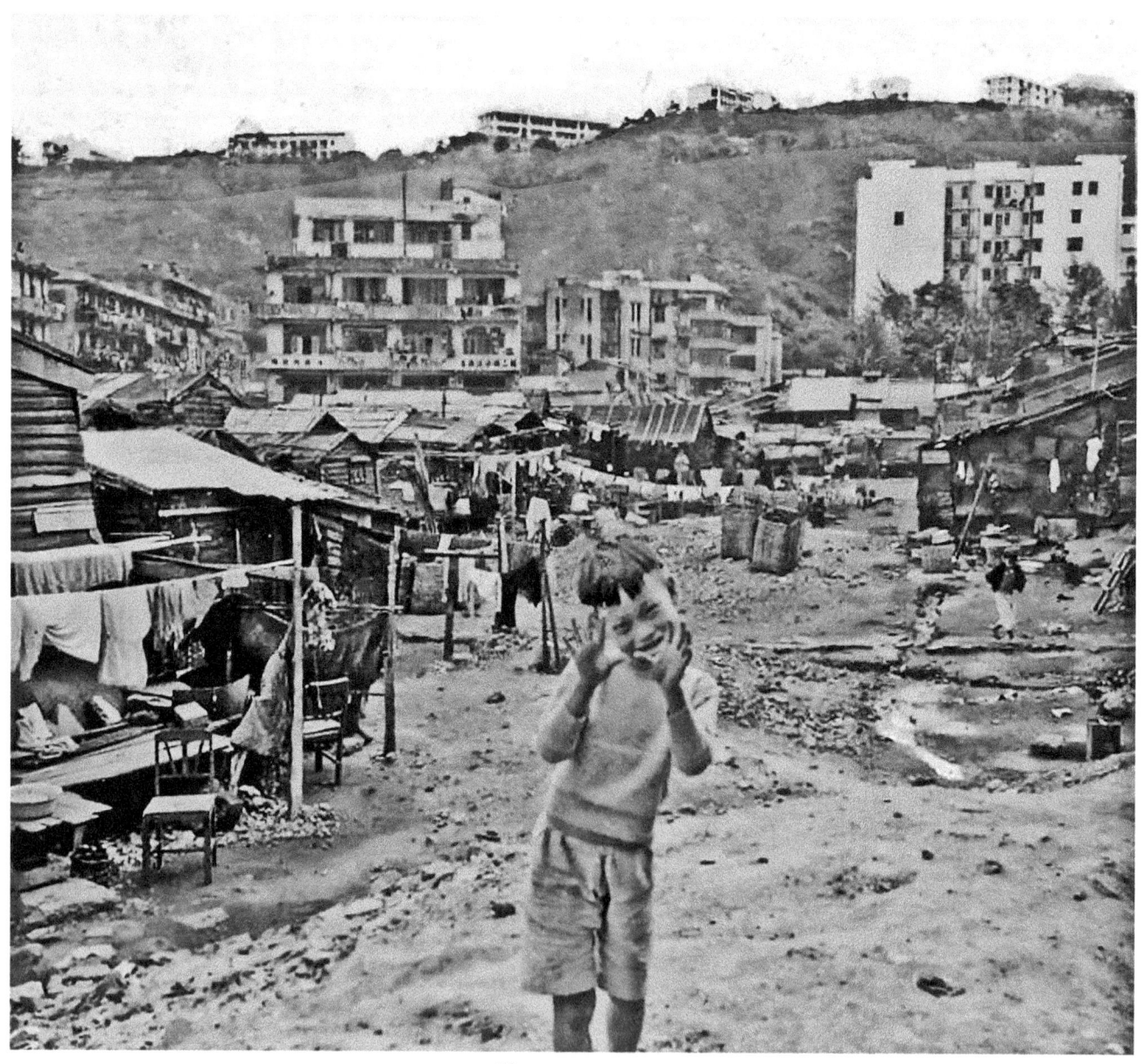

Shanty town.

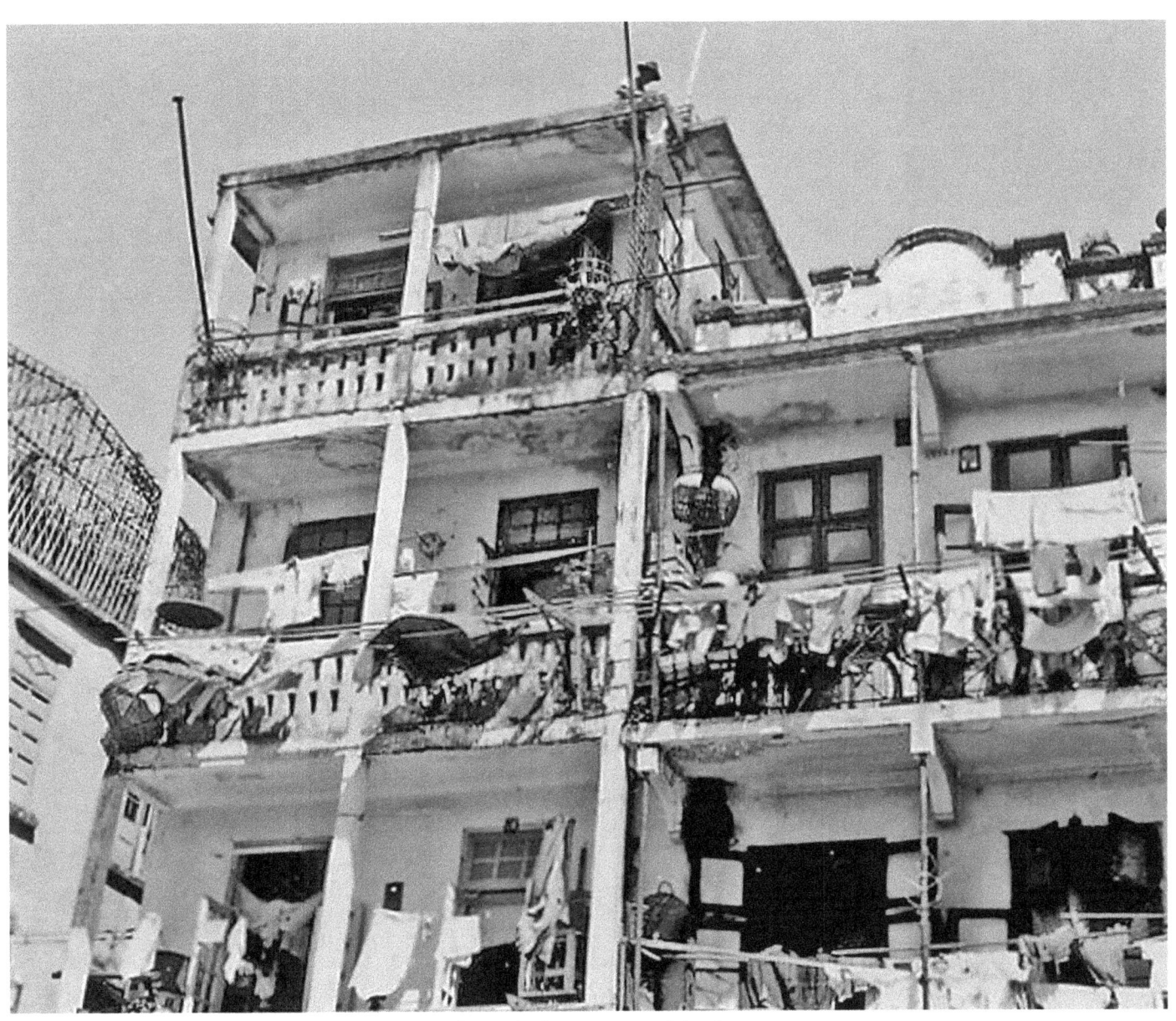

Crowded tenement block.

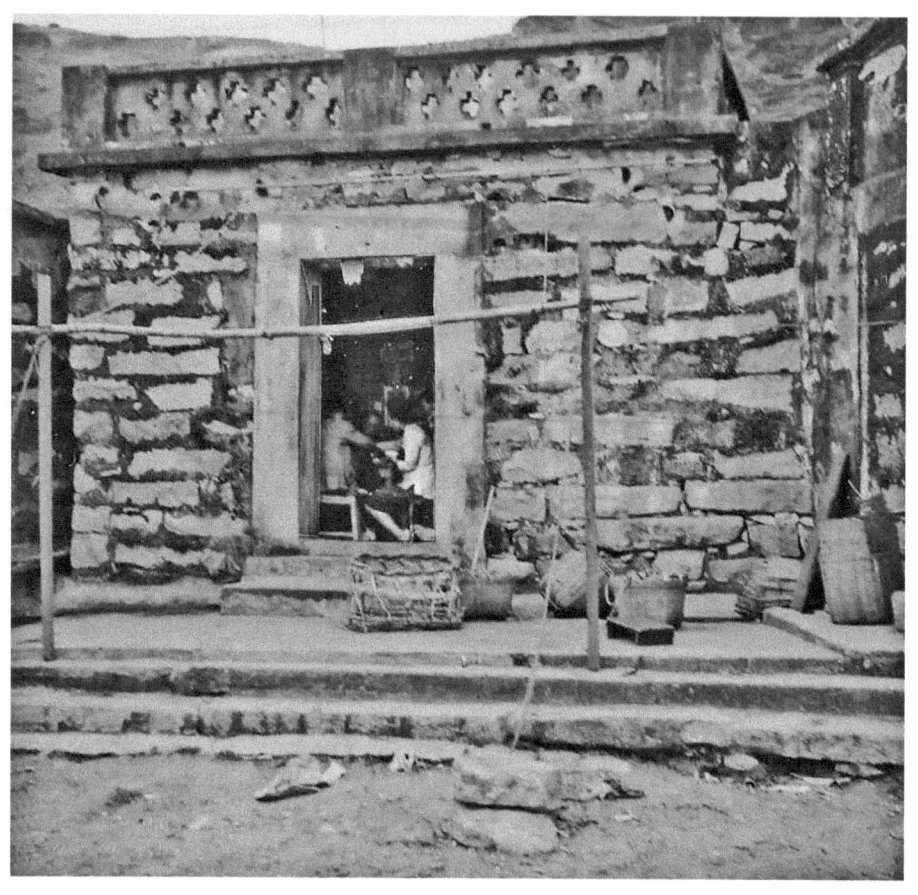

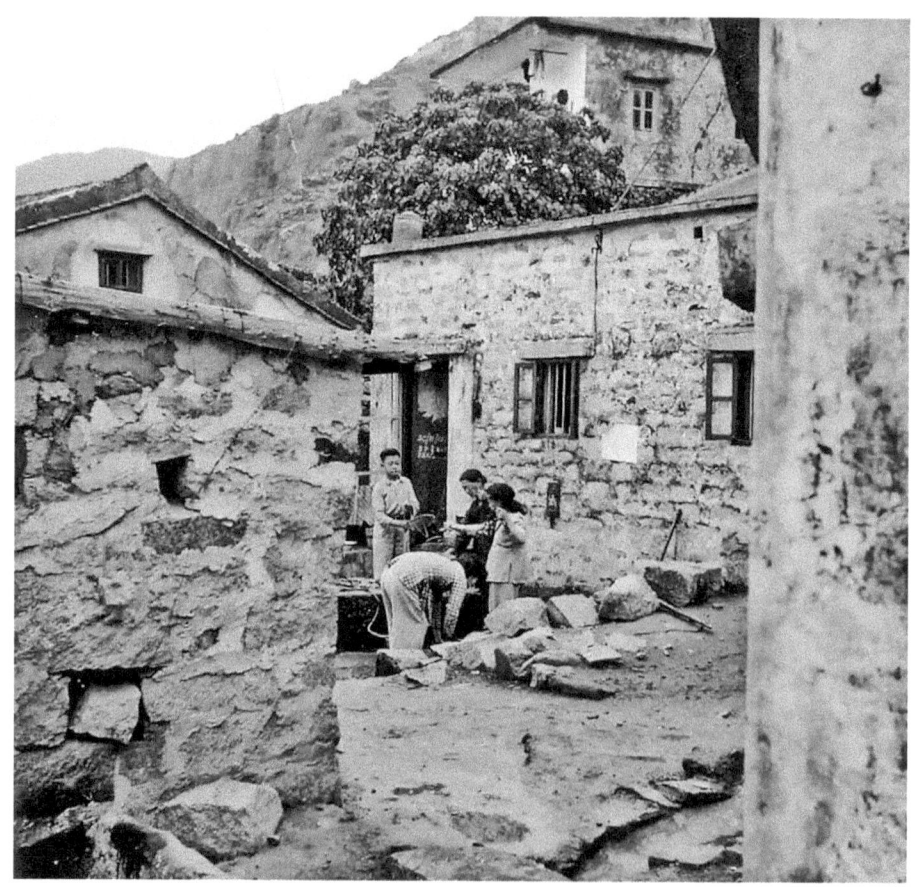

More permanent hill dwellings.

PRELUDE TO CHANGE: HONG KONG OF THE 1950S

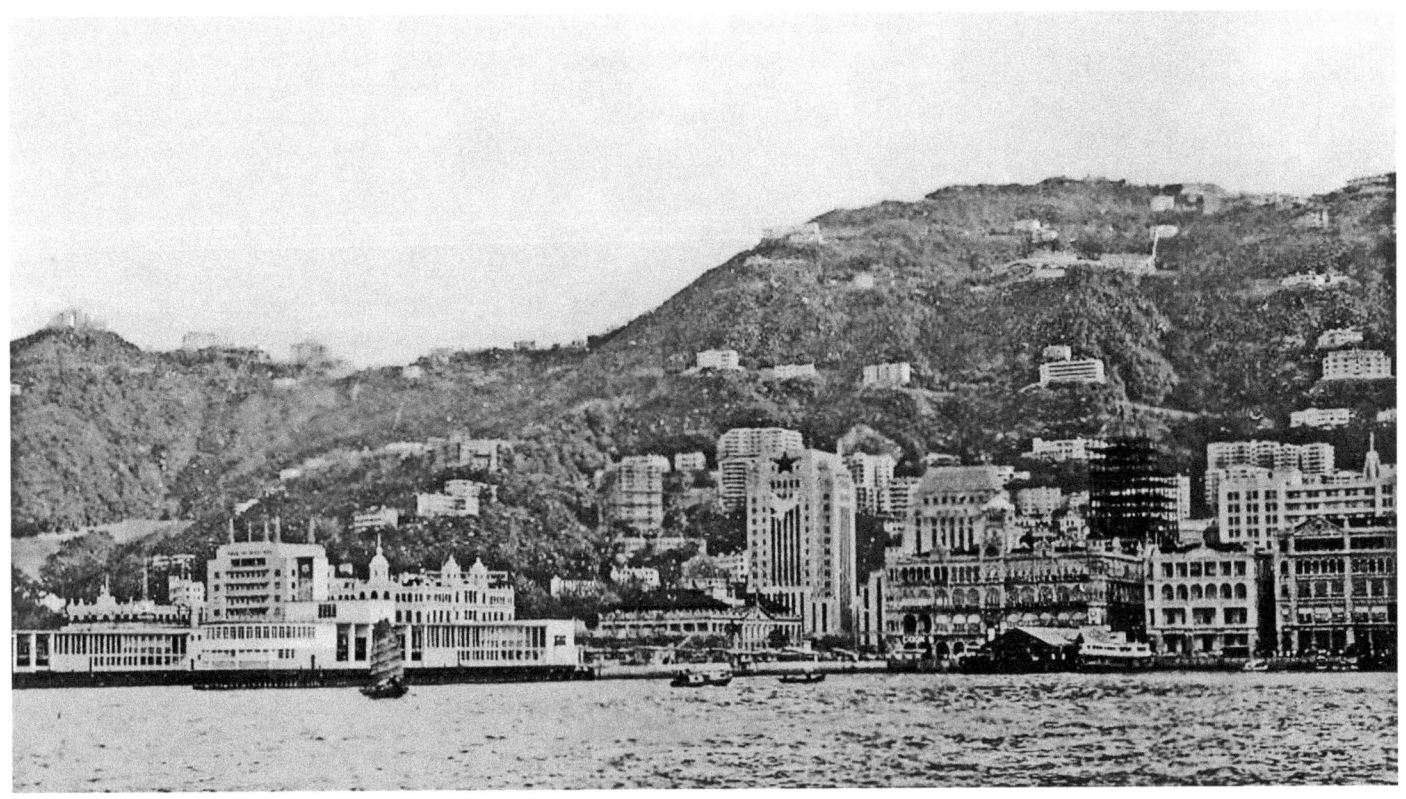

Victoria.

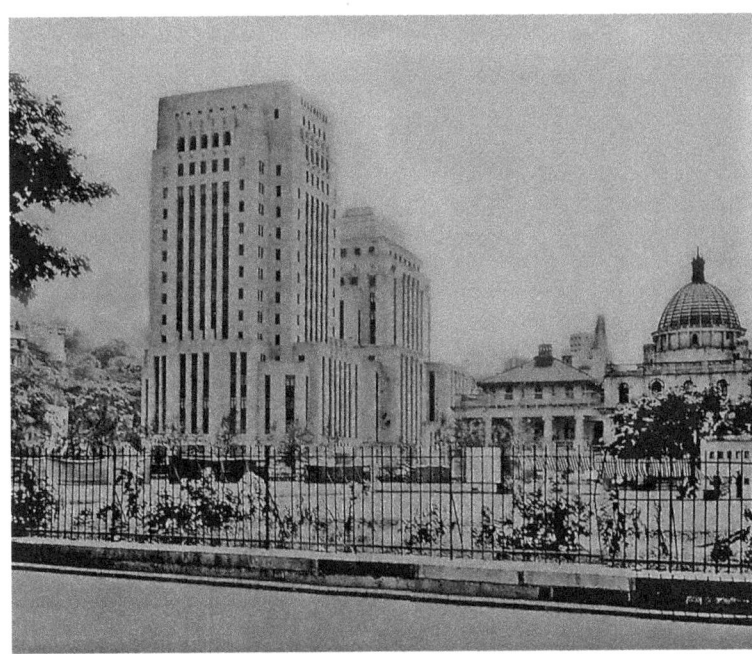
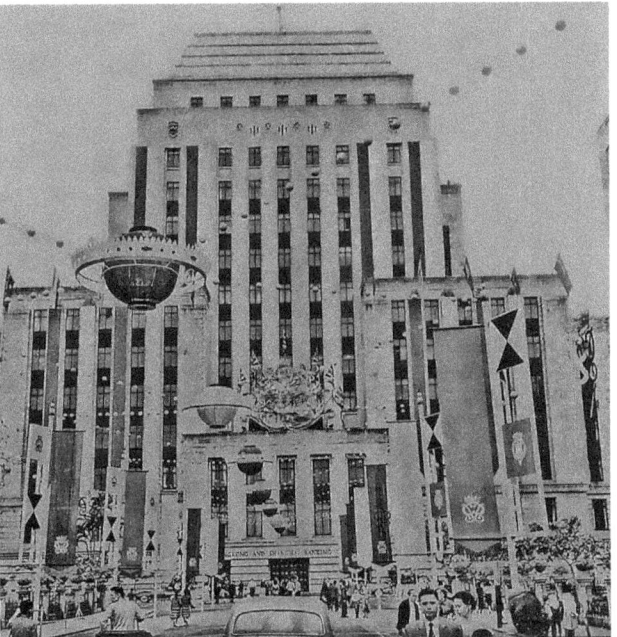

The Big Banks: After the 1950s, Hong Kong would expand its presence in the world of commerce exponentially, with the many tall multi-storey buildings dominating its skyline that we see today.

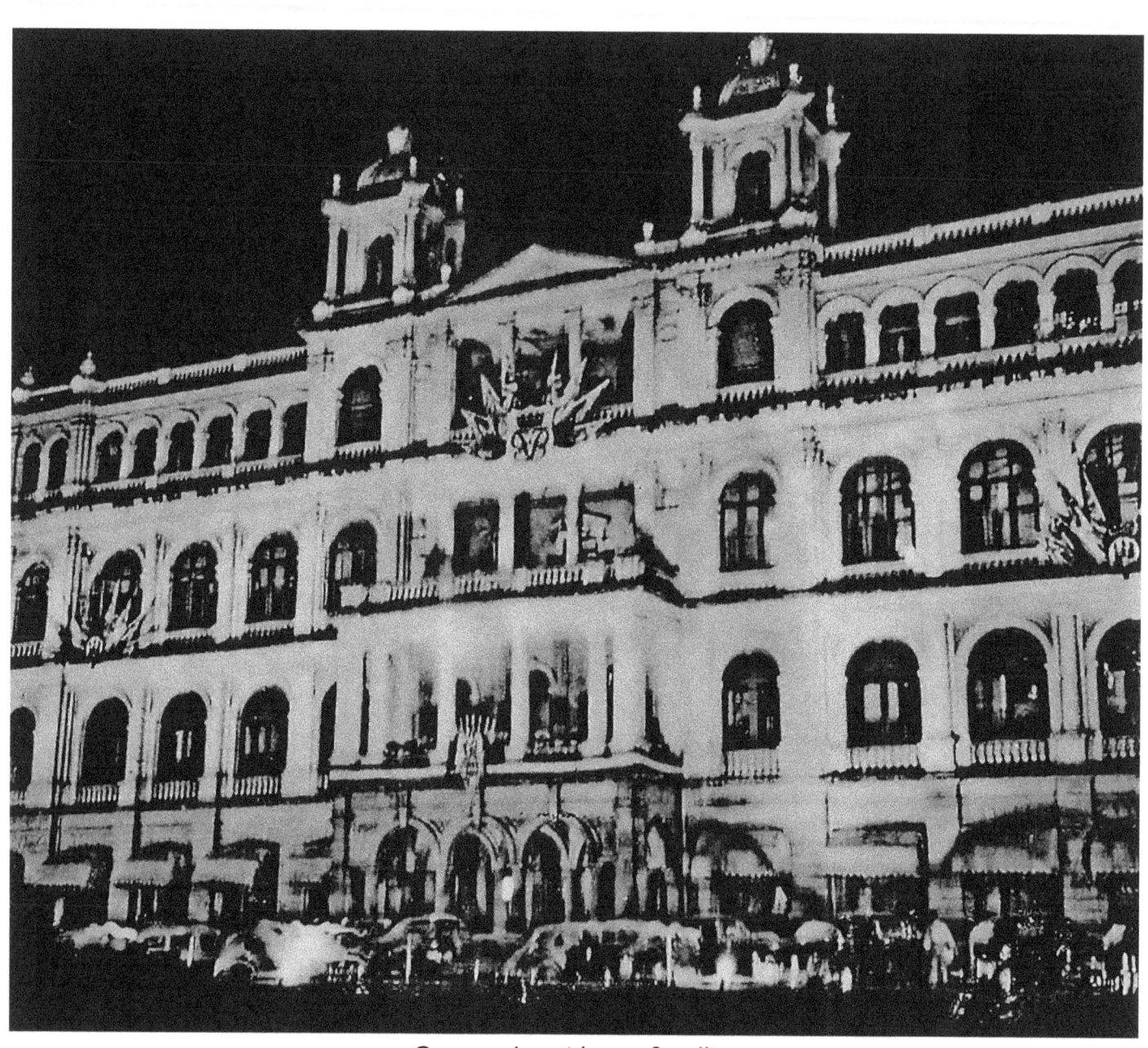

Governor's residence, floodlit.

New Territories Development

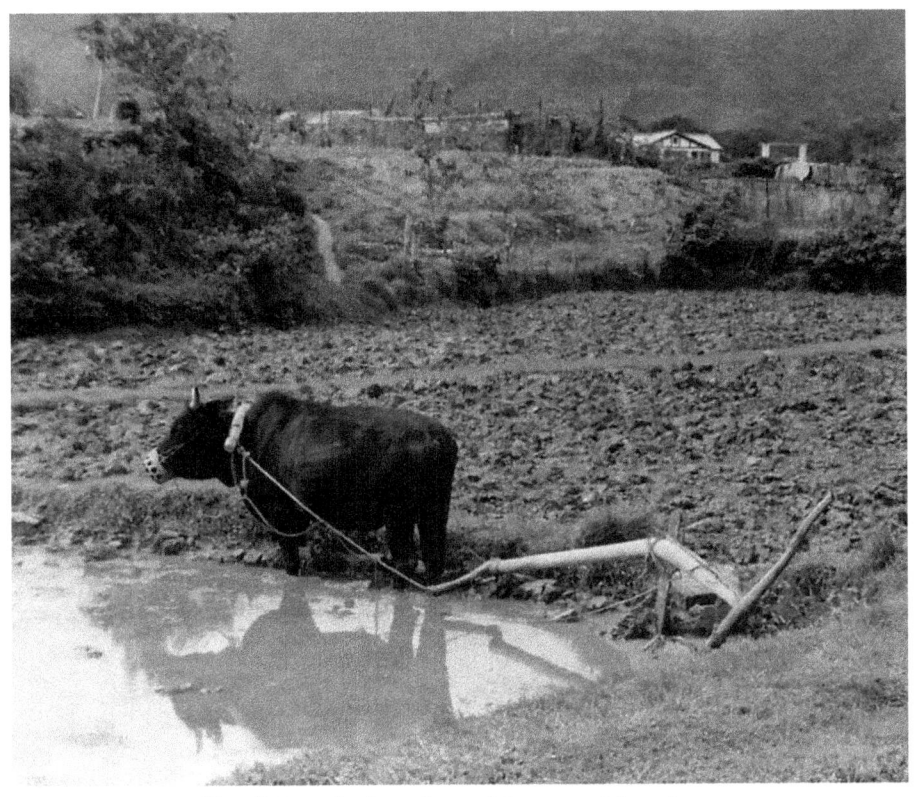

Traditional plough and beast of burden.

In the 1950s, the Hong Kong government started to build the first of its 'new towns', including one in the hitherto predominantly agricultural New Territories, as a policy designed to deal with Hong Kong's acute overcrowding due to the influx of refugees crossing over from Red China. This policy was accelerated in the 1970s, along with the rapid advance of Hong Kong's economy. A shanty town fire at Shek Kip Mai in 1953 forced the government to act when 58,203 people were rendered homeless, and to formulate plans for 'satellite towns' (as the new towns were later called) to be sited in various locations within the colony of Hong Kong.

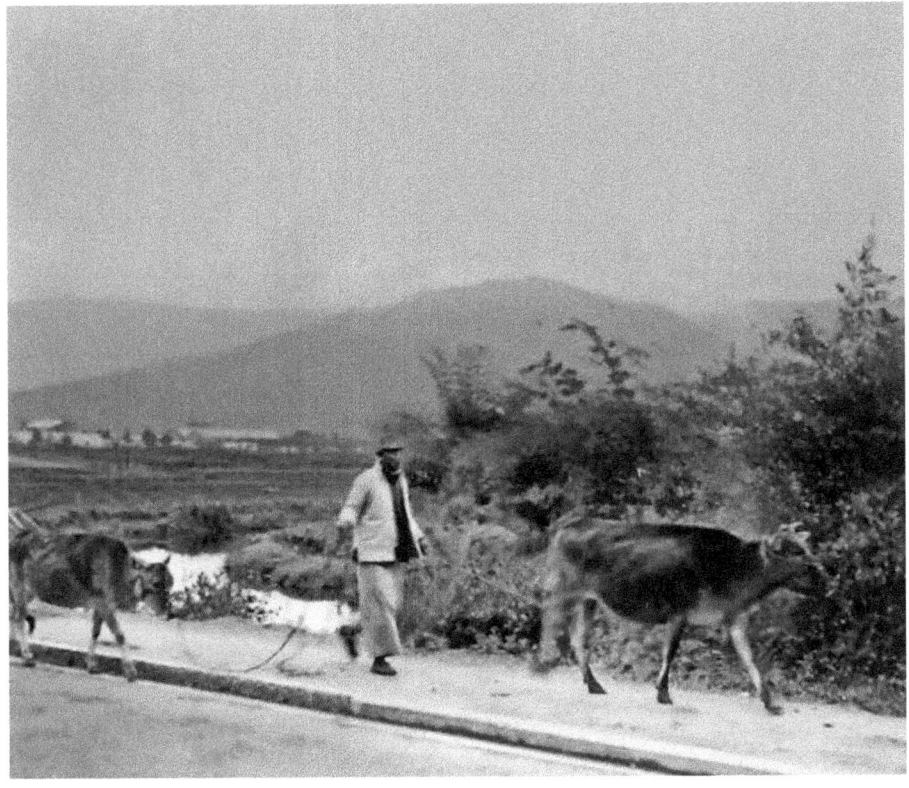

Taking cows to market.

In 1957, my pal Tony Campion and I decided to take a trip by ferry boat sixty-two miles east, across the mouth of the Pearl River, to the Portuguese colony of Macau. We planned to visit the casino in our hotel, see the sights and watch Macau's fourth Grand Prix which was, at that time, a major sports car event.

We would find a unique blend of Chinese and Portuguese to be seen in both its population and its architecture that added to its charm. At that time, no cars were allowed on Macau's streets, making it very quiet and restful.

Political & Economic History

Macau, with a present-day population of 680, 000 in an area of only 12.7 square miles, is today the most populated area in the world. Back in 1957, it was a tiny enclave administered by Portugal since it had been leased from China in 1557 as a trading post.

During the early 18th century, Macau had a significant role to play in the opium trade as a hopping-off port. However, once Hong Kong became established as a British port following the First Opium War in 1841, Macau's importance in the opium trade diminished. Portugal's hold on Macau was further strengthened, however, when, in 1887, the Sino-Portuguese Treaty of Peking was signed, giving Portugal colonial rights in return for Portugal agreeing to co-operate in efforts to end the opium trade.

As with Hong Kong, Macau's colonial status remained unchanged even during China's civil war and after the communists gained control in 1949. Unlike Hong Kong, though, Macau was not occupied by Japanese forces during World War Two.

With the influx of refugees during China's civil war, Macau was able to grow its economy by expanding its textile and clothing industries and with tourism after legalising casino gaming.

Post 1950s Macau

In 1966, Macau would see unrest at the time of China's 'Cultural Revolution', and Portugal had to relinquish some of its administrative powers to China. In 1974, Portugal formerly relinquished its colonial status by acknowledging Macau as a Chinese territory under Portuguese administration.

After full transfer to China in 1999, Macau's wealth grew exponentially with foreign investment being allowed into its thriving casino industry.

All of these changes were, for us, as we entered the waters of Macau's harbour, events that would unfold during later decades. We were about to explore somewhere very different in character to its colonial neighbour, Hong Kong.

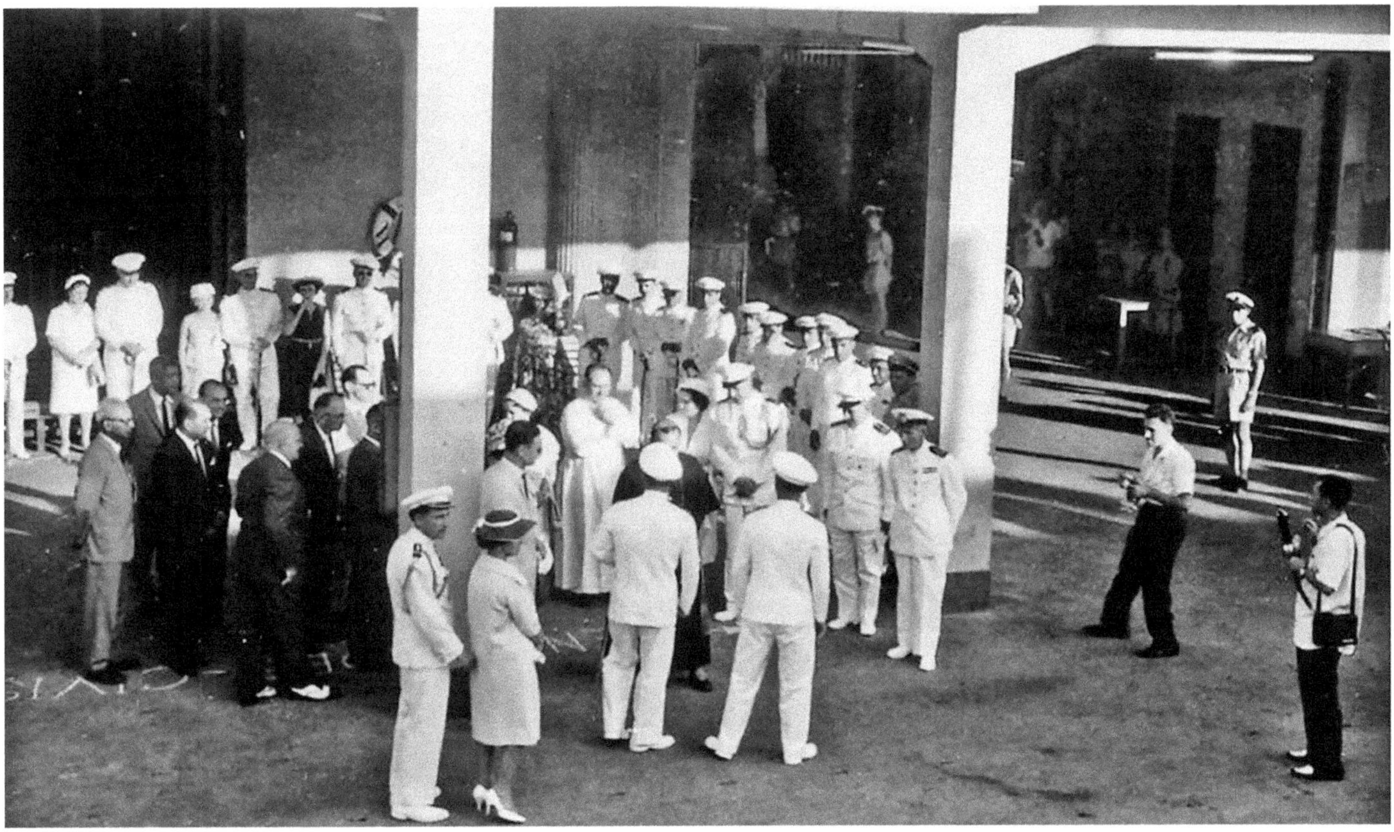

![The view from the ferry on our arrival in Macau of a welcoming party of dignitaries for what appears to be a senior church cleric.]

The view from the ferry on our arrival in Macau of a welcoming party
of dignitaries for what appears to be a senior church cleric.

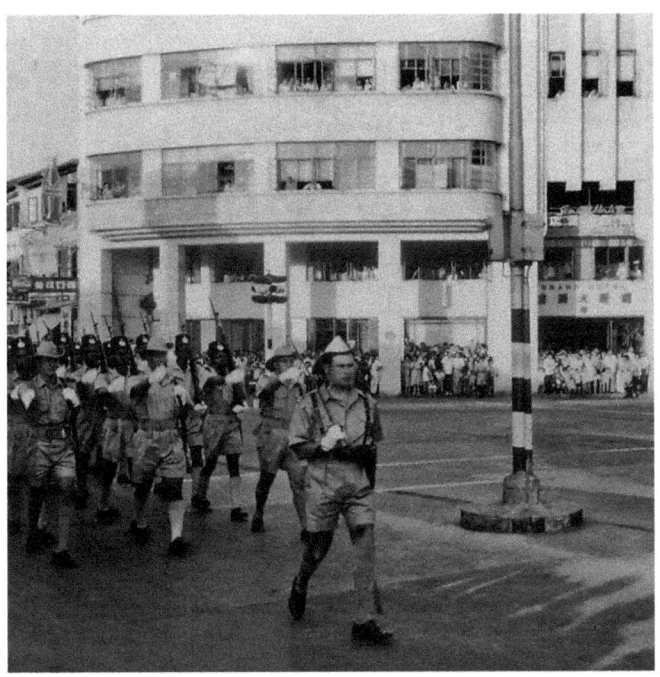

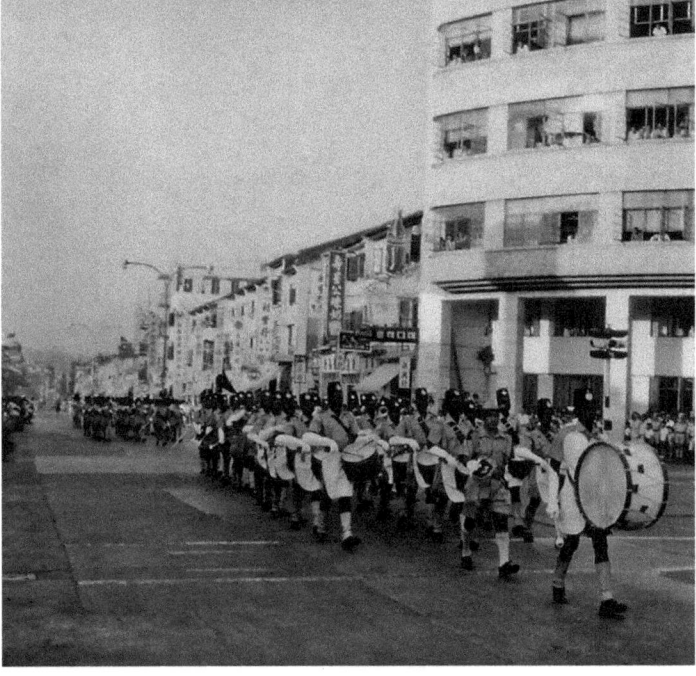

Macau's border gates crossing into neighbouring communist China
were manned by African soldiers from one or more of Portugal's African
colonies, seen here on parade through the streets of Macau.

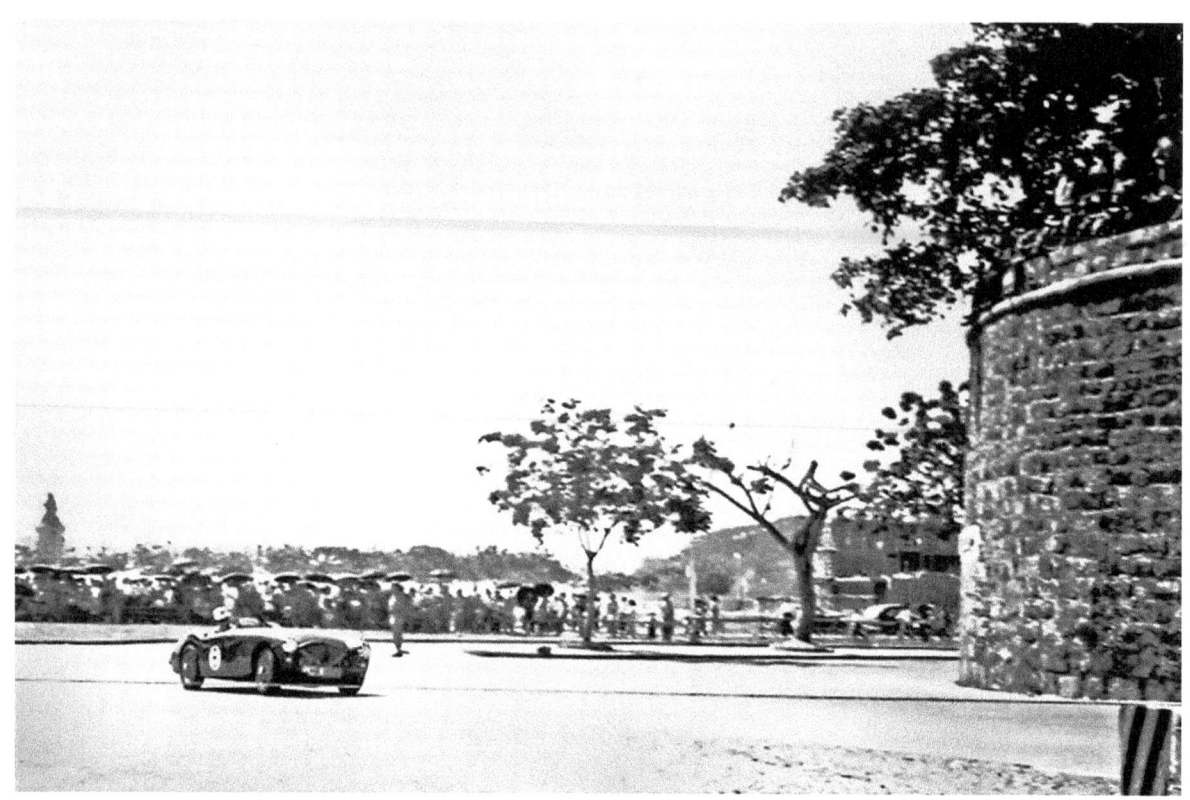

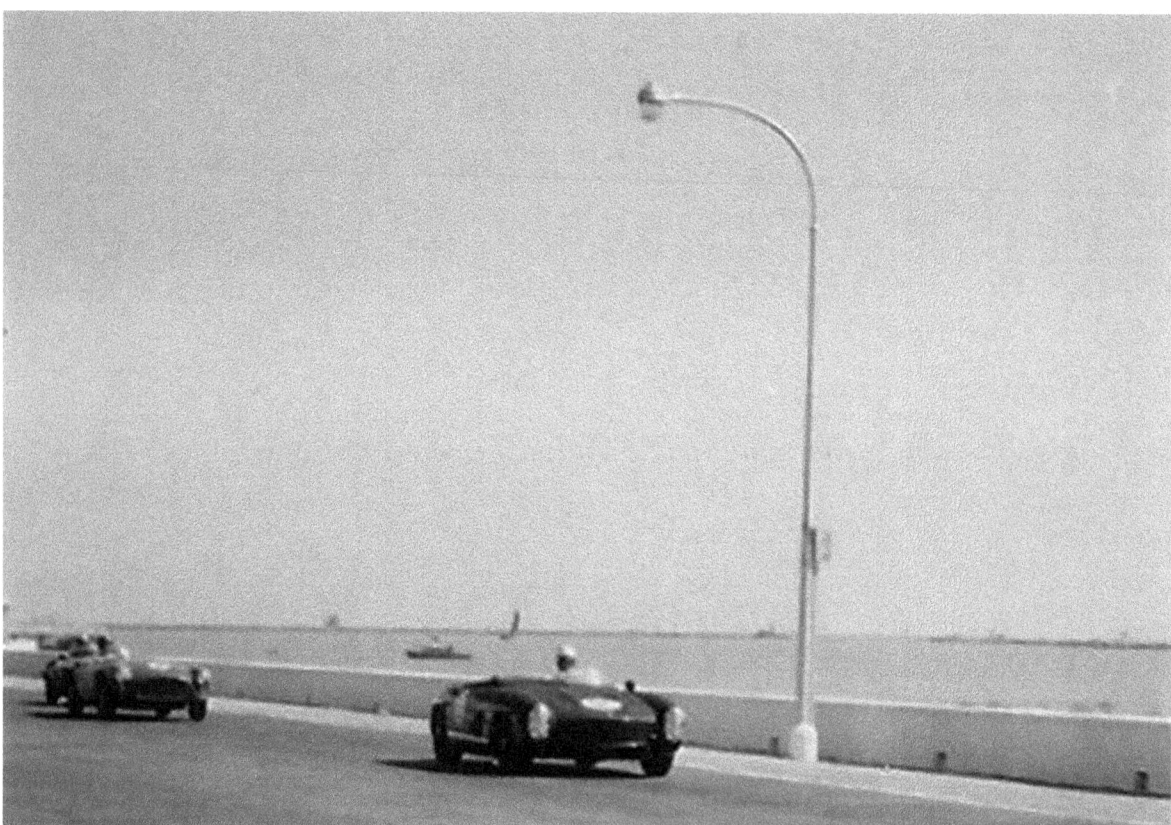

The Macau 1957 Grand Prix: the race, which had originally been conceived in 1954 as a treasure hunt, then became The Macau Grand Prix, a race for amateur drivers. This now world famous Formula Three event would, over the years, play host to some world-class drivers.

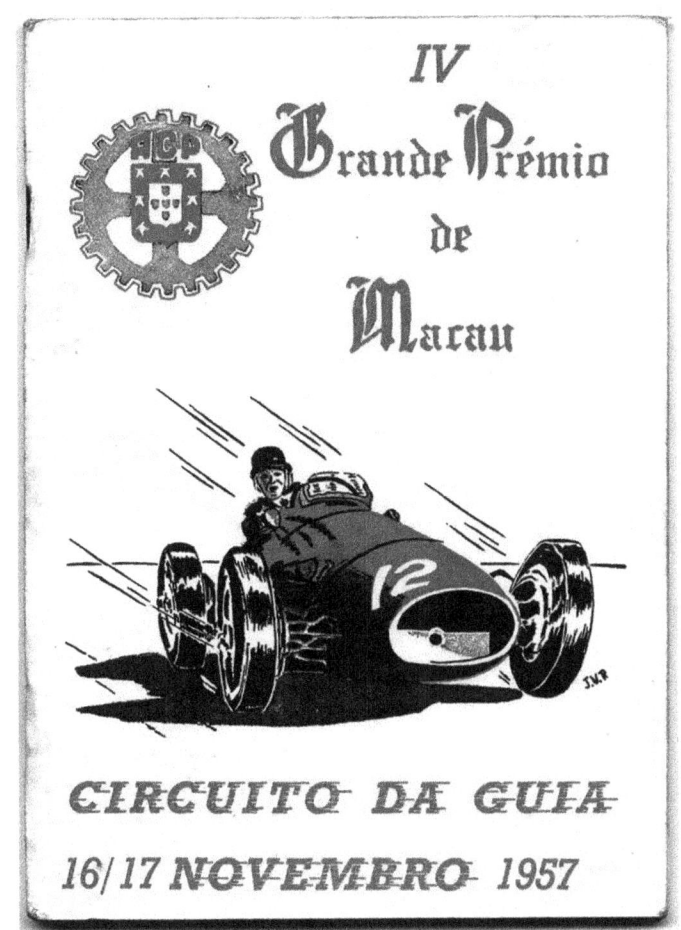
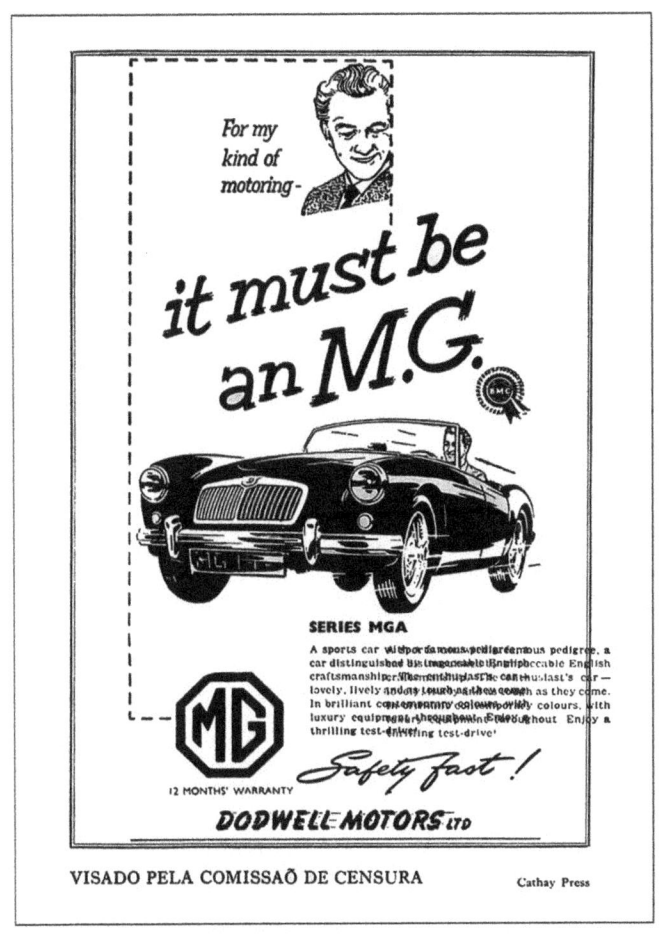

Race programme with a sample of advertising.

Macau: A Place Quite Different

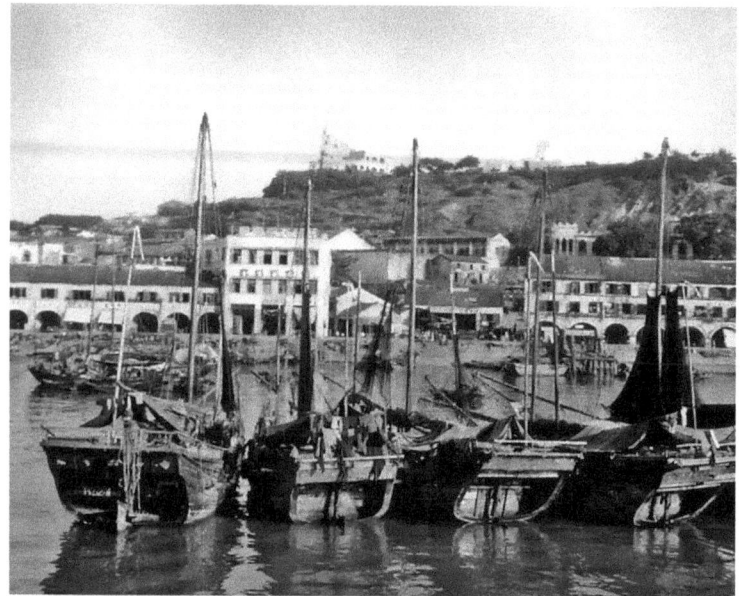

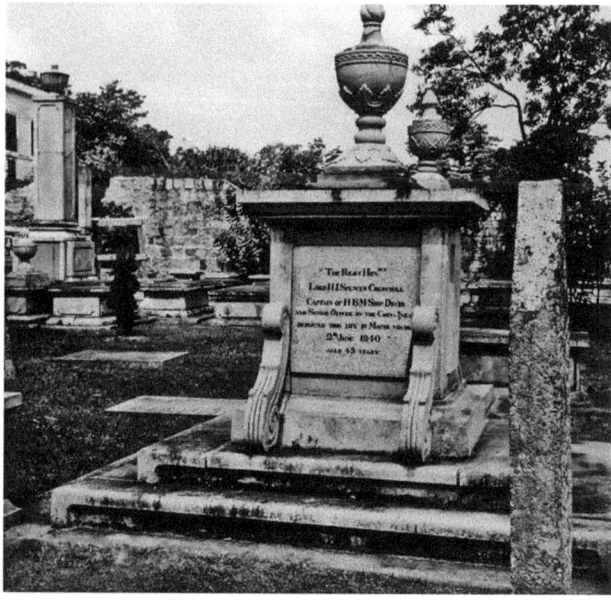

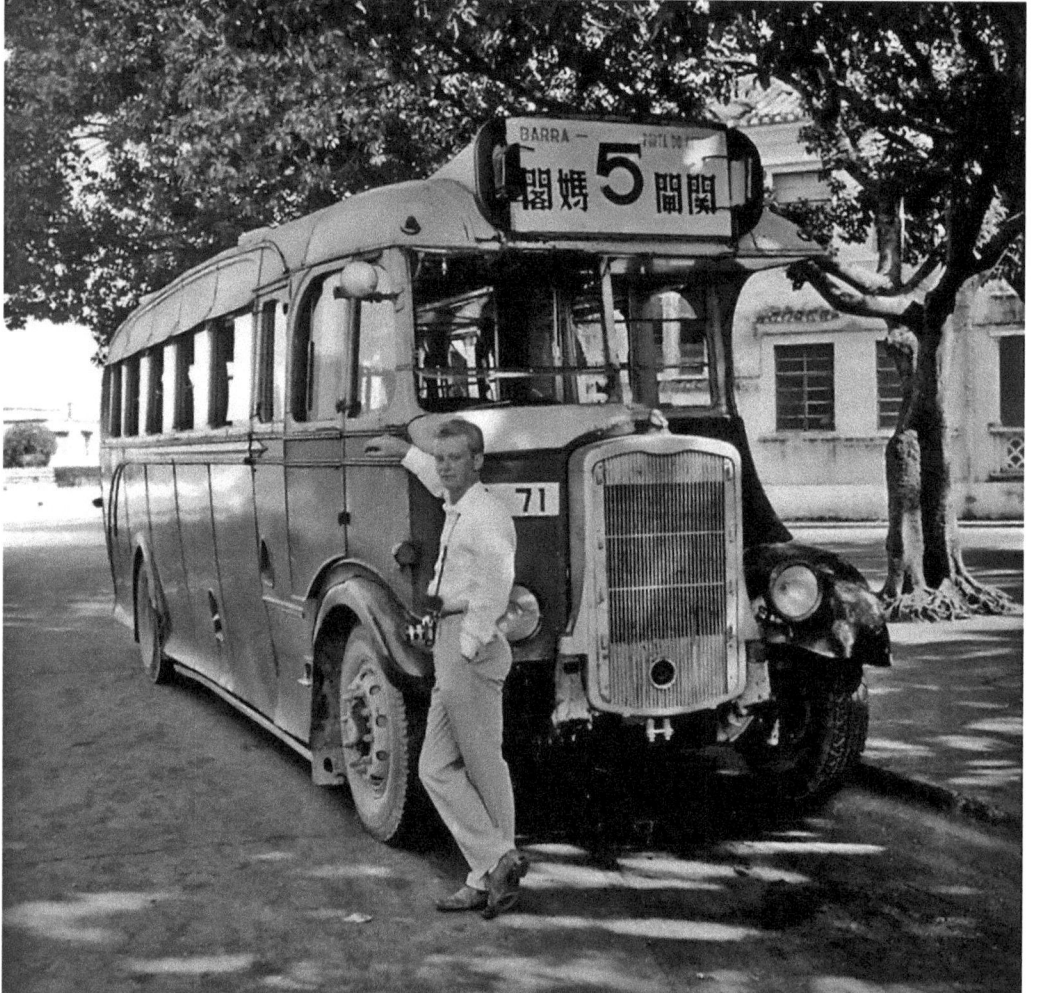

Top left: a fleet of fishing junks.
Top right: in a quiet churchyard we found this magnificent tomb of Lord Henry John Spencer Churchill, great-grand-uncle of Sir Winston Churchill, Captain of Her Britannic Majesty's Ship Druid and Senior Officer in the China Sea. Died 2nd June 1840.
Left: Tony, by one of the few motor vehicles allowed on the roads.

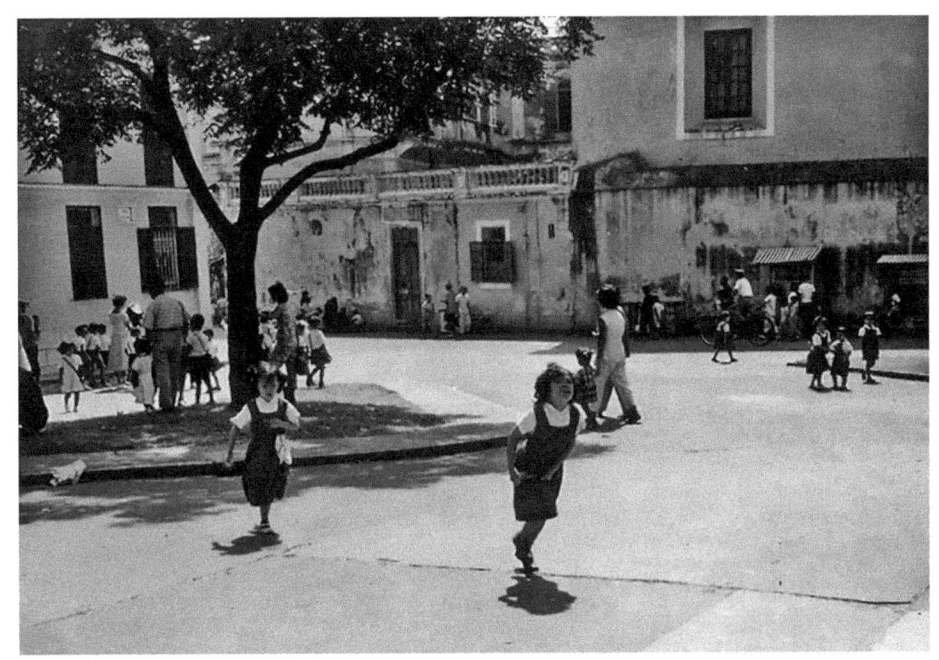

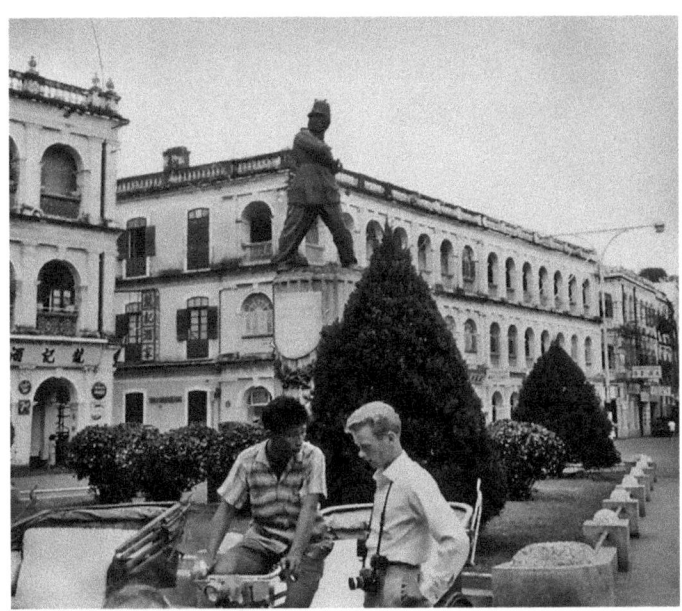

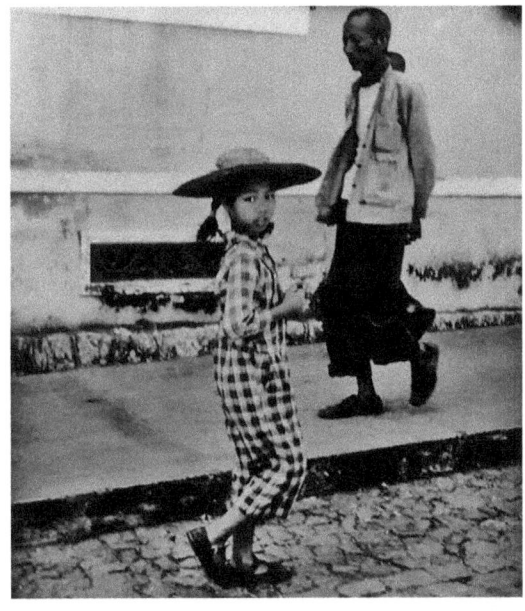

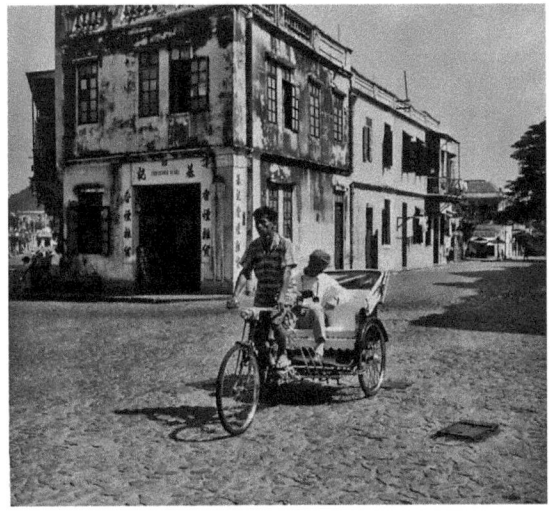

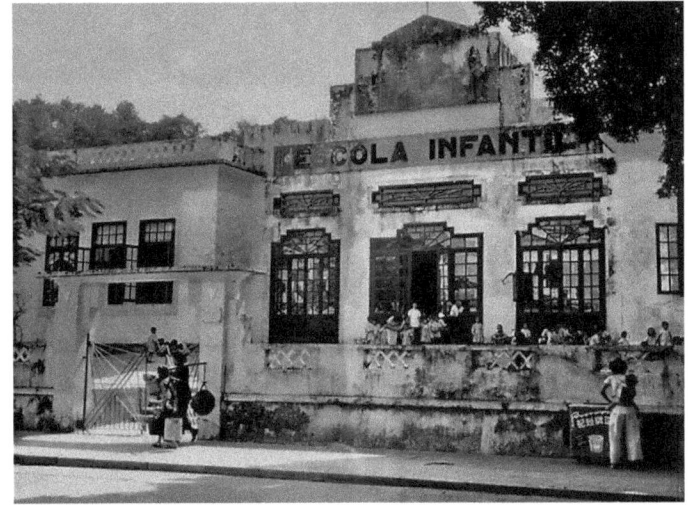

VISIT TO MACAU

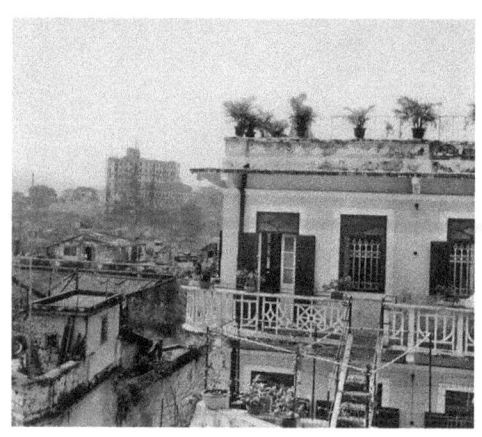
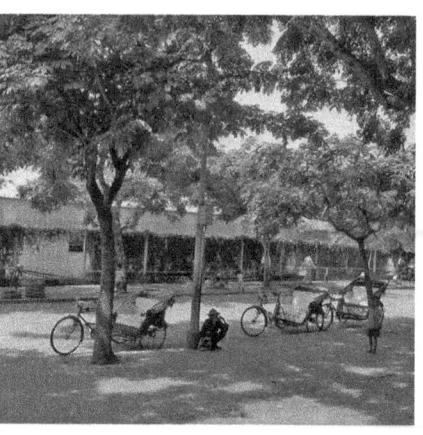
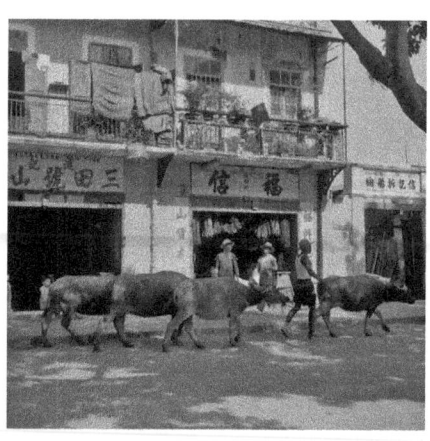

PRELUDE TO CHANGE: HONG KONG OF THE 1950S

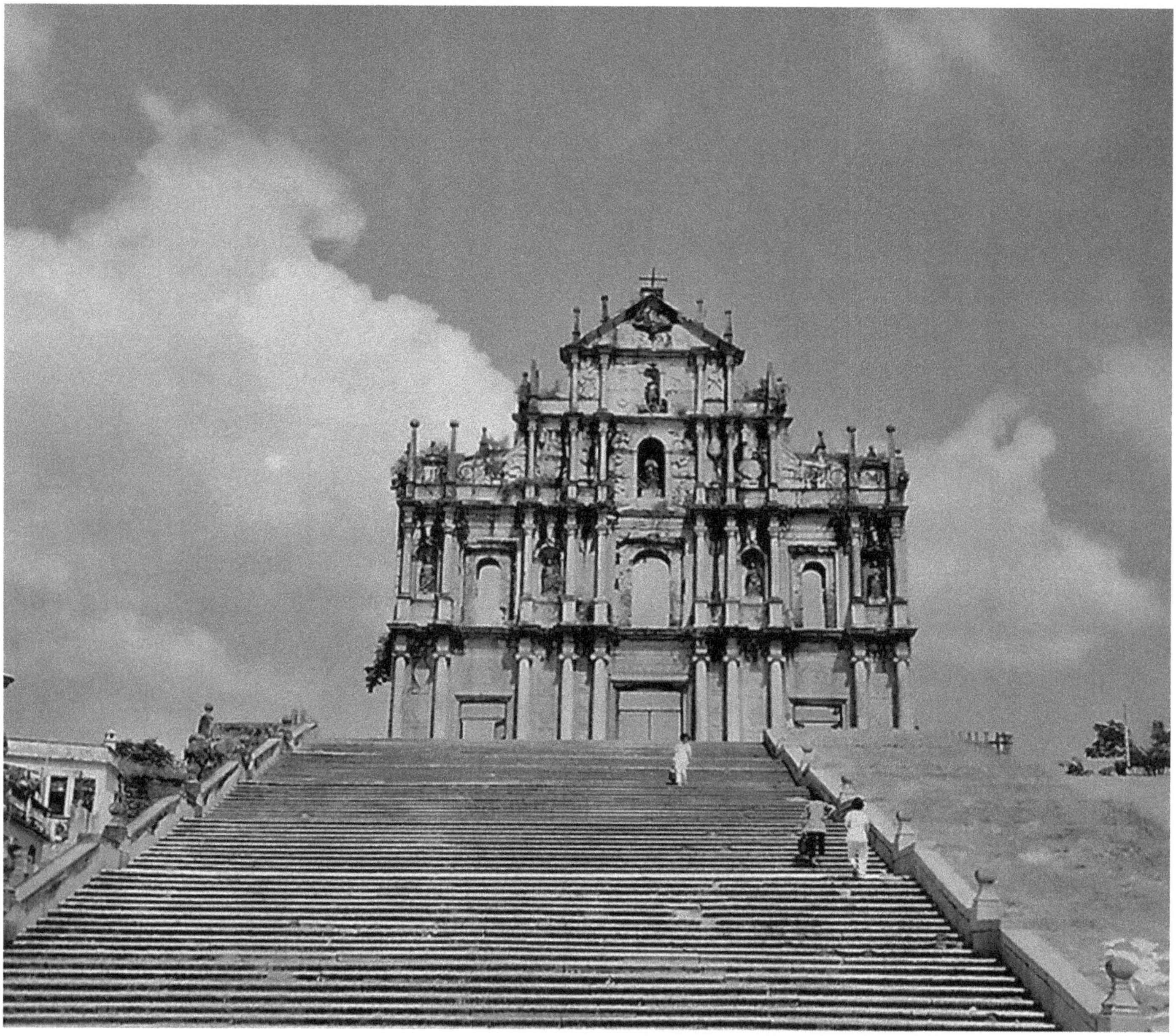

RAF Little Sai Wan

Political Landscape

In 1956, when I was posted to Hong Kong, the Cold War was in full swing, and brinkmanship was the jargon of the day. Therefore, hostility between the Western Powers, including Great Britain, and the Republic of China remained at their height, although actual hostilities between British and Chinese forces had ceased with the armistice signed in 1953 to end combat operations on the Korean Peninsula. However, hostilities between the new Communist Republic of China and Chinese Nationalists, who had retreated to the Island of what was then known as Formosa (now Taiwan), were still very much ongoing, in the form of air activity over the straits between them, and shelling of small offshore islands held by the Nationalists.

My arrival in Hong Kong in 1956 was just eleven years after Great Britain had reclaimed the colony from Japanese occupation, and it was a source of wonder to me, after my arrival, that the far more numerous Communist Chinese Red Army had not simply reclaimed Hong Kong as part of China after the Japanese surrender. I must admit to having felt, at first, quite nervous about the fact that a huge country hostile to Britain lay just a few miles to the north of us. I had certainly not signed up to be a hero!

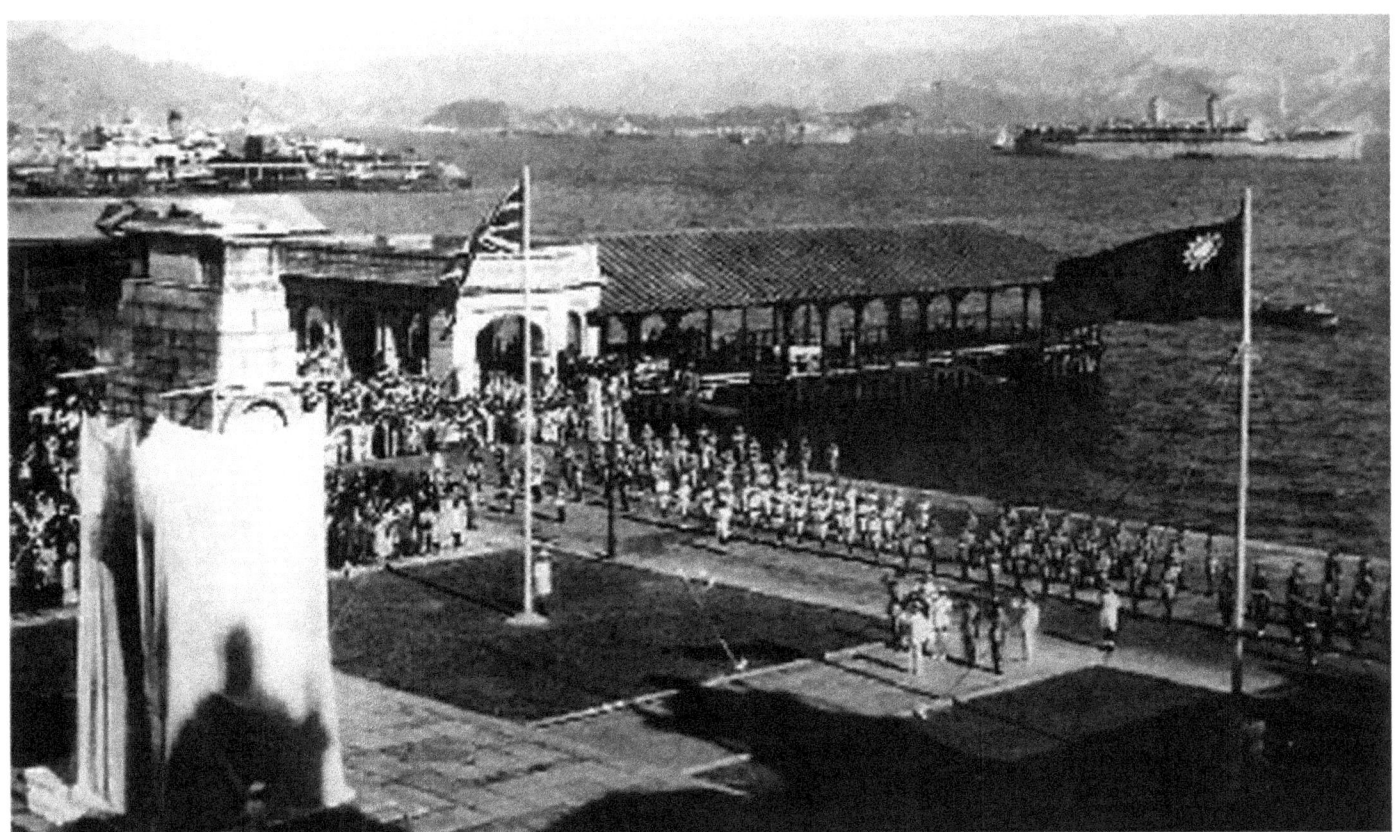

The Liberation Parade at the Cenotaph in Hong Kong in 1945 following the Japanese surrender (library picture).

Physical Landscape

In the foreground of my picture below is the Officers' & Sergeants' Mess building. To the west of this was our square doughnut-shaped secure signals centre. Hidden from view, further up and to the left, were the main entrance, guard room and medical centre, or sick bay as we called it.

Seen over the roof of the officer's mess is the NAAFI, below which was the airmen's mess hall and adjacent to them was the Astra Camp Cinema. The tall buildings at the rear were our barrack buildings.

The camp faced towards the north, where the vast communist country of the Chinese People's Republic lay. Most of us had been trained by the RAF as wireless operators to send and receive Morse code signals, and behind the buildings of our RAF camp were situated very large wireless masts, all clearly visible, especially to passing ships and smaller vessels out to sea. That it was very obviously a substantial intelligence-gathering facility could have been no secret to the Communist authorities to the north of Hong Kong.

All who worked inside our signals centre were subject to the restrictions laid down by the Official Secrets Act. Once off-duty, nobody spoke of what their job entailed or of anything to do with our work inside the signals centre.

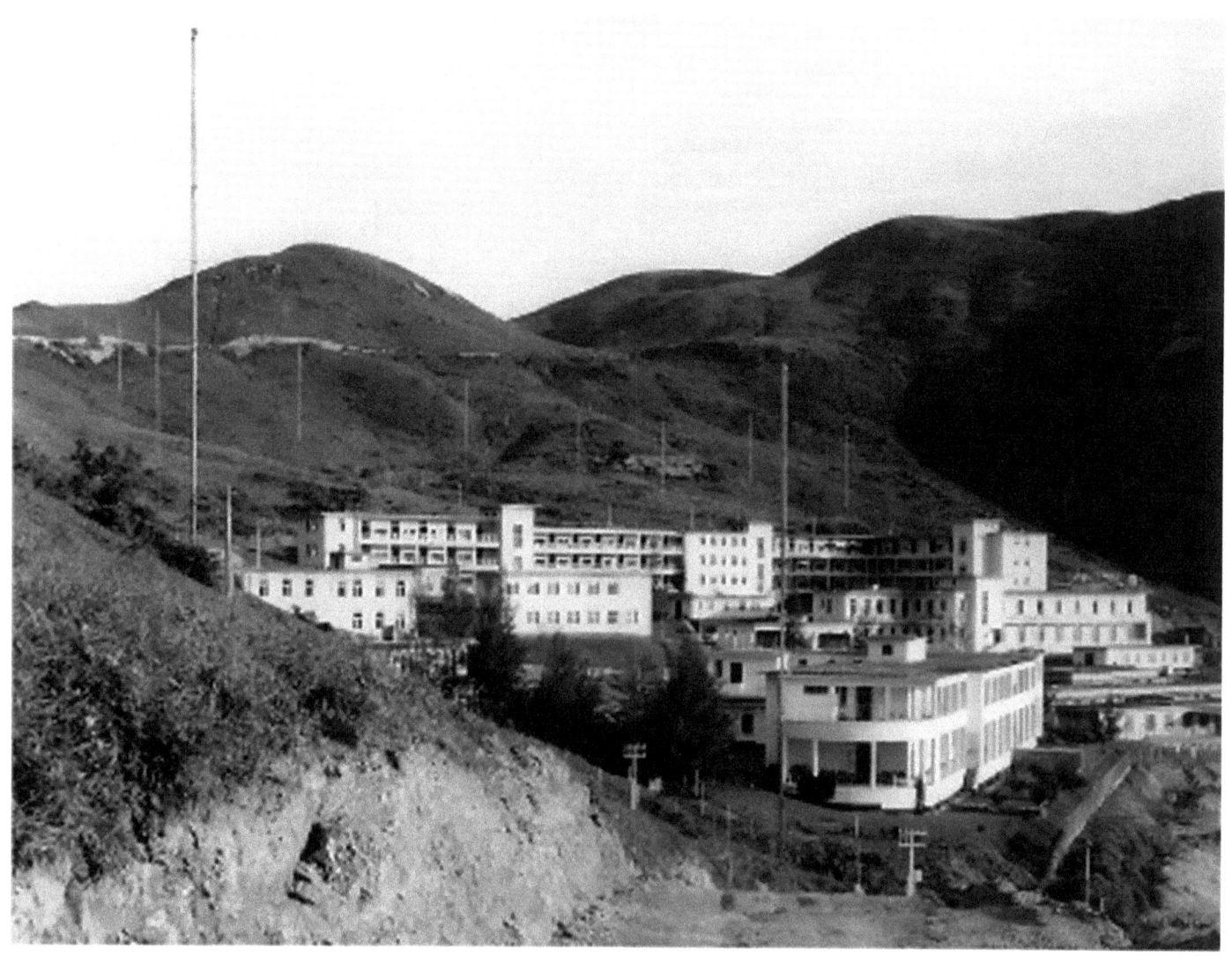

RAF Camp at Sui Sai Wan

The Communications Landscape

Sputnik 1 was launched by the Soviet Union in 1957 to orbit the earth. The American Telstar 1, launched in 1962, was the world's first active communications satellite. The world wide web would take until 1989 to be invented. So, communication by the internet and orbiting satellites, as we know it now, was some way in the future. Messages to and from our station were sent via buried cables using the now largely obsolete electro-mechanical teleprinters. It was more secure than using wireless signals, which could be easily intercepted.

Being so vast and largely undeveloped, communist China was at that time dependent on using Morse transmissions that could travel long distances and penetrate static interference caused by adverse weather conditions or cosmic radiation. Their radar and army units were therefore dependent, at that time, on wireless networks using Morse signals for reporting their activities. I was assigned to the radar section of our facility and after a while I was given the job of plotting all aircraft movements being reported by Chinese radar units in the south of China. This I did using different coloured Chinagraph pencils on a large sheet of perspex overlying a map of southern China. It was my job to collect the signals sheets from our wireless operators and, using the co-ordinates supplied by Chinese radar stations, plot the route taken by each aircraft. I therefore had access to all aircraft movements over southern China. Looking back now, it was quite a responsibility for a nineteen-year-old lad and something I could not talk about to anyone outside of my section.

We were doing the same job as had been done by British armed forces during WW2, when intelligence information gathered from wireless outstations would be analysed at Bletchley Park. In the 1950s, all intelligence gathered would be analysed at GCHQ in Gloucestershire, as it still is. Our wireless room was equipped with AR88 wireless receivers as used during WW2, albeit modified to have barrel tuners that could more speedily search the airwaves for incoming signals. Each operator had two sets, one above the other, allowing him to match up traffic between an outstation and its control station when callsigns and frequencies were changed each month by the Chinese. The position of each transmitter could then be triangulated by direction-finding equipment at RAF Little Sai Wan and our American allies on the island of Taiwan.

During the 1960s, Little Sai Wan would be manned entirely by civilians and our barrack rooms would be converted into apartments for them. As technology changed and the political tension between China and the West eased, the need for a large facility like Little Sai Wan lessened, and in 1982 it was closed for good.

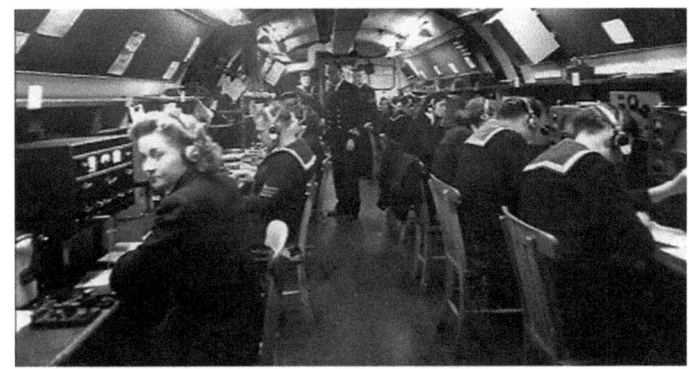

Naval wireless operators intercepting Morse signals during WW2 using old style AR88 wireless receivers (library picture).

Duty up at The Peak

Towards the end of my tour of duty in Hong Kong, our jobs were being taken over by civilians. National Service was being phased out, and there would not be the ready supply of young men to train up as 'WOPs' (wireless operators). I believe that we young guys, from all walks of life, had done a great job. Having worked as a backroom boy during most of my service at Little Sai Wan, when I was told that I was being put back to my original wireless operating job I was a bit apprehensive, to say the least. I wasn't even sure I could remember the Morse Code, let alone read it over the crackle of a wireless receiver!

My fears subsided when I was told that I was being assigned to duties at the station's satellite station atop the Peak, overlooking Victoria, Hong Kong harbour and beyond. So, for my last few weeks in Hong Kong I boarded the gharry, as the camp bus was known, to take an early morning ride through town and up to the dizzy heights of Hong Kong's lovely mountain, The Peak, where the colony's very rich had their homes. The early morning views could be stunning, and you could see for miles into the Chinese mainland. The mist-shrouded mountains were so reminiscent of classical Chinese watercolours.

Truth is, it probably changed morning by morning, but that early morning experience of arriving for duty up at the very top of The Peak has been an enduring memory of my time in Hong Kong.

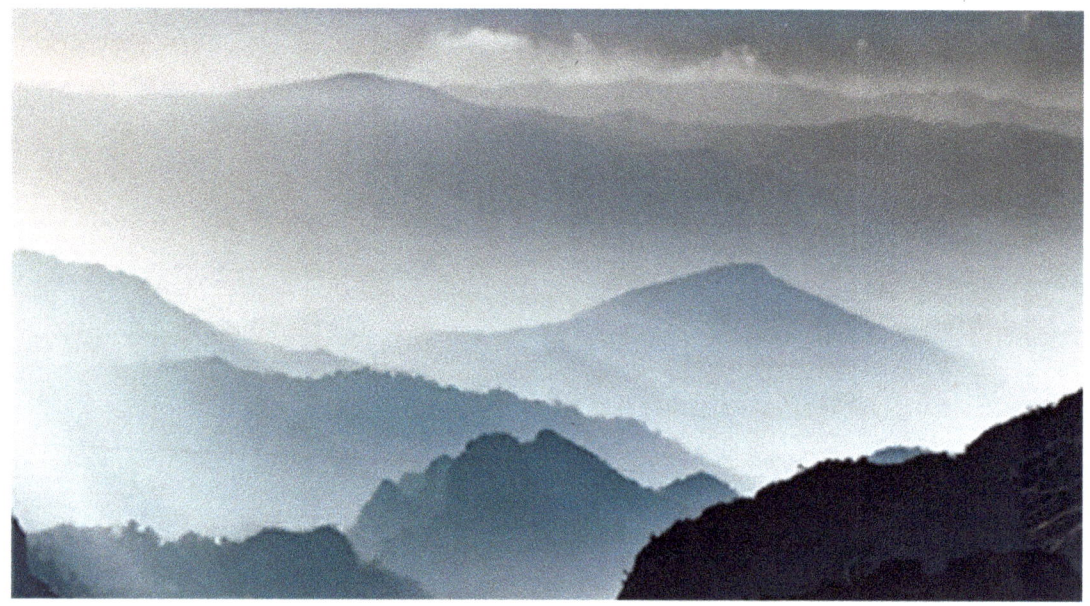

Sunrise from The Peak: The image in my mind

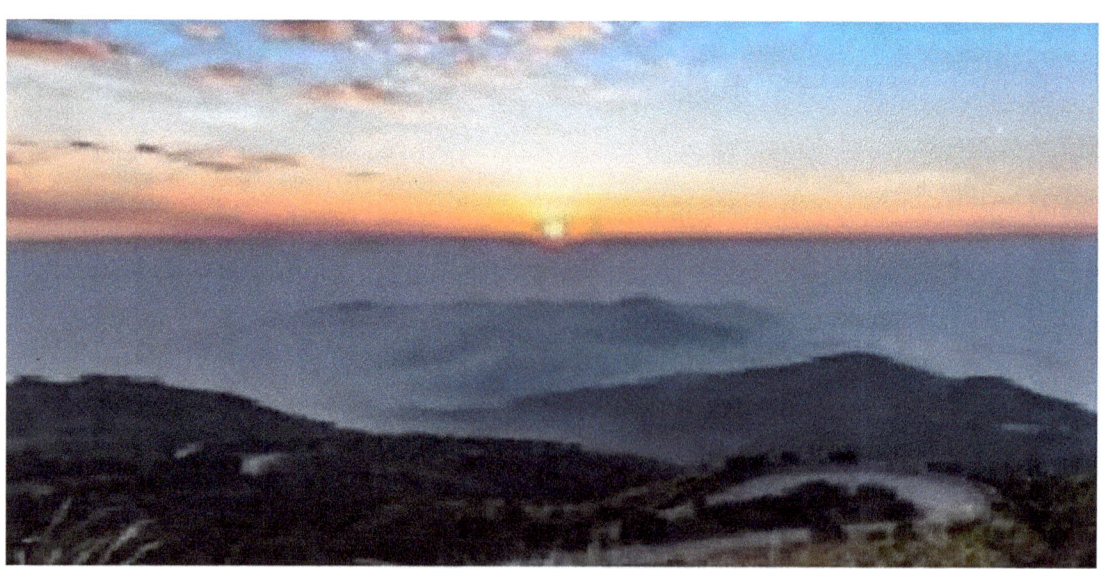

Or was it more like this?

The Day We Were Invaded

We were told that on a certain day the army guys would attack our camp to test our ability to defend ourselves against attack. It would prove convincingly that as a part of Her Majesty's armed forces we were woefully incapable of doing so.

On the given day, all off-duty airmen were ordered to draw rifles from the armoury, which I and the other guys not on duty duly did. We were then told later in the day to assemble in the camp cinema with our guns to await the impending attack. It was a large camp and had a long shoreline, plus an even longer, fenced-off boundary. There were two gates: the main gate, where the guard house was located; and a small gate on the west side, where the camp's 'amahs' (female domestics) came and went with their baskets of washing.

In theory the army could attack from anywhere along this perimeter, so it seemed that our means of defence would be to await the attack and surge out from the camp cinema to oppose the attacking forces. We were given no blanks to fire but were told that if we aimed at marauding soldier we were to shout, 'Bang! You're Dead!' That, we all agreed, would be sure to stop them in their tracks!

It grew dark and all of us off-duty airmen were assembled in the camp cinema chatting and smoking cigarettes, with our heavy Lee Enfield rifles propped between our knees, under the command of a sergeant and three corporals. Suddenly, we could hear loud bangs coming from outside.

'Lights!' shouted the sergeant, and from a brightly lit space we were plunged into blackness. 'Doors!' came the next command, and two squares of light appeared at opposite sides of the cinema. 'Out!' came the next shouted command. Easier said than done, with about two hundred airmen in the pitch dark trying to make their way down gangways or over seats, lugging their heavy rifles to their nearest square of light. There were yelps and curses as heavy rifles caught many of us painfully in places they were not intended to go! It was more a drill in how to escape from our cinema than in defending our camp.

Eventually, I managed to 'escape' and, just as I did, eight soldiers wearing khaki woollen hats and with blackened hands and faces, raced along the concrete path leading from the west gate, just above the level of the cinema. They stopped at an entrance to our multi-storey barrack block and four went in whilst the remainder stayed guard at the entrance. I could hear blanks being fired, so I went up to the four on guard at the entrance and asked if they could let me have a couple of blanks to fire. How could I have been so stupid? They looked at me in total amazement!

Just then their sergeant returned down the stairs and said, pointing at me, 'Who the hell is he?'

'Don't know, sarge,' came the reply.

'Right, take 'im along. He's our prisoner,' replied the sergeant to his bren-gunner, and with that I was prodded hard in the back with his light machine gun, followed by a burst at my heels. Whereupon I performed a high-stepping march, in absolute terror, towards the guard room, while my captor fired blacks alternately up towards our barrack block and down at my heels.

When we reached the guard room gate, the eight soldiers piled into a waiting lorry, and it was all over. RAF Little Sai Wan had proven convincingly that it would be unable to defend itself in the event of an attack from just a very few well-trained soldiers!

Leisure-time & Friends Remembered

On camp we had two tennis courts and a football pitch, plus the sea to swim in and a small weight-training room. So, for those of us who enjoyed sport and keeping in shape, there was opportunity to do so. There was also the challenging walk over the steep hill and down onto the sandy beach at Big Wave Bay, where beach football and more opportunity to swim and sunbathe could be had. During the evenings we could visit the on-camp cinema The Astra or enjoy a drink at the NAAFI.

Of the many friends I made at Little Sai Wan, there was Stacey Davis, who went on in civilian life to become a stage and TV actor; Neville, who would return to his job as an advertising executive in Manchester; and Barry, who would stay on in Hong Kong, marry his Chinese girlfriend and find work as a DJ on local radio. Then there was Nick, who had a job at the bank waiting for him back home in Devon; my pal Frank, with whom I enjoyed what was termed an 'indulgence trip' to Japan, travelling by passenger-cargo tramp steamer first to Tokyo and then to the port of Kobe further south, where it would pick us up again. It was a wonderful experience. We met up with two other RAF lads on the ship so explored Japan together. Then there was my pal and tennis opponent Tony Campion, with whom I enjoyed that visit to Macau.

Our section sergeant was Ernie, a great guy who had been awarded the OBE for his work at Sai Wan and who rode in each day on his Lambretta scooter from Victoria where he lived off camp with his Chinese wife and their new baby.

Last but by no means least, a mention for our lovely Amah, Amoy, who did all our washing and ironing, cleaned our room, and even prepared our webbing and brasses for the monthly CO's parade. She was, as always, cheerful and, as my picture shows, our little ray of sunshine.

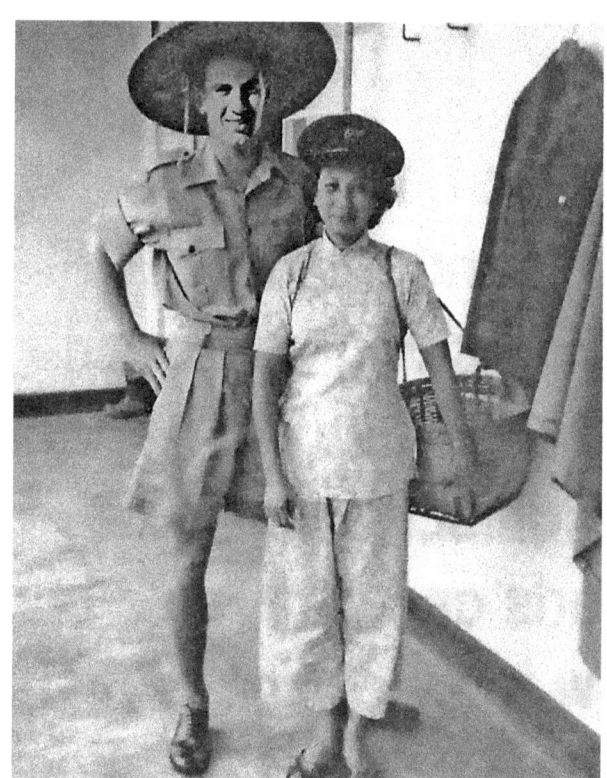

Amoy and I swapped hats for this picture taken on the balcony outside my barrack room.

Satellite Image of Hong Kong Island Today

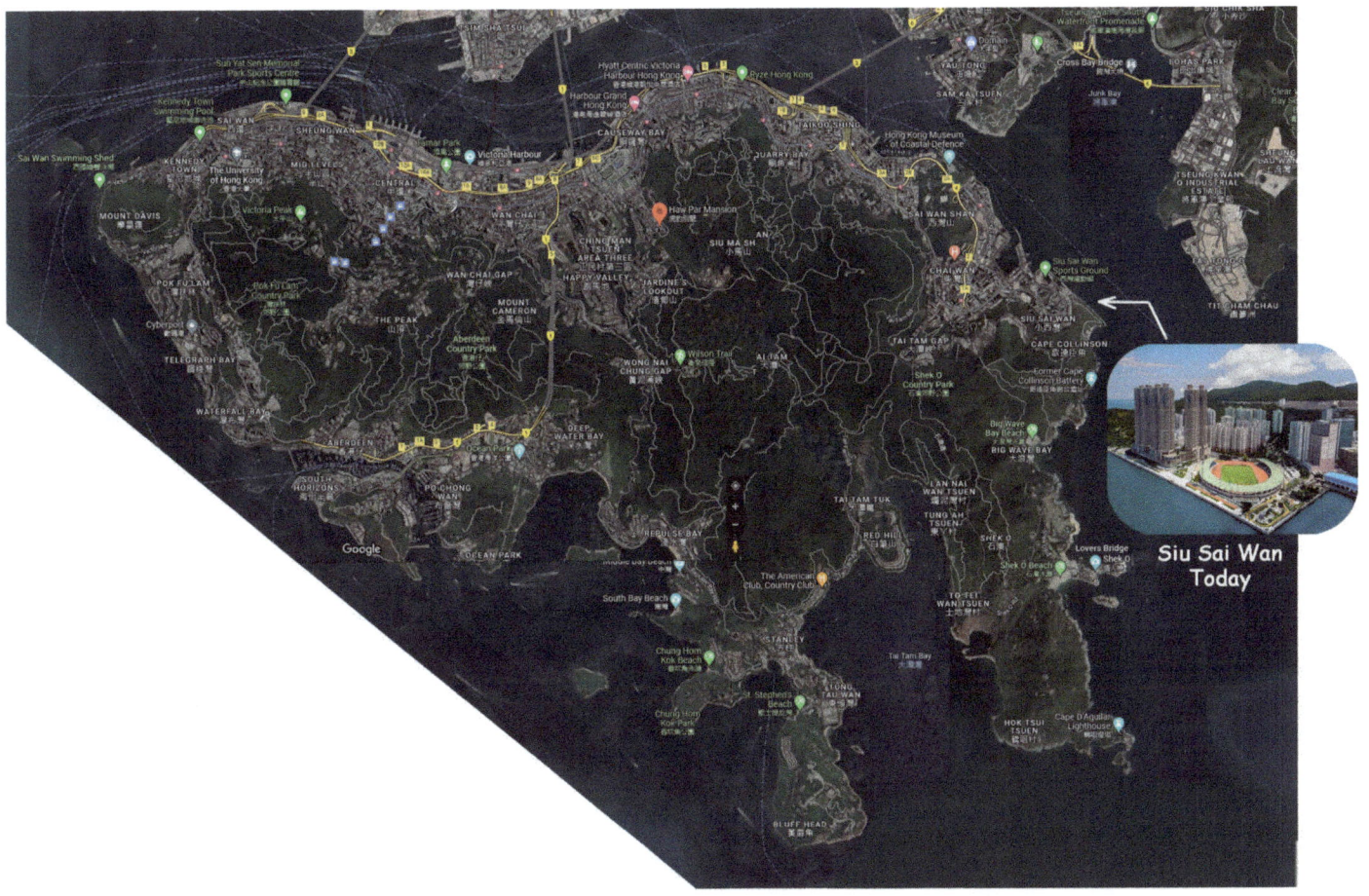

Much of the coastline of Hong Kong Island has been extended out with reclamation schemes. Many more roads and high-rise buildings are now in evidence, and the Hong Kong that I remember is gone for ever.

Reminders of Japanese Occupation

It has been said that history tends to be written by the victors and, in the case of recent history, I believe that is very likely to be true. I also believe that it is a mistake to try to make amends for how our forebears saw things, because, in what is hopefully now a kinder world, some things that were once accepted by society at large are often seen not to be the way we should now behave towards our fellow humans.

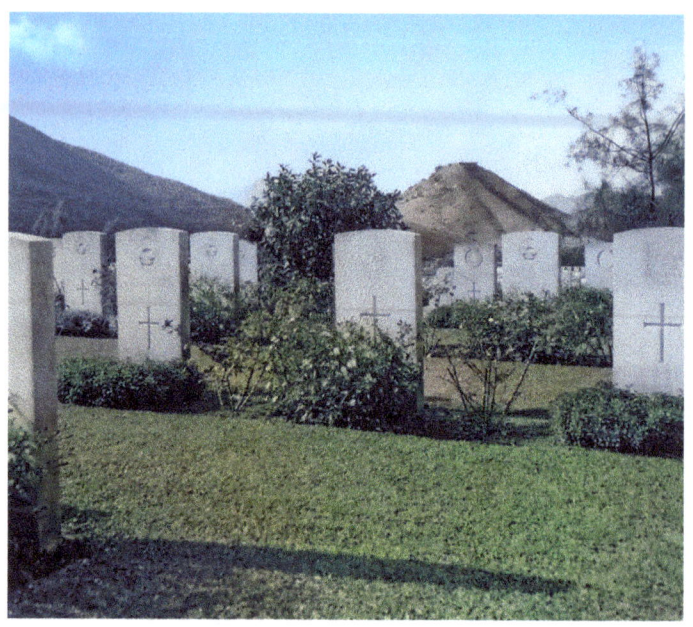

If we try to look dispassionately back at WW2, there can be no doubt that bad deeds were committed by all sides during those troubled times. It is therefore not my place or intention to judge but to show here a little of the evidence that remained of the Japanese occupation during that time.

Although a brave resistance to invasion by Japanese forces was put up by British, Canadian and colonial troops with only minimal support being possible from the Royal Navy and RAF, Hong Kong was forced to surrender on 25th December 1941. Over two thousand defenders were killed or reported missing, and the Sai Wan Cemetery (top right) was a sad reminder of the price paid by these mainly young men.

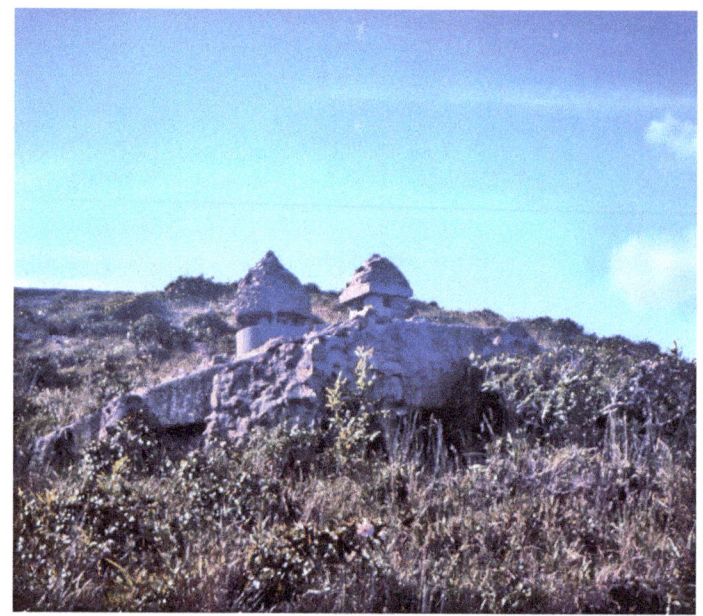

On a walk, I also came across what appears to have been perhaps a Japanese machine gun box built into the hillside (bottom right). The narrow road to our camp, cut into the mountain sides, was reportedly originally built by prisoners of war.

(The picture of the war cemetery was taken from a scanned-in black and white print and 'colorized' using Photoshop, whereas the picture of the machine gun box was scanned directly from a colour slide.)

Digital Enhancement

As a young airman in Hong Kong, and now as a retired engineer, my endeavours to produce photographic imagery have been self-taught and entirely amateur by nature. What has astounded me, since starting, after retirement, to try to master skills in the use of digital software, in the form of Adobe's Photoshop Elements, is the way that, with such modern-day technology, even as a self-taught amateur, I have continued to be able to unlock details stored in the original images that were created over sixty years ago.

The process used in film photography is in essence a chemical one whereby light, focused through a camera lens, makes chemical changes to a roll of film positioned at the back of the camera. This is then processed in a dark room to 'fix' the images chemically into a developed film, which are termed negatives. From the negatives, prints can then be made of the images that have been photographed.

Many years later I 'scanned' these images onto the 'memory' contained within my computer, thus converting them from their original form of information stored chemically either as prints or as colour slides, into digital or binary format, the numerical language of computer technology.

A scanned image is transformed by computer technology into one made up thousands of tiny squares called pixels. The human eyes see a total image as the brain blends all the individual pixels to form a complete picture. 'Resolution' refers to the quality of an image, and a resolution of 300 ppi (or 300 pixels per inch in each direction, giving 90,000 pixels per square inch) is a fair resolution for most images.

What I have found to be so remarkable is how film camera images, taken and processed so many years ago in Hong Kong, can now yield up hitherto indistinct details by means of having been converted into a digital format, thus rendering them capable of being 'digitally enhanced' so that details concealed for so long are brought back to life again.

For most of the images that I have presented in this record of life during the 1950s in Hong Kong, I have used such tools that Photoshop has to offer to enhance the details contained in my original mainly black and white photography, to produce 'grayscale' pictures, plus a few samples from colour slides. On the following pages I have endeavoured to demonstrate how images can also be 'colorized', to use Photoshop's terminology, and how a black and white image can be enlarged to produce an interesting close-up.

On this and following pages:
By use of the enhancement tools offered by
Adobe Photoshop Elements, the original image has
revealed greater detail and colour has been added.

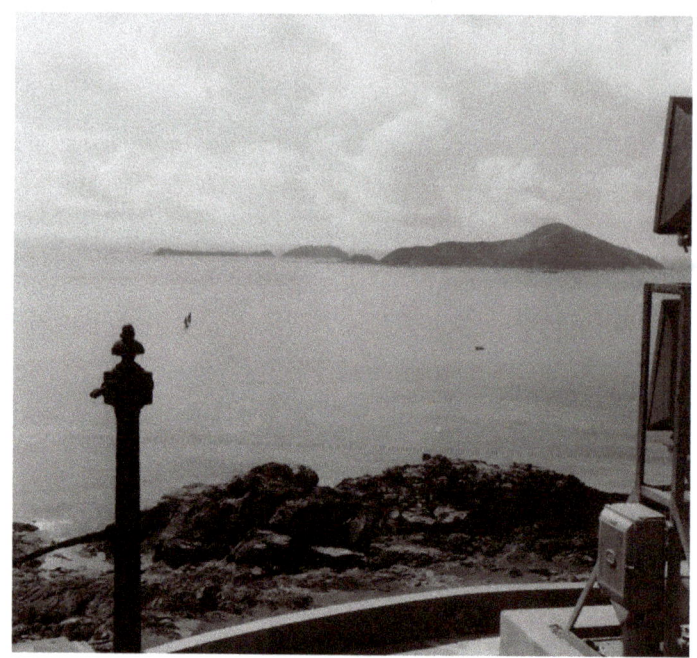

Original image

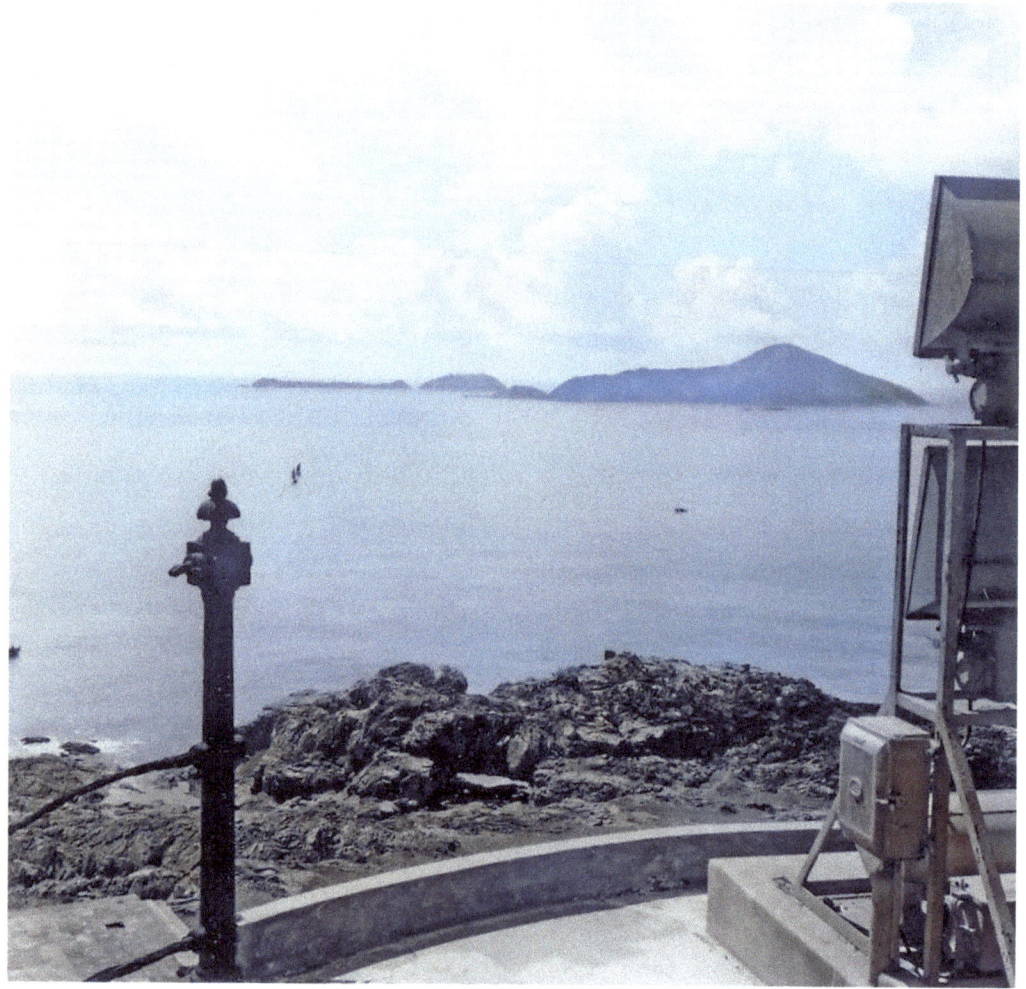

Enhanced image

PRELUDE TO CHANGE: HONG KONG OF THE 1950S

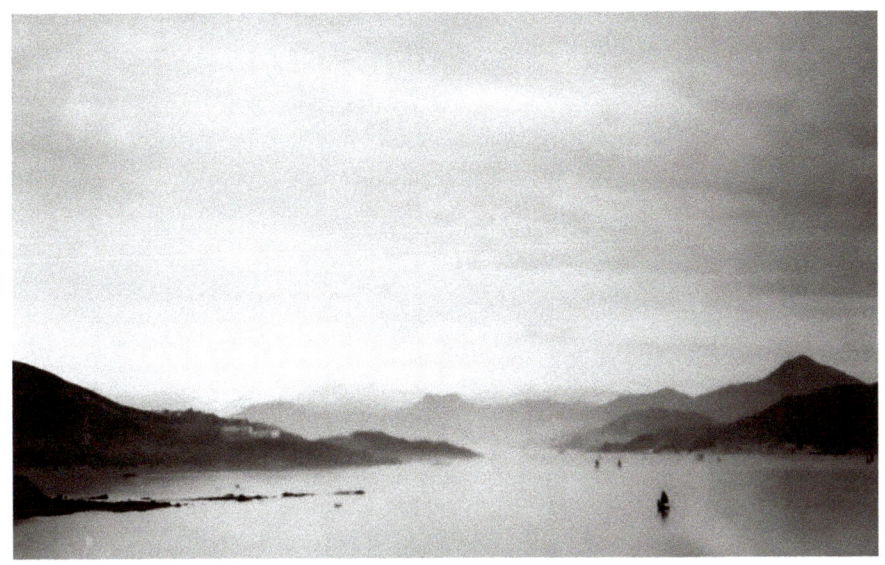

Original image: Looking out from Little Sai Wan on misty morning.

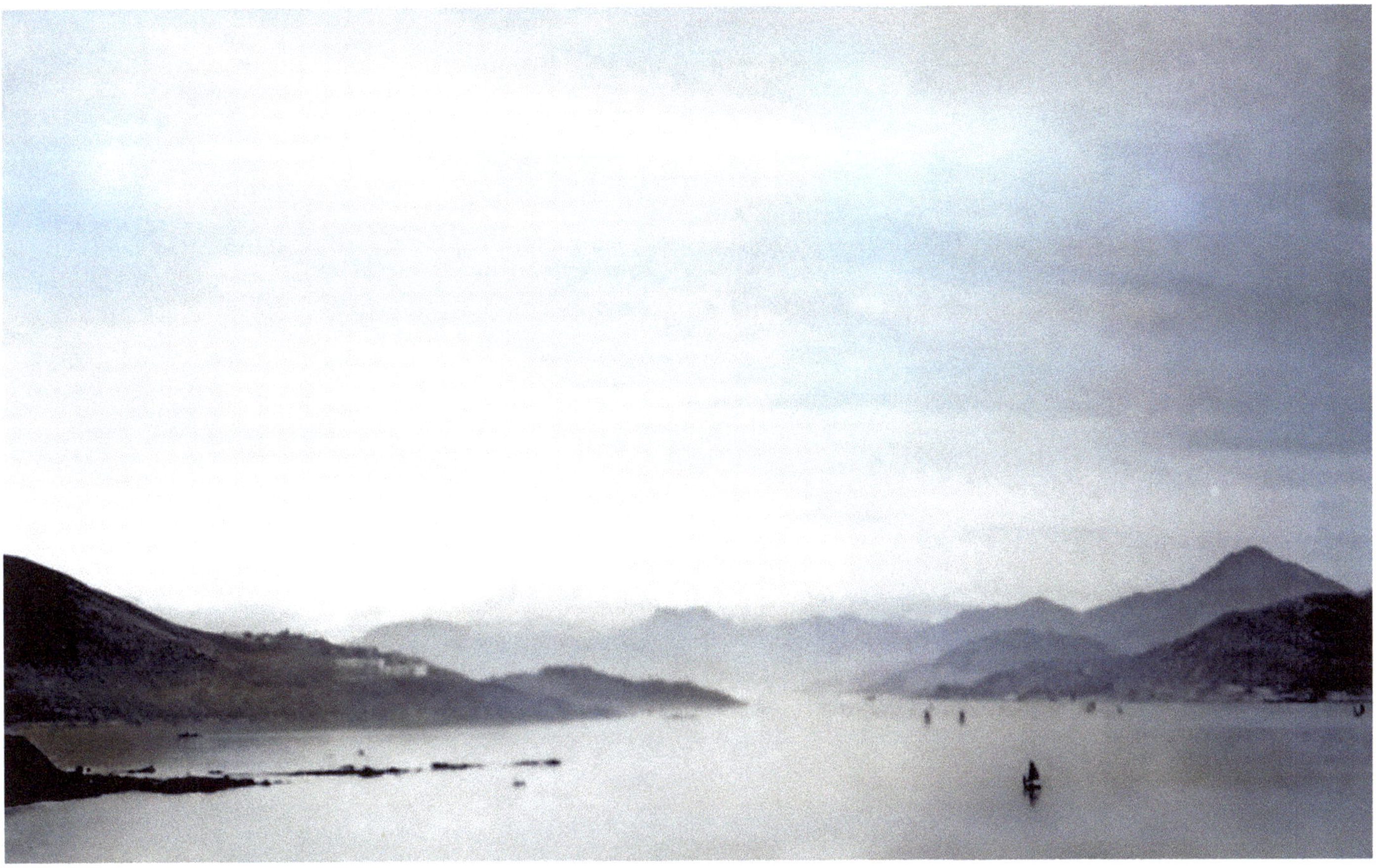

Colorised image

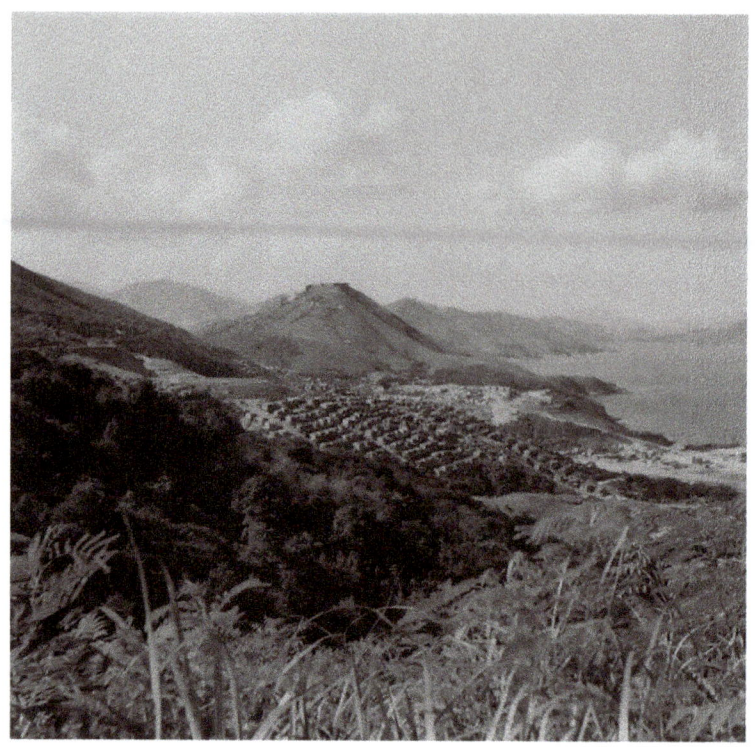

Original Image

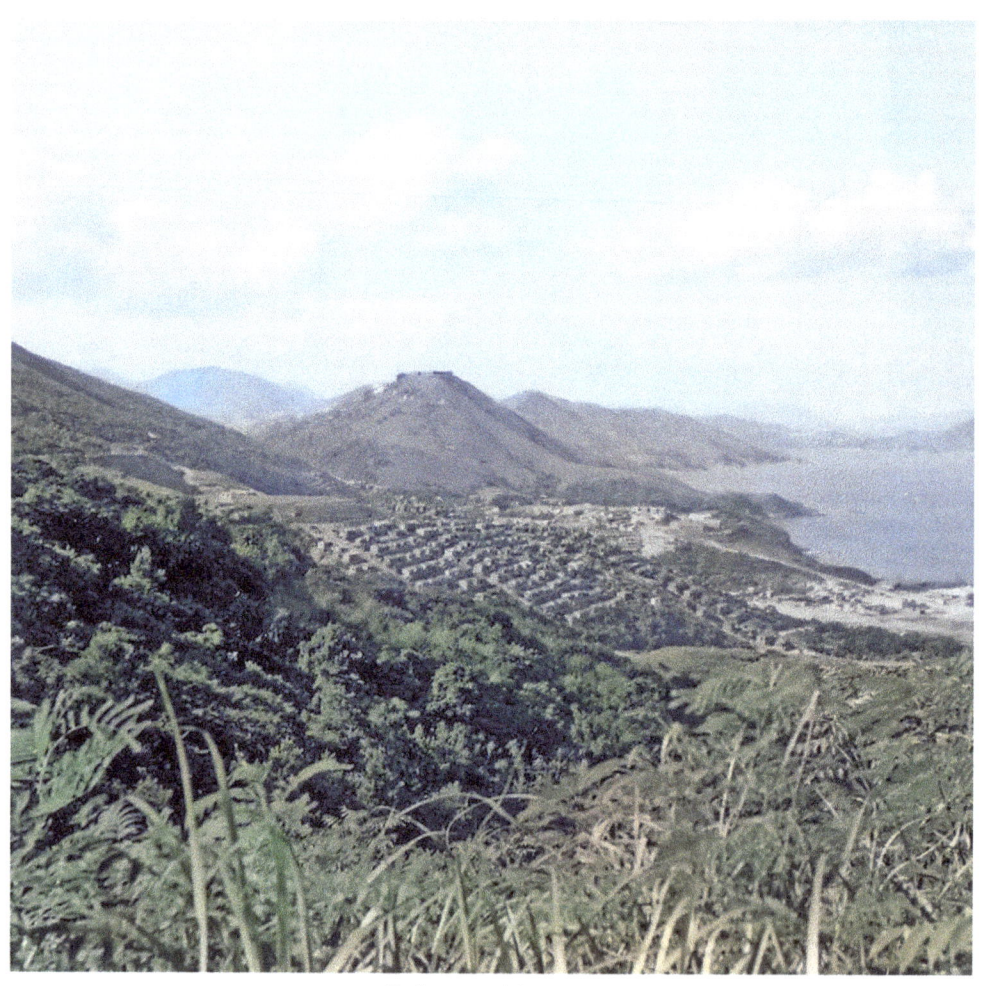

Enhanced image

PRELUDE TO CHANGE: HONG KONG OF THE 1950S

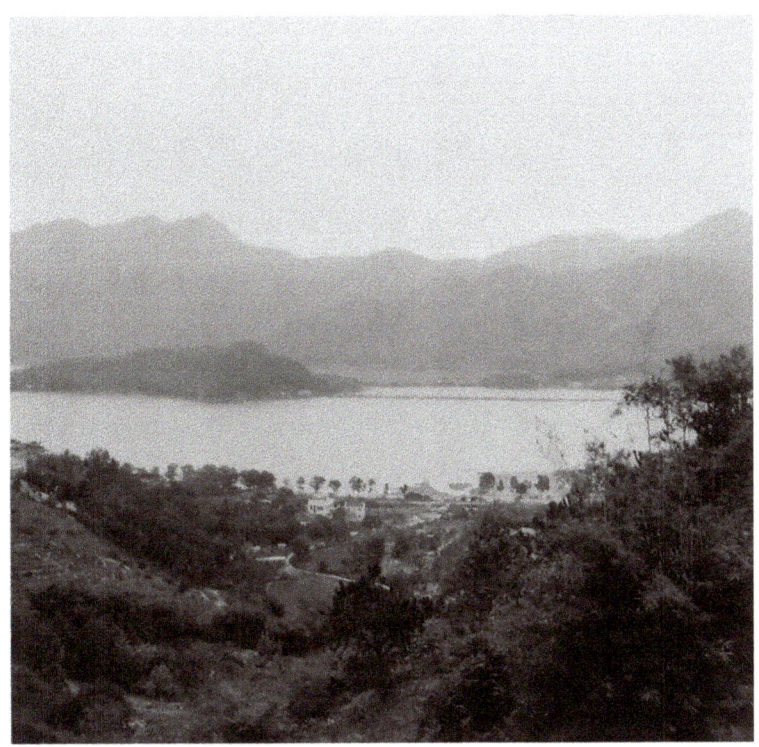

Original Image

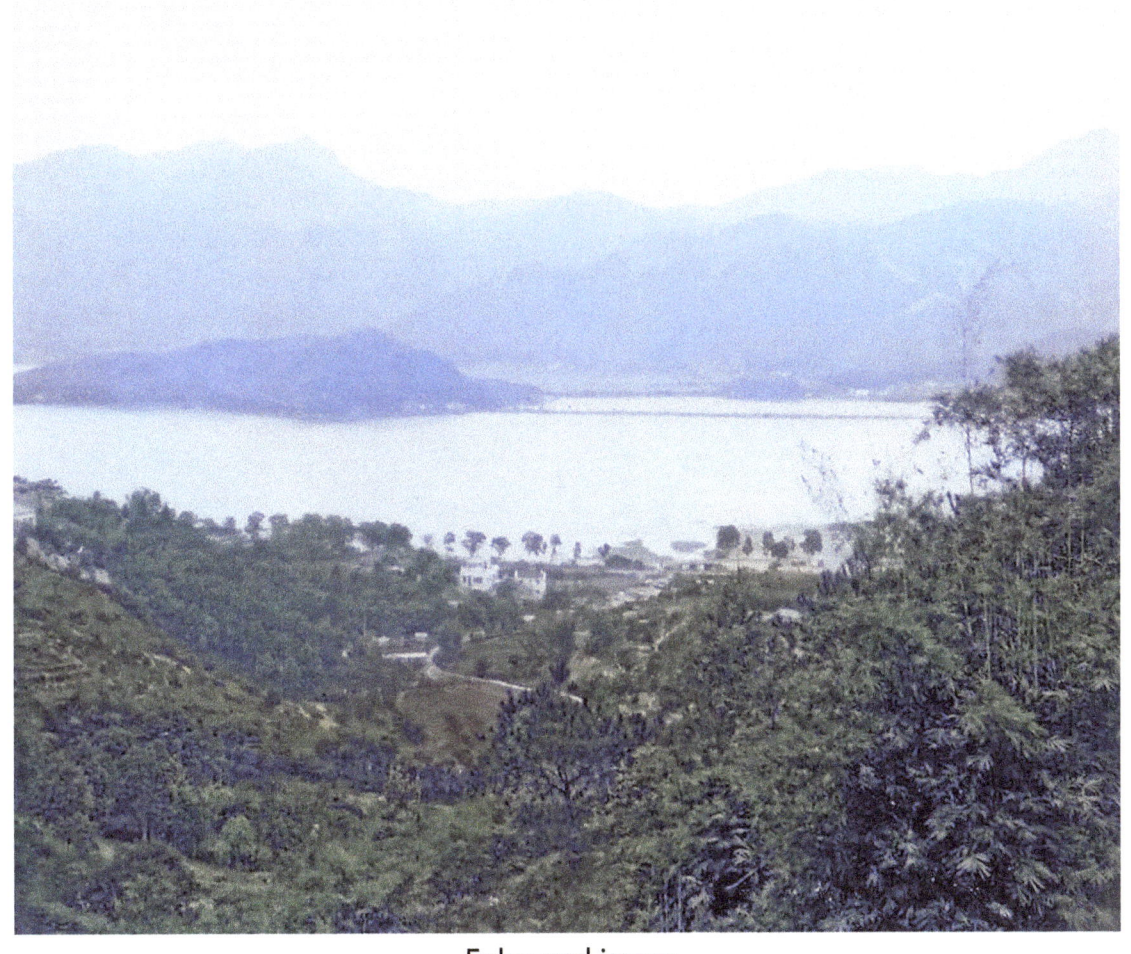

Enhanced image

DIGITAL ENHANCEMENT

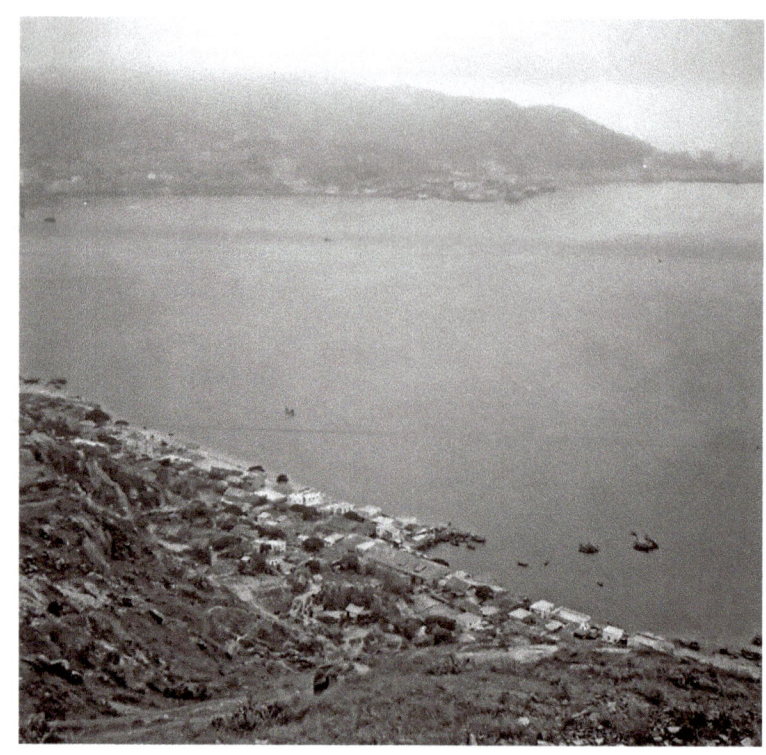

Original Image

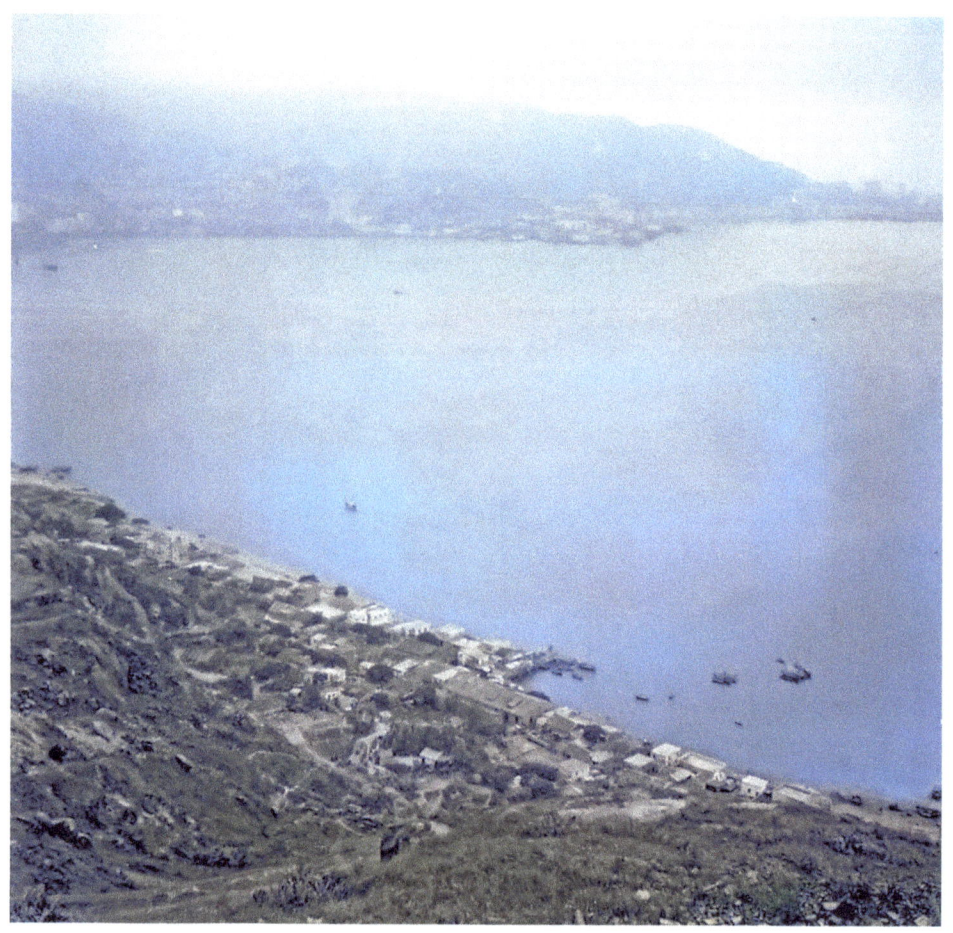

Enhanced image

PRELUDE TO CHANGE: HONG KONG OF THE 1950S

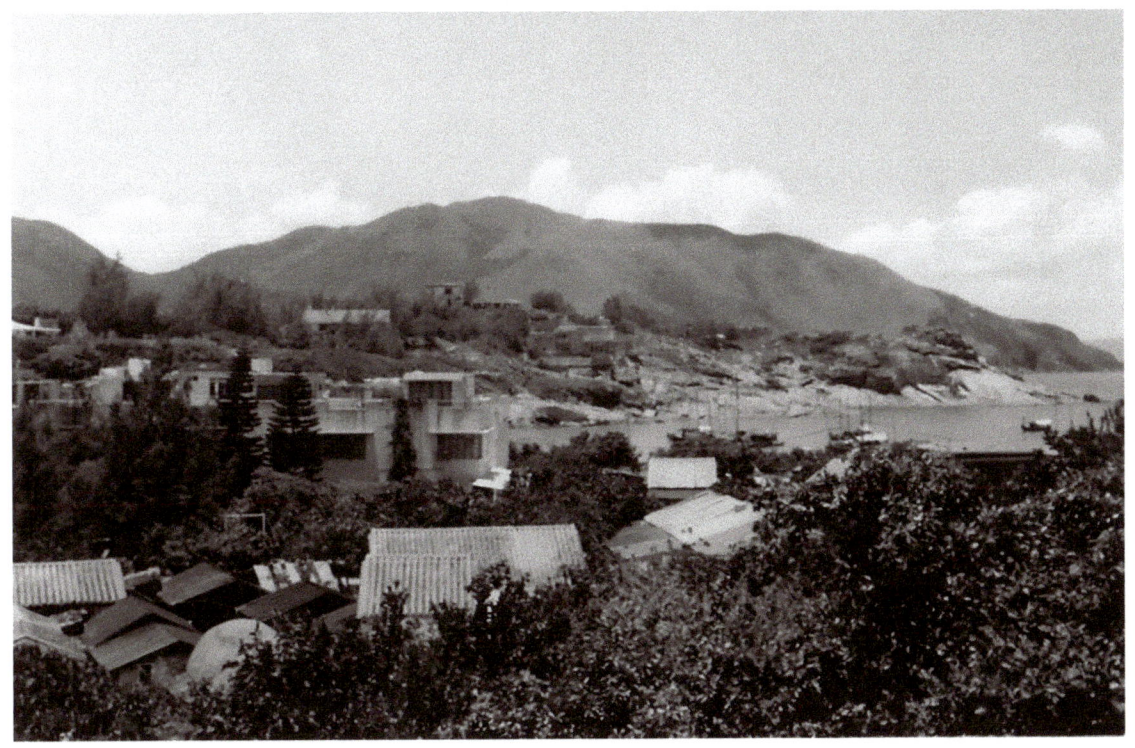

Original Image

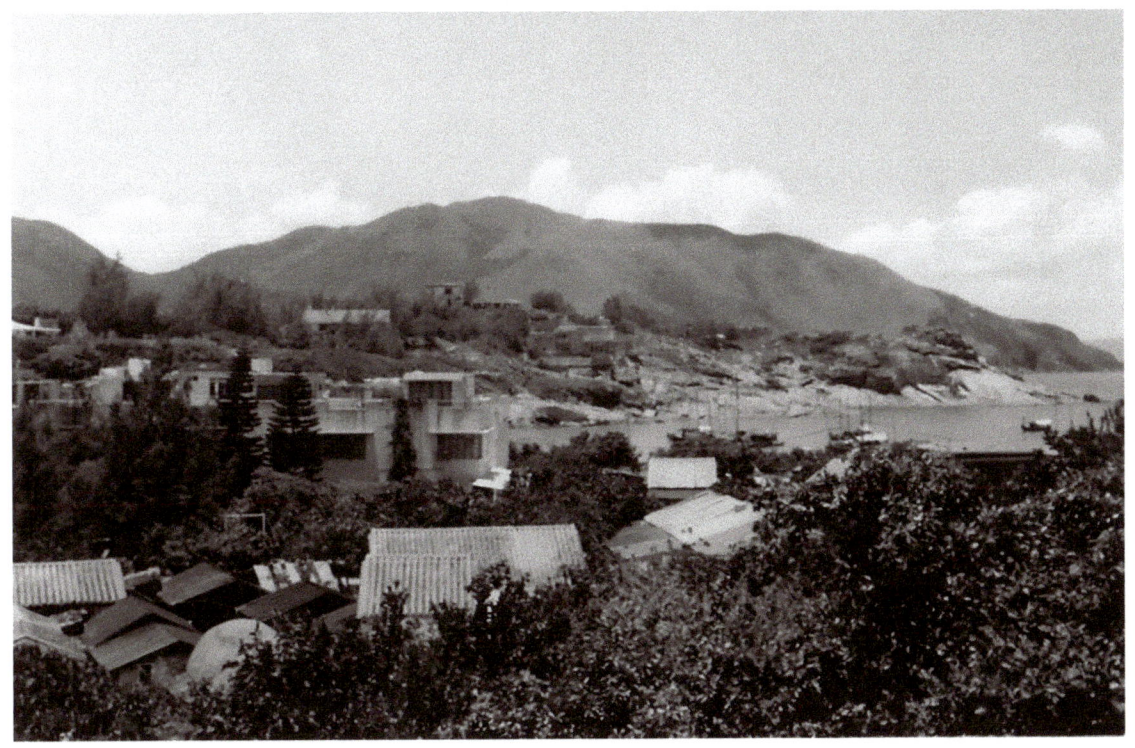

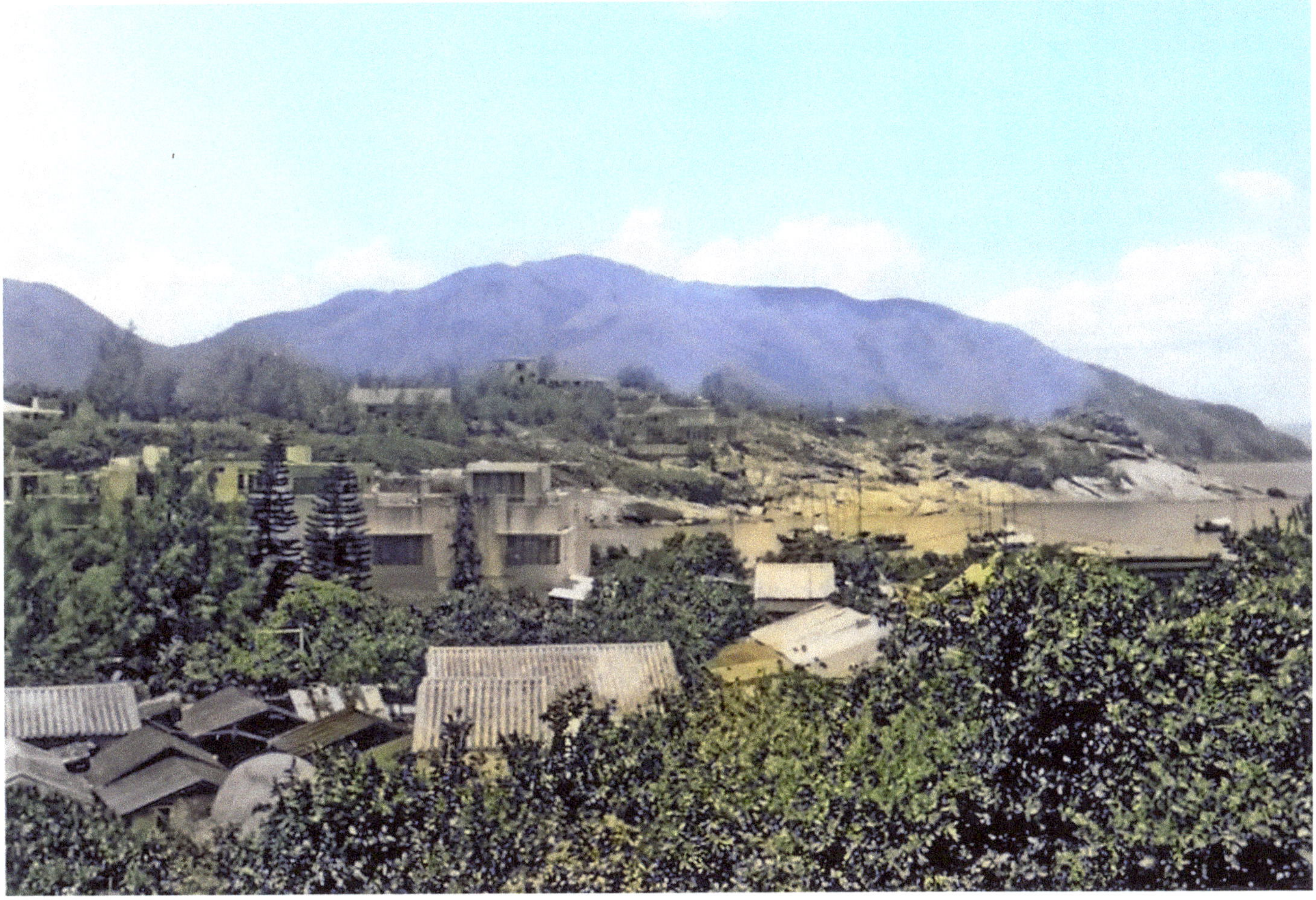

Enhanced image

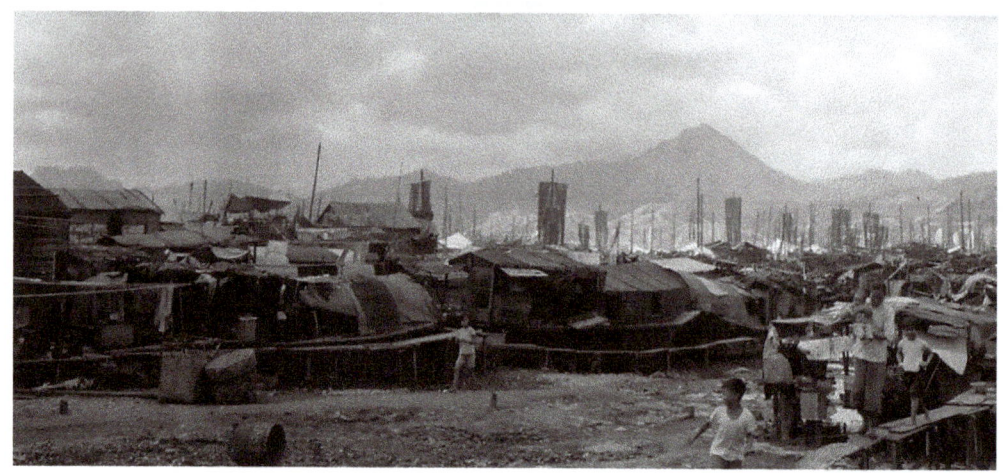

Original Image

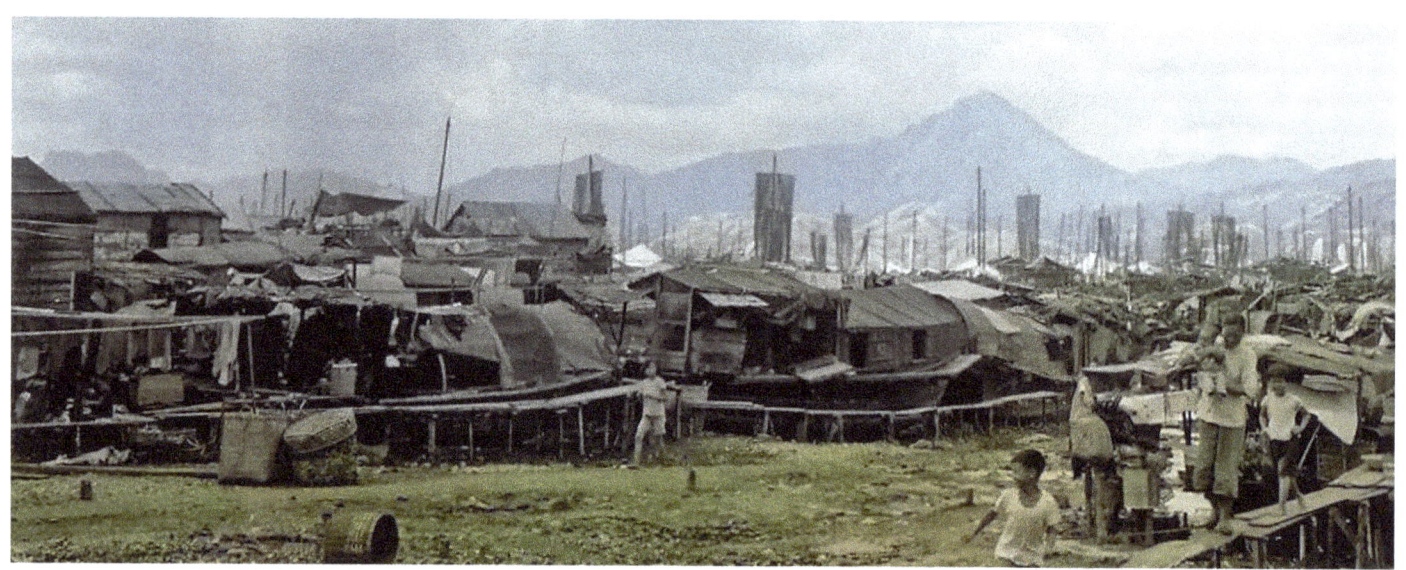

Enhanced image

PRELUDE TO CHANGE: HONG KONG OF THE 1950S

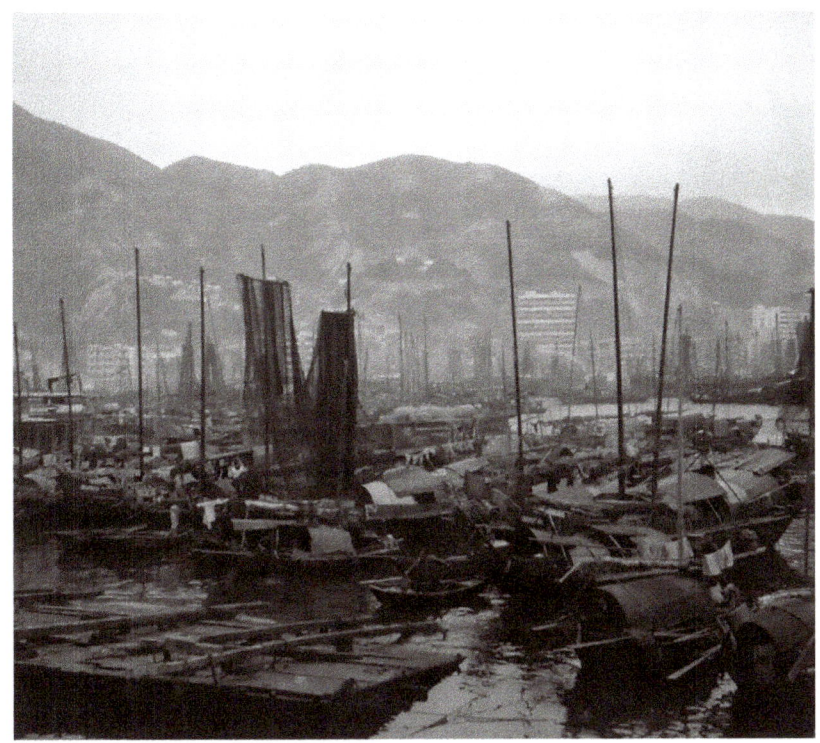

Original Image

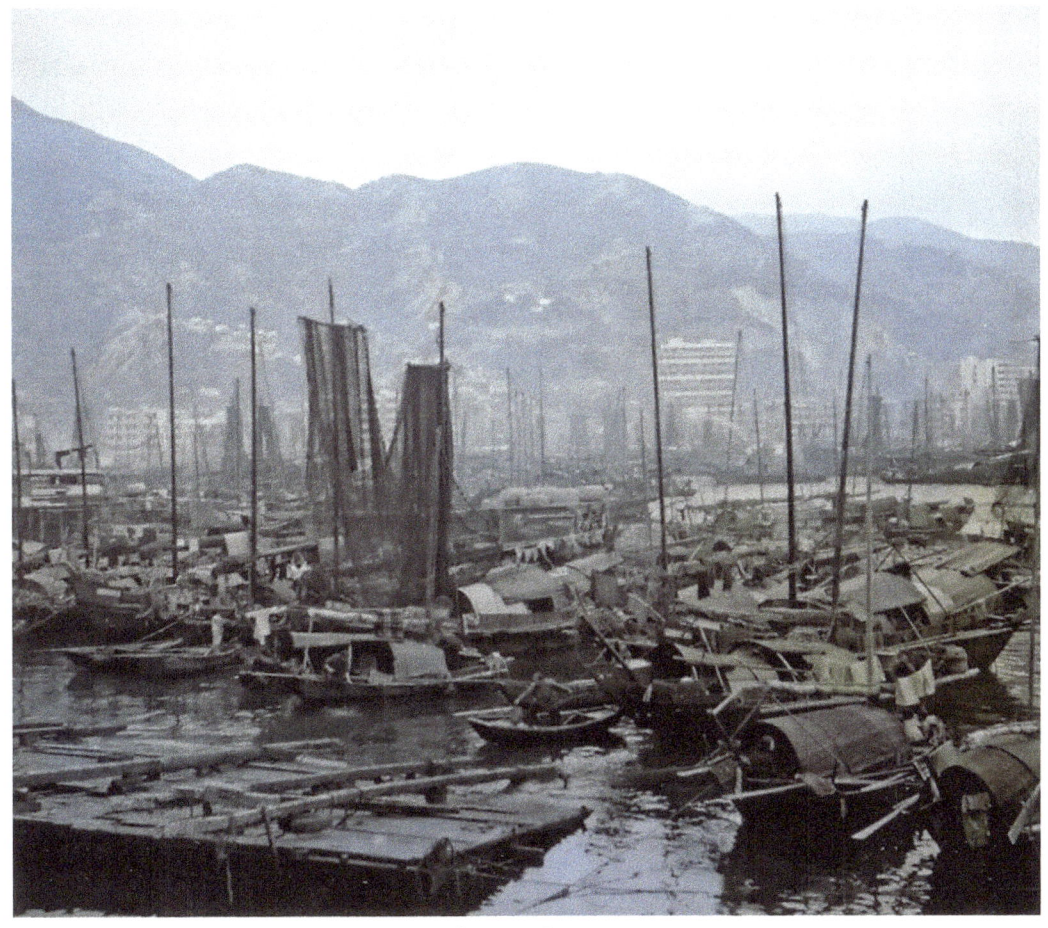

Enhanced image

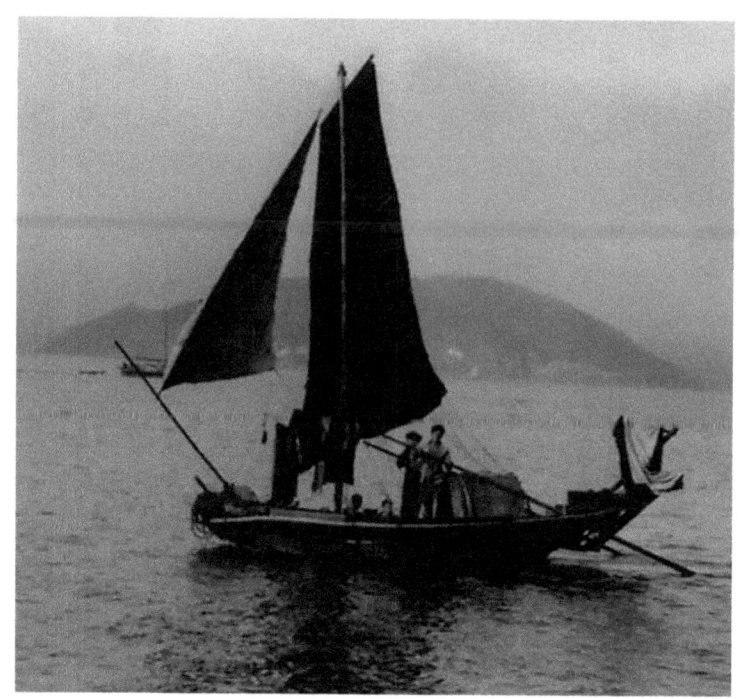

Original Image

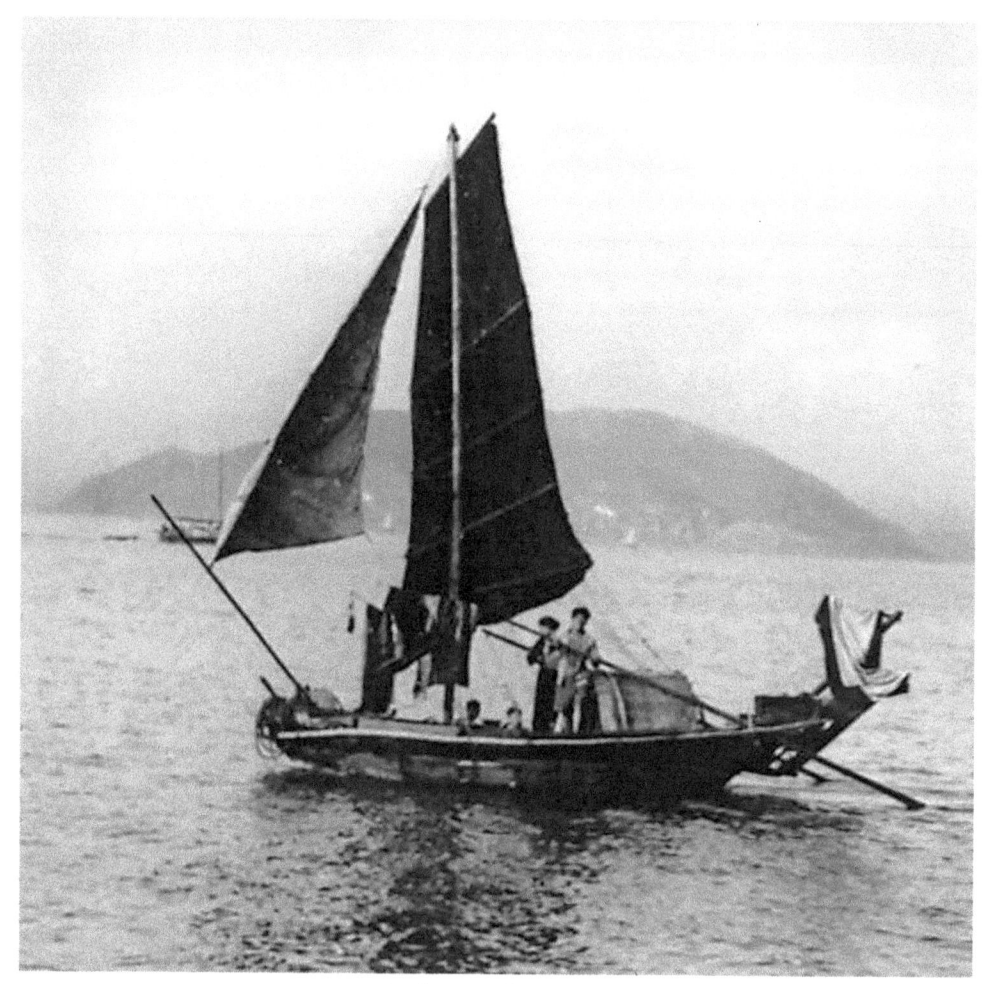

Enhanced image

PRELUDE TO CHANGE: HONG KONG OF THE 1950S

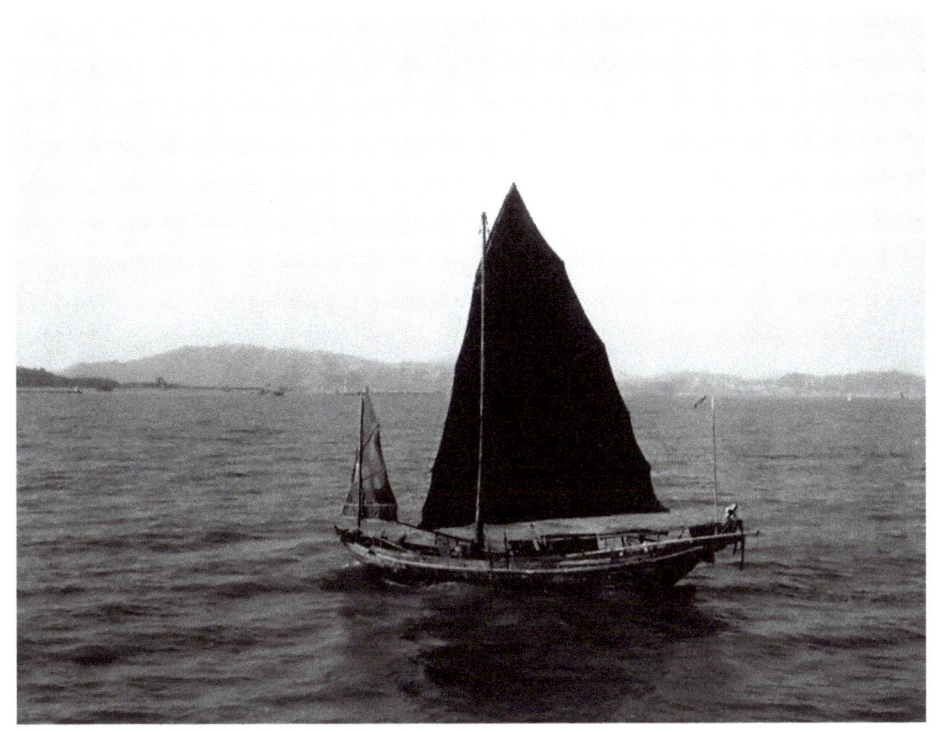

Original Image

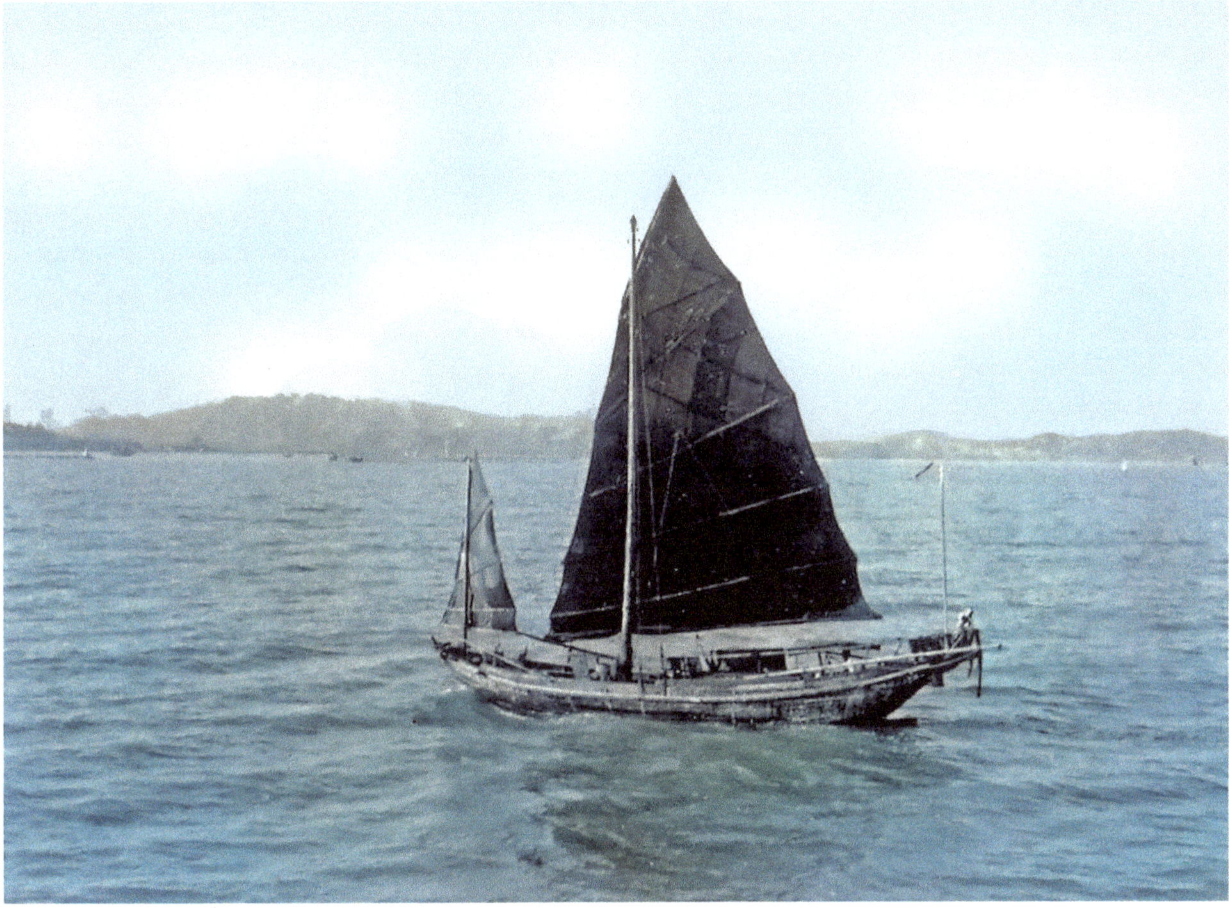

Enhanced image

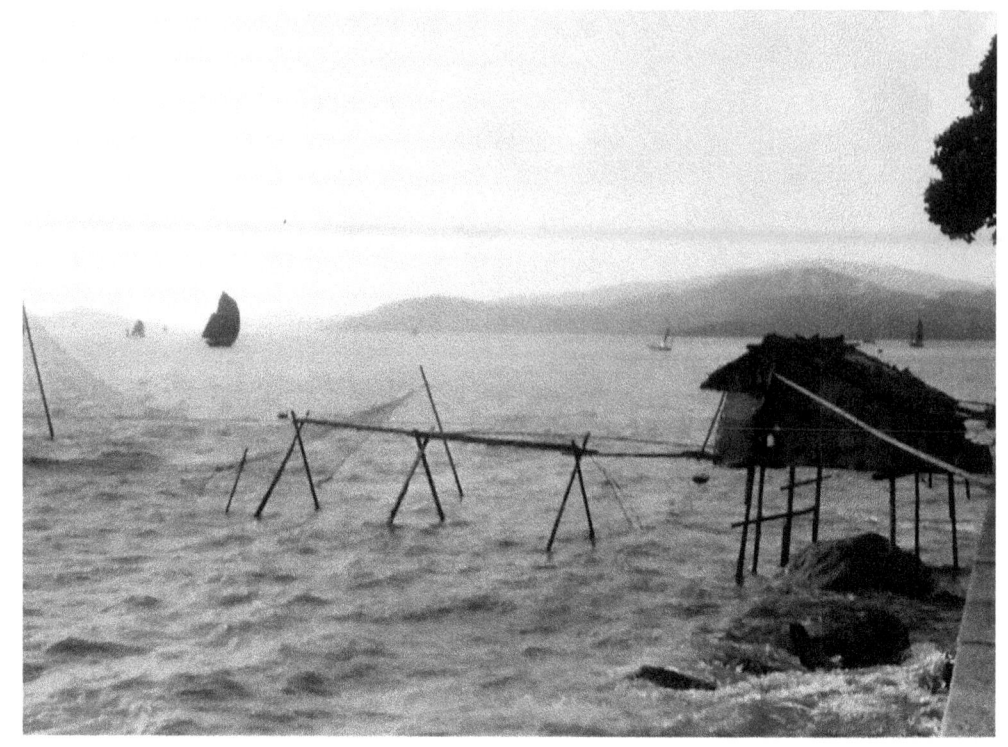

Original Image

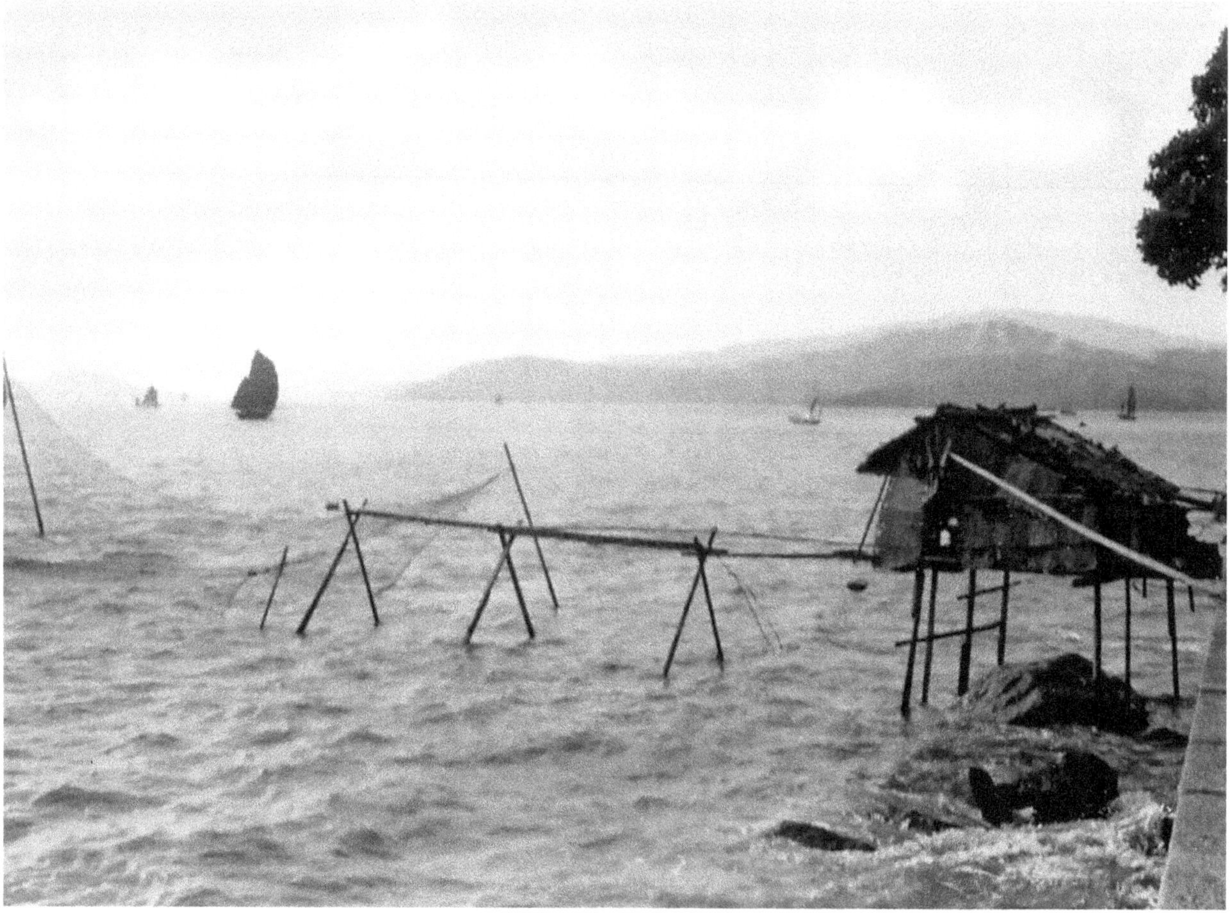

Enhanced image

PRELUDE TO CHANGE: HONG KONG OF THE 1950S

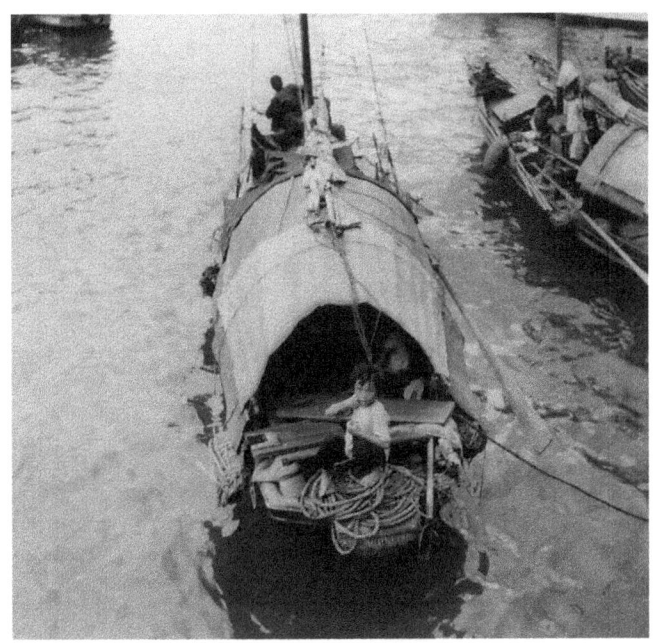

Original Image

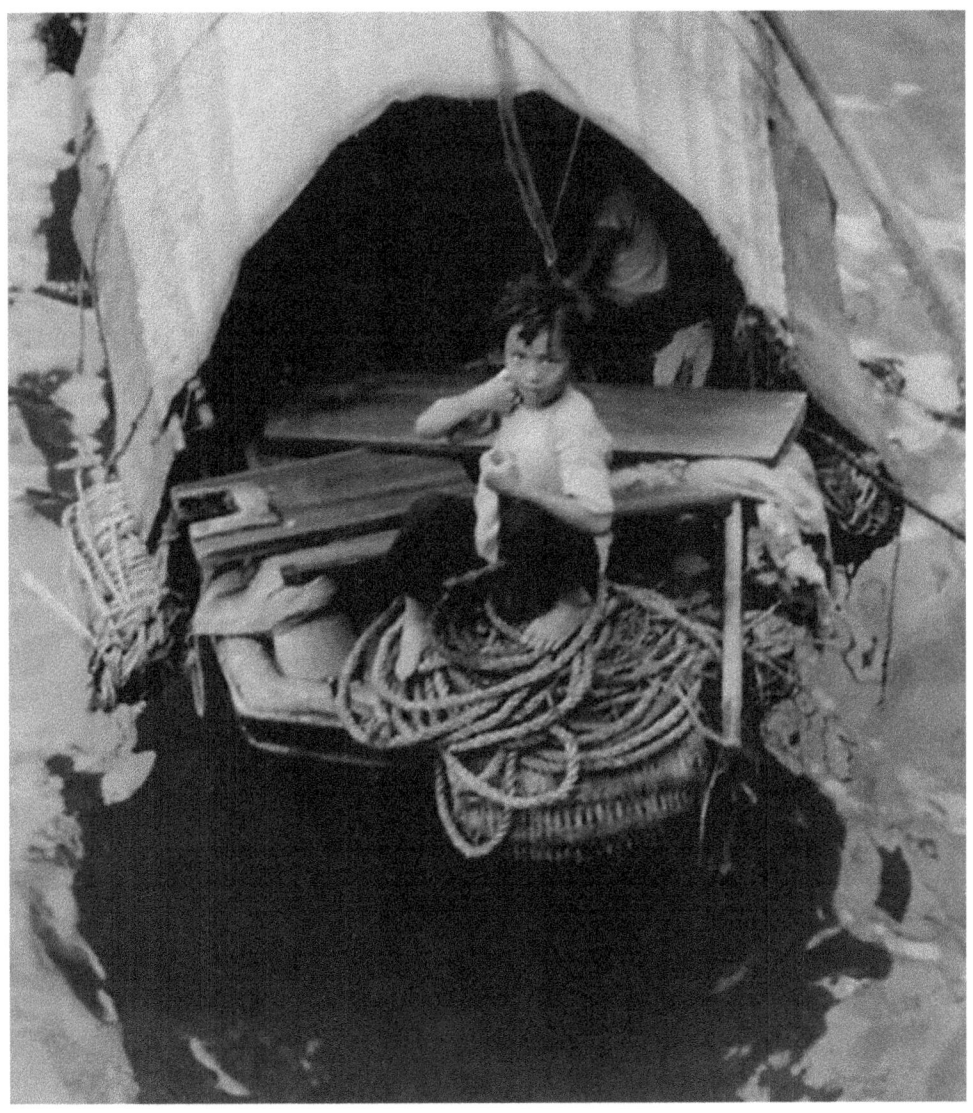

Enhanced enlarged image of young sampan dweller.

Farewell to Hong Kong

To get a posting to Hong Kong was a young serviceman's dream if, like me, he had a thirst for travel and adventure. From my photographs, the Hong Kong of the '50s clearly did not disappoint. The Hong Kong that I remember is not the Hong Kong of today. My Hong Kong was a colonial one, where the authorities struggled to cope with terrible overcrowding and inadequate housing. But it was also very vibrant and beautiful. My Hong Kong is the place depicted in my photographs and locked for ever in my memory.

In July of 1959, I took my last look at the place that had been home for the past two and a half years, from the deck of HMT Empire Fowey, the ship that would take me, and many other servicemen, back home. It was, for me, a prospect every bit as daunting as when I had taken off from RAF Lyneham all of those months past.

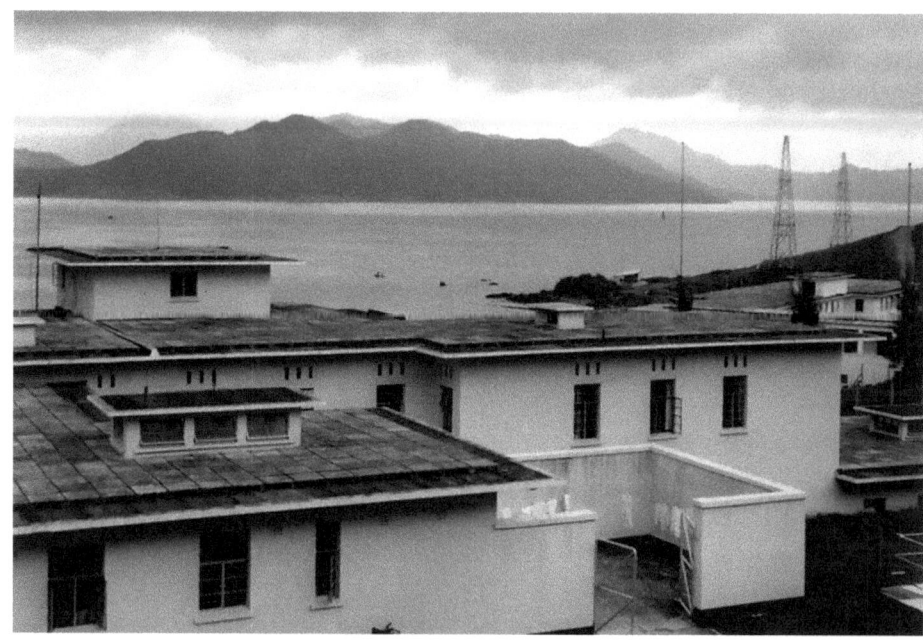
Sai Wan as it was

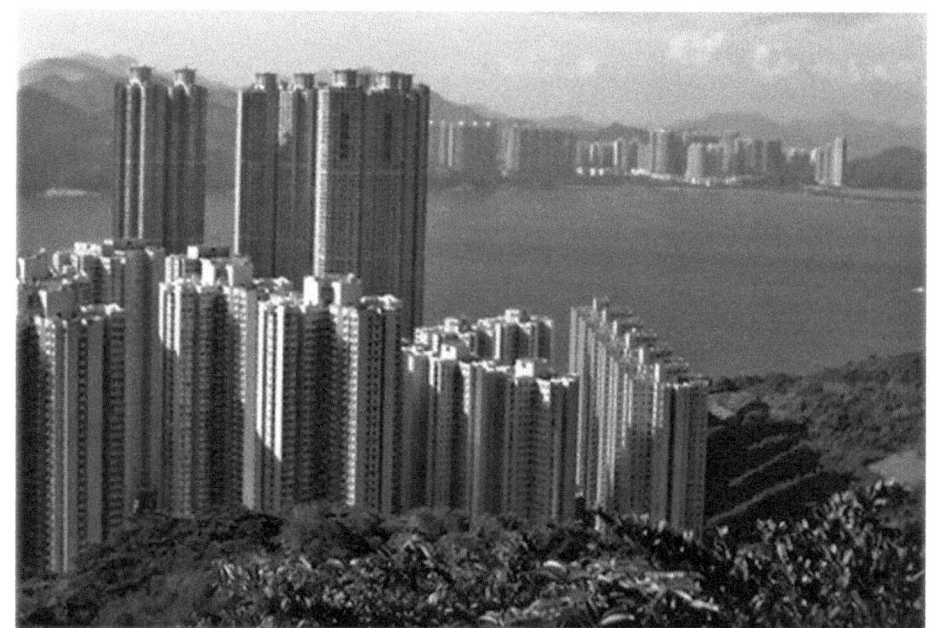
As it is today (library picture)

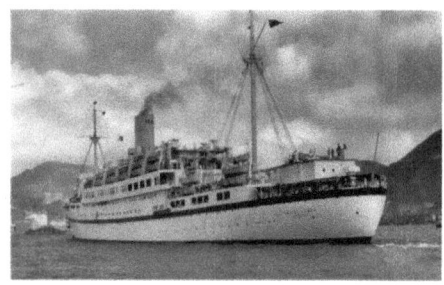
HMT Empire Fowey, Hong Kong Harbour 1959 (library picture)

As it was for so many servicemen and women, becoming a civilian again was a total shock to the system. Not only did I find that I missed the ever-present companionship of service life, but late 'fifties Britain seemed, by comparison to Hong Kong, drab, and uninteresting, while no employer needed someone whose only skill was to be able to send and receive Morse signals. All the people I had known in Dover where I had grown up, were dispersed, my parents had divorced and there was no longer a bedroom for me at the flat my mother and sister had rented. I got a job selling advertising space to small shops and other businesses for a local agency representing various parish magazines. It was lonely and soul-destroying, travelling by train to all parts of England and Wales to put up for a few days at a bed and breakfast while I tried to persuade small business owners to part with their hard-earned money. My failure to succeed was probably due to my own lack of belief that advertising in a local magazine would do anything to increase their profits. It was a lonely, miserable existence that lasted only a couple of weeks.

I persuaded my sister, who lived with her husband and two toddlers in Old Windsor, to let me rent their boxroom and found a job as a progress chaser at an injection-moulding plastics factory in Slough on a huge commercial estate. My new employers soon discovered that my heart was not in checking the number of 'widgets' produced per day, so my daily trips to Slough soon came to an end. By this time, I had formed a burning ambition to pass my car driving test and become a sales representative with a Hillman Minx car, just like our friend and close neighbour. Had I joined a different sales team in the company I might have fared better, but my small, niche team sold electronic conductors, and my lack of knowledge in this area was soon exposed. My immediate superior, the guy supposed to ease me into the job, had gained a commission during his National Service and flown jet fighters. He reminded me of this superiority frequently and not entirely to my surprise, after my six-month trial period ended, so did my dream of being a 'rep' driving around in a Hillman Minx car.

At this point I resolved that never again would I lose a job due to a lack of appropriate training and qualifications. It had been a pipe-dream from back in my RAF days that I would like to become a civil or structural engineer. I had even sent off and paid my first instalment of a correspondence course. Hong Kong had held too many distractions and too few inducements for me to stick at it, but this time I was determined to succeed.

I went to the library in Windsor and managed to find the addresses of over sixty civil and structural contractors and consultants – and I wrote off to every one of them. Only one came back with the offer of a job, but it was in Manchester. It was for me to start at the very bottom to work and study part time to become a structural concrete designer-detailer. So off to Manchester I went and as soon as the new academic year started, I signed up for a two-year evening class course for an ONC in Building Technology.

I had learned that within five or six years I could take the Institute of Structural Engineers examination paper to become a Chartered Engineer. So, in short, that is what I did, but not without the support and companionship of my wife Sue. Sue had moved in next door to us at Old Windsor, just as I was about to move to work and train in Manchester. We married in 1962 and she joined me to live in the tiny attic room I had by then rented at the top of a very large unheated old house on the outskirts of Manchester. That winter of 1962 was the longest cold spell on record. Sue had become pregnant, and I had to help her 'skate' across an ice-covered driveway to our small car. Without Sue's wonderful support and help, I fear that my resolve to overcome all obstacles and qualify as an experienced design engineer might have wavered, but just before my 30th birthday I was informed that I had passed my final examination set by the Institute of Structural Engineers and so became a Chartered Structural Engineer. It was truly a turning point in our lives.

I was soon to accept a post to work in the design office of a large structural steel company in Johannesburg, and within a year I was offered the post of Chief Designer. During my career in construction, I was involved in some very large and interesting projects.

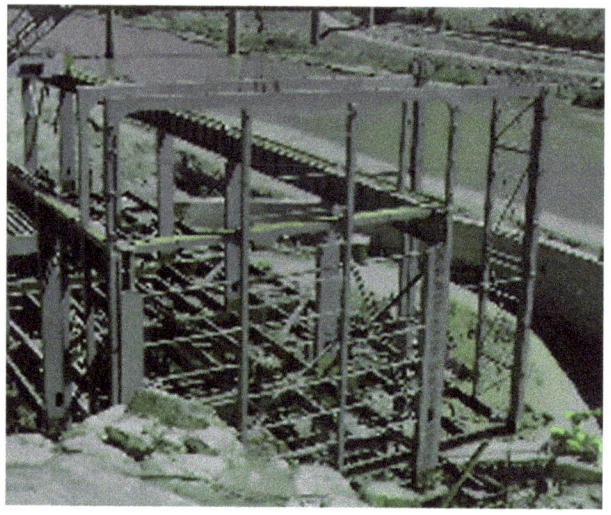

Gariep Dam Power Station Steel Framework: hydro-electric power station under construction.

In pride of place is the steel framework that I designed to win, for my company, a competitive tender for the design and construction of the framework for a hydro-electric power station for Eskom, the South African electricity supply company. It was required to not only support a massive overhead crane to take the weight, when required, of the turbines for maintenance but also to transmit the forces that would be generated by the river in full flood, to the rock face, into which the power station was to nestle.

Perhaps in some way my interest in still photography reflects something in my DNA of that same desire to create something – be it an image that captures something of Hong Kong's life in the 'fifties, or the framework of a major steel structure like the one here.

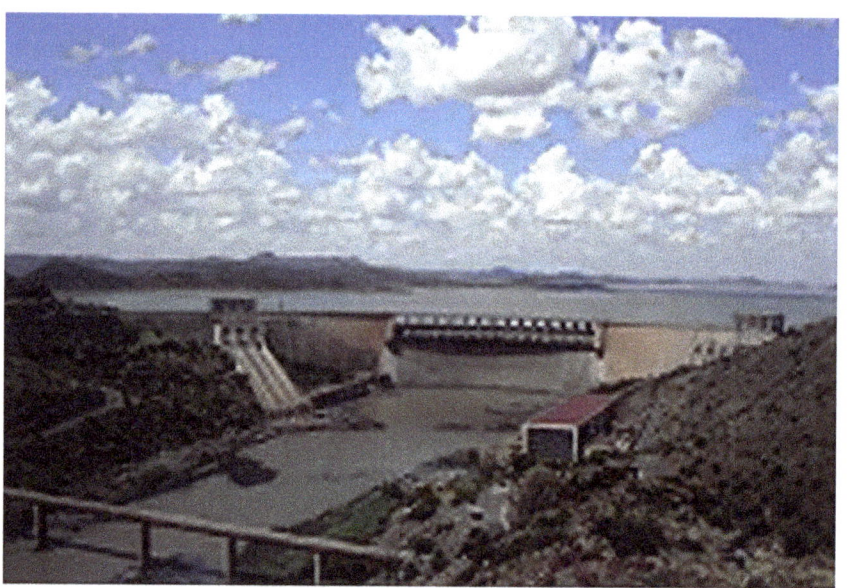

Finished dam and power station.